Employment Relationships

The second half of the twentieth century witnessed a quite dramatic shift in the nature of white-collar employment, from lifetime tenure, often in a very hierarchical work structure, to a new model defined by flatter organizations, job insecurity, shorter tenures, declining attachment between employer and employee, and contingent work. Managing employment relations has become an issue of huge strategic importance as businesses struggle to respond to the pace of change in management systems and working practices. *Employment Relationships: New Models of White-Collar Work* traces the latest developments in employment arrangements drawn from a number of business contexts. These include the rising role of outside hiring and lateral moves in shaping and managing careers, increased career uncertainty, and much greater variety in organizational structures – even within industries and professions – as employers struggle to meet the diverging demands of their product markets.

Employment Relationships offers an authoritative resource for students and scholars wanting to understand the role of employment relations in real-world business settings.

PETER CAPPELLI is the George W. Taylor Professor of Management and Director of the Center for Human Resources at the Wharton School, University of Pennsylvania.

Cambridge Companions to Management

Cambridge Companions to Management is an essential new resource for academics, graduate students, and reflective business practitioners seeking cutting-edge perspectives on managing people in organizations. Each *Companion* integrates the latest academic thinking with contemporary business practice, dealing with real-world issues facing organizations and individuals in the workplace, and demonstrating how and why practice has changed over time. World-class editors and contributors write with unrivaled depth on managing people and organizations in today's global business environment, making the series a truly international resource.

FORTHCOMING IN THIS SERIES

Brief *Diversity at Work*
Saunders *et al* *Organizational Trust*
Sitkin, Cardinal and Bijlsema-Frankema *Organizational Control*
Smith *et al* *Global Challenges in Responsible Business*
Tjosvold and van Knippenberg *Power and Interdependence in Organizations*

Employment Relationships

New Models of White-Collar Work

Edited by

PETER CAPPELLI
The Wharton School, University of Pennsylvania

CAMBRIDGE
UNIVERSITY PRESS

CAMBRIDGE UNIVERSITY PRESS
Cambridge, New York, Melbourne, Madrid, Cape Town, Singapore, São Paulo, Delhi

Cambridge University Press
The Edinburgh Building, Cambridge CB2 8RU, UK

Published in the United States of America by Cambridge University Press,
New York

www.cambridge.org
Information on this title: www.cambridge.org/9780521684088

First published 2008

Printed in the United Kingdom at the University Press, Cambridge

A catalogue record for this publication is available from the British Library

ISBN 978-0-521-86537-1 hardback
ISBN 978-0-521-68408-8 paperback

Contents

Figures

Tables

Contributors

Matthew Bidwell is Assistant Professor of Strategy and Management at INSEAD.

Forrest Briscoe is Assistant Professor of Labor and Employment Studies and Sociology at Pennsylvania State University.

John C. Dencker is Assistant Professor at the Institute of Labor and Industrial Relations, University of Illinois at Urbana-Champaign.

Isabel Fernandez-Mateo is Assistant Professor of Strategic and International Management at the London Business School.

Peter D. Sherer is Associate Professor of Human Resources and Organizational Dynamics at the Haskayne School of Business, University of Calgary.

Steffanie L. Wilk is Associate Professor of Management and Human Resources at the Fisher College of Business, Ohio State University.

Margaret Yap is Assistant Professor in the School of Business Management, Ryerson University, Toronto.

Foreword

We are pleased to introduce Peter Cappelli's *Employment Relationships: New Models of White-Collar Work*, as part of the Cambridge Companions to Management series. The series is intended to advance knowledge in the fields of management by presenting the latest scholarship and research on topics of growing importance. Bridging the gap between journal articles and student textbooks, the volumes offer in-depth treatment of selected management topics, exploring the current knowledge base and identifying future opportunities for research. Each topic covered in the series is one with great future promise, and one that also has developed a sufficient body of research to allow informed reviews and debate.

Management scholarship is increasingly international in scope. No longer can scholars read only the work conducted in their own countries, or talk only to their near neighbors; creative and innovative work in management is now being conducted throughout the world. Each volume is organized by one of our most prominent scholars, who brings researchers from several countries together to provide cross-national perspectives and debate. Through this series we hope to introduce readers to scholarship in their field they may not yet know, and open scholarship debate to a wider set of perspectives.

We feel fortunate to be working with Cambridge University Press. Their rigorous independent scholarly reviews and board approval process helps ensure that only the highest-quality scholarship is published. We feel confident that scholars will find these books useful to their own research programs, as well as useful in their doctoral courses.

Here, in *Employment Relationships*, Peter Cappelli and his chapter authors take the field of employment relations beyond its roots in the study of blue-collar jobs and unionization to address new models of office and professional work. Since such jobs now dominate the rich economies, we see this book as leading an important historical shift in the field of employment relations.

Further, those in office and professional jobs now face frequent corporate restructuring, unstable careers, and complex employment relationships with worksite supervisors but off-site contract employers, among many other upheavals. These topics are widely discussed in the popular press, and are gaining more attention from those in diverse management fields. The field of employment relations brings a history of rigor and intellectual depth to these changing patterns of work that will enrich the work in such diverse fields as organizational behavior, corporate responsibility, industrial and organizational psychology, and strategy. We are pleased to bring this exciting book to all of those interested in today's changing work and organizations.

Cary Cooper, Lancaster University Management School
Jone L. Pearce, University of California, Irvine
Series editors

1 | *Introduction*

PETER CAPPELLI

The context of new models of white-collar work[1]

The Organization Man, the famous book by *Fortune* editor William H. Whyte written in 1955 about corporate careers, defined for a generation the career experience of managers entering the business world, as well as the effects of that experience on society. It provided the details for practical issues such as how corporations made hiring decisions (even detailing how to "cheat" on personality tests), how executives thought and acted, and how they got ahead in their careers. In those days, virtually all the good jobs in business were in large corporations.

When *The Organization Man* was published, and for the generation that followed, business careers began with college recruiting, when employers looked for candidates who could be molded into executives with the values and characteristics appropriate for their company. They looked for potential, and the key component of potential was their personality. Once hired, the company set about training and developing the skills of the young manager – not just their business skills but their social and interpersonal skills. Pressures to conform were considerable, and those pressures extended to their family and to their life outside work. Managers were groomed to see their interests and identity as defined by their organization, hence "the Organization Man." The defining attribute of careers was that they were governed by the company's rules and interests. All senior positions were filled by promotions from within, which made it essentially impossible to quit because no other company would hire managers from the outside. The company decided who would advance, often based on elaborate assessment exercises, when they would move, and where they would go. The hierarchy of authority and the rewards associated with it were clear, as was the

[1] This book looks at workplace changes primarily in North America. These trends are generally mirrored throughout the world, however, particularly in Europe, and more recently in Asia.

1

path through which one got there. Candidates climbed well-defined ladders of advancement, and no deviations were allowed. This included relocations, which were frequent, and the failure to accept them was a "career-ending move." The skills crucial to getting ahead involved good performance but also managing internal politics – especially fitting in and cultivating superiors. The companies also took care of their managers however. No one was laid off and virtually no one was ever fired. Managers who were passed over were shunted to marginal positions and retired with generous pensions.

The system Whyte described took root first in these large corporations, but it was copied across all but the very smallest businesses. Many people still believe that the model he outlined is the one to follow, but in fact the Organization Man died a while ago. The fact that this approach continues to be used as a model has less to do with any evidence that it still exists and more to do with the difficulty in coming up with alternative descriptions of how careers are in fact operating. The chapters in this volume suggest some of the different models of how careers look now. Before getting to them, however, it is important to describe the ways in which the old model is coming apart.

Models of talent forecasting

In the mid-1960s a study of personnel departments found that 96 percent had a dedicated manpower planning function that was charged with forecasting human capital needs and then developing the approaches to meet them (Allen, 1966). Hiring at the entry level was a key part of that process but more important, and more complex, was the process of developing talent and moving candidates through organizational charts to arrive at the right roles at the right time. Virtually every company had an executive called "the manpower planner" who headed that functional area. The most crucial job in the entire human resources (HR) organization, some would argue the most powerful job in the entire company, was the position informally known as "chess master." That was the person who decided how executives would move around the chessboard represented by the company's various assignments. The favored few would find themselves with plum jobs in corporate headquarters; those out of favor would see the moving van come to take them to the greenfield plant in East Nowhere.

James Walker has described the manpower forecasts of the American Oil subsidiary of Standard Oil Corporation as extending out ten years

(Walker, 1970), a figure that may have been typical. Estimates of demand for talent in the future were then matched against estimates of supply. The assumption in these models was that the supply of talent was within the control of the company, an internal function (see, for example, Rowland and Sovereign, 1969). Because the supply for all but entry-level jobs came only from within, managing that supply involved adjusting the rate at which candidates progressed from one job to the other in the firm.

The first serious model for understanding the movement of employees within organizations was based on the work of the mathematician Andrei Markov, who developed procedures for understanding the movement of items from one state to another, in this case the movement of individuals from one job in a promotion hierarchy to another.

The practical use of Markov chain analysis was in forecasting the number of people who would be in different positions in the hierarchy at some future point. It began by calculating historical averages of the percentage of individuals who moved from one position in the organization to another each year. By applying those percentages to the employment levels in each job, it was possible to estimate how those levels would be different in future years. More sophisticated models attempted to calculate the rates of movement from one position to another by seeing how they varied with factors such as company growth rates and the attributes of the individuals in each position, such as average tenure (see Walker, 1970, for examples). As models began to accommodate the variety of arrangements possible for advancement in an organization (e.g. "flexible" hierarchies, whereby one could move across functional silos), their complexity – and the amount of mathematics required to describe them – expanded considerably (see, for example, Dill, Gaver, and Weber, 1966).

Armed with these estimates of what the supply of talent would be for particular jobs, the planners altered promotion paths and rates of development to help get the right number of people to the right positions at the right point in time. A 1966 report by McKinsey and Company suggests how companies were tackling the problem of talent management even for the more straightforward functional areas, in this case sales. At least initially, the job structure for sales positions was reasonably flat: salesmen and their managers. The complication was getting individuals with the right abilities into the appropriate sales jobs and, particularly, to fill the management jobs. As with other jobs, the new model began with an "audit," essentially a replacement table, that looked at the performance and attributes of incumbents and fore-casts of how many individuals would be in which position in the future. This was compared to an estimate of demand, which included assess-ments of the characteristics of salesmen that the companies needed for each position. In the process, the companies were able to forecast where shortfalls would occur.

The McKinsey report details the problems that companies were having with sales, and they sound incredibly contemporary. First, shortfalls in talent were happening in large measure because of turnover. Promising salesmen were leaving at an especially high rate before their first promo-tion. Second, there was real concern about the large number of mediocre performers who stayed in place and clogged the middle stages of the career. What was not contemporary was the solution. The companies developed a new model for careers (seen in figure 1.1), a career path that began with "up or out" promotions to weed out poor performers within eighteen months and continued with forced career decisions every two or three years.

Several aspects of this new career path are extraordinary. What had been a straightforward sales job became a complex hierarchy with ten distinct positions, all organized along a promotion path. Candidates were either promoted or reassigned every few years, and every job had a tenure requirement associated with it. It was impossible to remain in those jobs longer without being moved in one direction or another. The candidates apparently had little choice in the matter. It was also clear that the implicit priority in this model was to develop managerial expertise. Individuals ended up in sales careers by default, when they were not promoted up the management hierarchy. Those who stayed in customer sales were not left alone, however. They faced a separate, five-step career hierarchy with a series of up or out promotion decisions.

The report also quotes a vice-president of sales about the priority placed on development, saying that, for every promotion in their com-pany, the president wanted to know the names of the individuals who that candidate has developed. "And if he can't cite examples of men he has helped bring along, the chances of him getting promoted in this organiza-tion are pretty slim" (Pearson, 1966, p. 46). Remember, this is for *sales* jobs, a function we now think of as being individual-oriented and brutally competitive among the individuals involved. The arrangement above, which played out in different ways across a range of jobs and companies, transformed what had been a haphazard employment system into one that was highly regimented and bureaucratic.

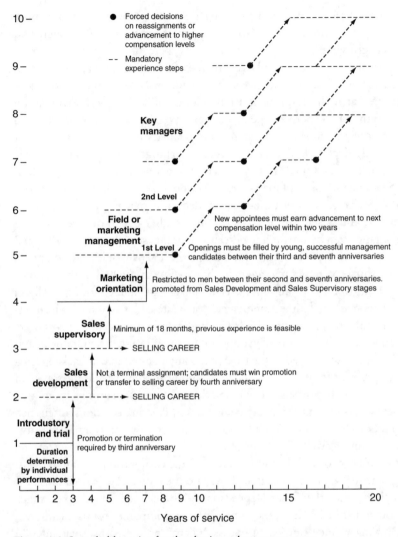

Figure 1.1 Sample blueprint for developing sales management
Source: Pearson (1966).

Collapse of the old models

Workforce planning, succession planning, and the Organization Man approach to careers began to fall apart when the ability to forecast the overall level of demand in the economy collapsed following the oil price shocks, first in 1973 and then in 1979. The economy grew far more slowly than anticipated. Gross national product (GNP), which had been growing at a rate of about 5 to 6 percent in real terms during most of the 1960s, actually declined in 1974, 1975, and again in 1980. The 1970s became known as the decade of "stagflation" – low economic growth despite inflation. Companies that had planned on growth of 6 percent per year on average suddenly discovered that their business demand not only failed to meet that target but actually declined. Talent management arrangements ran into trouble because of the long lead time inherent in a system of internal development. The number of managers who were ready for director positions, for example, was set in motion by decisions made ten years or more earlier and based on forecasts of much higher demand. Overshooting demand even by only a few percentage points soon begins to add up; 3 percent per year over a decade such as the 1970s would lead to having one-third too many managers in the pipeline at the end of the decade.

What to do with all those excess managerial candidates, especially in the context of lifetime employment for white-collar workers, which virtually all companies practiced? Commenting on the decline in corporate growth and the slowdown in opportunities that resulted, Sandra Beldt and Donald Kewell noted at the time that companies had been backed into a corner, as promotions were the most significant reward and the source of motivation. In response, they found that "the need to continue promoting people has been met in many companies by creating positions; often such positions have a title without commensurate responsibility and authority" (Beldt and Kewell, 1980). In other words, they added management and executive jobs, and the bureaucracies of the corporations began to bloat.

The recession that began in 1981 was the worst downturn in business activity since the Great Depression. GNP declined by two percentage points just in 1982. At the same time, the companies found themselves carrying a huge burden of excess "talent" produced by their internal development systems because, over the past decade, they had vastly overshot the actual demand for human capital. It also brought to a head a number of even more significant changes in the environment for business, which had a profound effect on talent management practices.[2]

---

[2] Among the more influential arguments that the US economy had undergone fundamental and painful change in this period was that of Michael

The era of downsizing

Facing the internal glut of talent, the sharp recession of 1981, and the changes in the economic environment noted above, employers moved aggressively to break the lifetime employment arrangements with their employees. As late as the end of the 1970s survey evidence from the Conference Board indicated that management's priorities in setting employment practices were to build a loyal, stable work-force. A decade later, however, by the end of the 1980s, that priority had clearly shifted to increasing organizational performance and reducing costs (these surveys are discussed in Belous, 1989). The most powerful evidence in this regard is another Conference Board survey, which found more than two-thirds of the large employers in the sample reporting that they changed their practice and no longer offered employment security; only 3 percent in the mid-1990s said that they still offered job security to employees (Conference Board, 1997).

The most important manifestation of this new relationship was downsizing. The term "downsizing" was at first a euphemism for lay-offs, but later it came to mean something different. Whereas layoffs had been seen as a temporary response to downturns in business resulting from recessions focused on hourly workers, downsizing was a perma-nent reduction in jobs, and it did not appear to differentiate between levels in the organization. The US Bureau of Labor Statistics (BLS) did not even measure permanent job losses (as distinct from recession-based and temporary) until after 1984, because of the assumption that workers who had lost their jobs would get them back once business recovered. Similarly, the level of "contingent work," defined by the BLS as jobs that are expected to end soon, was not measured before the 1990s. Contingent work by this definition remained roughly constant at about 4.3 percent of the employed workforce through the late 1990s, even as the overall unemployment rate fell and the labor market tigh-tened (Hipple, 2001).

The American Management Association (AMA) surveyed its mem-ber companies about downsizing during the 1990s, finding that the

L. Dertouzos, Richard K. Lester, and Robert M. Solow (1989). Peter Cappelli *et al.* (1997) suggest that the economic restructuring of the 1980s had a range of negative consequences for employees.

incidence of downsizing had increased virtually every year through 1996, despite the economic expansion of the decade. Roughly a half of the companies reported downsizing, and 40 percent had downsizing in two or more separate years over the previous six (American Management Association, 1996). Other surveys reported roughly similar rates of downsizing. The scale of these job cuts was unprecedented in a period of economic expansion.

White-collar and managerial employees experienced the most fundamental change from this new approach, because they were the ones with the most protections to lose. There was a sharp rise in unemployment for white-collar employees relative to other groups beginning in the 1980s, as well as an increased risk of job loss for individuals (for an explicit comparison, see Cappelli, 1992), which is certainly among the strongest evidence that whatever special protection this employee group had had in the past was now gone. White-collar and managerial employees now face much the same insecurity and instability as production workers, a profound change that undermined what had been the very basis of the distinction between white-collar and blue-collar. That distinction stems from the New-Deal-era Fair Labor Standards Act, which was based on the assumption that production workers needed legislative protection that white-collar workers did not because the latter were already protected by the firm. White-collar employees who kept their jobs also saw internal careers evaporating as job ladders shrank, restructuring disrupted the promotion tracks that remained, and external hiring blocked advancement by filling senior positions. In that situation, most employers abandoned virtually everything about the old system, even the rhetoric about their responsibility to employees.

The causes of downsizing also changed over time. Job cuts had been associated with recessions in the past, but a growing number of companies toward the end of the 1990s reported that job cuts resulted from internal management decisions – restructuring (66 percent) and outsourcing (23 percent). Virtually none cited overall economic conditions as an explanation, and most of the companies that cut were profitable in the year they were cutting. Further, downsizing was no longer necessarily about shrinking the size of the workforce: 31 percent of those firms in the AMA surveys were actually adding and cutting workers at the same time in 1996, and the average firm that had a downsizing was in fact growing by 6 percent (American Management Association, 1996). This development suggests that firms were relying on the outside labor market to restructure, dropping skills that were no longer needed and bringing in new ones.

Data on workers who have been permanently displaced from their jobs since 1981 confirms the fact that job security declined. The overall rate at which workers were permanently displaced backed down somewhat in the late 1980s from the peak of the recession period, 1981–3, but then rose again – despite the economic recovery – and jumped sharply through 1995. The rate at which workers were thrown out of their jobs was about the same in 1993–5, a period of significant economic expansion and prosperity in the economy as a whole, as compared to the 1981–3 recession, the worst downturn since the Great Depression (Farber, 1998). It is difficult to find more compelling evidence that the nature of the employment relationship had changed. About 15 percent of the workforce saw their jobs go for ever during that 1993–5 period of growth. The cause of the job losses reported in these surveys of individual workers mirrors the developments in the firm surveys – shifting away from economy- or company-wide reasons such as downturns in business or plant closures toward eliminating particular positions associated with restructuring. Further, the costs of job loss since the 1980s actually increased, especially for older workers who otherwise found it difficult to locate new jobs, even as the improved economic picture saw it decline for other workers (Farber, 2003).

The following chart describes the downsizing experience of the most stable workers, those who had been with their employers for more than twenty years. It compares the experience in the steepest downturn in modern times, the recession of 1981–2, to the period of the most rapid growth in a generation, 1999–2000. It is no surprise to see the displacement rate for blue-collar workers roughly twice as high during the recession as during the boom. What is quite remarkable is that *there is almost no difference in the rate of layoff for white-collar workers in the two periods.* Reengineering and restructuring generally explains why white-collar job losses remained high even in the period of economic expansion.

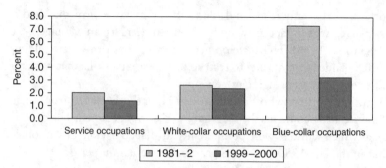

Figure 1.2 Displacement rates of long-tenured workers twenty years and older by occupation group of lost job, 1981–2 and 1999–2000
Source: Monthly Labor Review (2004).

Reengineering to shed talent

Companies began to find new ways to get work done with fewer people after the 1981 recession and to get rid of the management roles that had been created during the 1970s, a process that became known as "reengineering." Work systems that empower employees, such as cross-functional teams, eliminated supervisory positions and widened spans of control. Information systems eliminate many of the internal control functions of middle management positions, and decentralizing operations through the creation of profit centers and similar arrangements further reduce the need for central administration. Corporate hierarchies flattened in the 1990s (Rajan and Wulf, 2006), and with them job and career ladders, in part as headquarters were deflated and power was decentralized.

The net consequence of these developments was to reduce the need for managers just at the time that companies had an excess supply of managerial talent carried over from the 1970s. As a result, the priority inside companies shifted from developing talent to getting rid of talent. New companies that started in this period found a plentiful supply of managerial skills and talent available on the outside market. There was no need to develop talent when it could easily be acquired "ready to go." Manpower planning was not exactly a challenging exercise when companies were cutting back jobs; nor was it even necessary when companies had the option of bringing in experienced hires from the outside: just wait and see what was needed and then go get it.

New paradigms for finding talent

Despite the mass shedding of high-level jobs and management positions, companies still needed to cultivate talent. The shifts in management careers described thus far reflect similar changes in how companies recruit new talent.

Outside hiring

When companies did have vacancies and needed talent to fill them, they now turned to the outside market. This was particularly so for leadership positions when they were looking to change direction or strategy. New strategies frequently require different competencies that do not exist internally, and companies quite understandably looked outside to find employees with those competencies. The extent of outside hiring in the United States was quite large during this time period: 2.7 percent of the US workforce changed employers every month, about 30 percent each year (Fallick and Fleishman, 2002). At the executive level, boards and chief executive officers (CEOs) often brought in outsiders precisely to change the strategies and practices of the company. Evidence from Deloitte Research suggests that the average US employer spent about fifty times more recruiting an average middle manager with a salary of $100,000 than he/she spent on training his/her average employee (Deloitte Research, 2006).

Greater use of outside hiring emerges as both a cause and a consequence of the decline of the traditional model of talent management. Outside hiring reduced the need for internal development and caused retention problems that made internal development too expensive (see chapter 5). Once the internal development models were gone, companies had no choice but to look outside for talent. Studies of larger, publicly traded firms traditionally associated with internal succession found that outsider CEOs were prominent – approximately 25 percent in the 1990s (Ocasio, 1999). A different study, also of larger firms, reports that outsider CEOs represented 30 percent of all CEOs in the late 1990s (Murphy and Zábojník, 2004). At least one argument suggests that both the rise of outside hiring for CEOs and the sharp increase in CEO pay are related to the rising demand for managerial skills that translate across organizations, as opposed to company-specific skills, in those positions (Murphy and Zábojník, 2004).

At the executive level

One of the factors driving outside hiring at the executive ranks is the greater pressure on executives to perform, a consequence of the shareholder value movement, and manifested by more CEOs being pushed out of companies. In 2001 annual CEO turnover was 9.2 percent, a 53 percent increase from 1995, while the average CEO tenure declined from 9.5 years to 7.3 years (Lucier, Kocourek, and Habbel, 2006). A recent study found that worldwide turnover of CEOs in the 2,500 largest publicly held corporations broke records in 2004 and again in 2005, with more than 15 percent of CEOs leaving, a figure 70 percent higher than in the previous decade. The region with the highest turnover of executives (just under 20 percent) was Japan, the alleged home of lifetime employment. One-sixth of those who departed did so as a result of a merger or acquisition. Reports suggest that about a third were pushed out because of failure to meet performance targets (see Lucier, Kocourek, and Habbel, 2006), but these estimates are likely to be wildly understated, as companies go to great lengths to cover up the real reasons why executives leave.

Looking more broadly beyond the CEO to executive positions in general, a recent study found that 53 percent of all executive vacancies at the level of vice-president (VP) in large US companies had retained an executive search firm to find an outsider to fill them (a description of the search and staffing industry is provided in Cappelli and Hamori, 2005). My colleague Monika Hamori and I compared the careers of the top ten executives in the Fortune 100 companies in 1980 and 2001. These companies are not only the largest and most complex but traditionally the most wedded to models of internal development, and these jobs are at the absolute top of the succession process. What we saw in the comparison was sharp declines in the percentage of these executives who had been lifetime employees and even sharper declines in tenure – in part also because executives were now advancing more quickly.

These overall figures mask some interesting patterns however. Is there a difference in the important outcomes associated with attachment to the firm, for example, in the experience between younger and older firms? None of the Fortune 100 firms are especially new, but if we look at the twenty-six oldest firms, the ones that were in the Fortune 100 in 1980 as well as 2001, we see quite a different picture.

In these twenty-six firms, there appears to be little, if any, difference in outcomes associated with attachment to the firm. The top executives

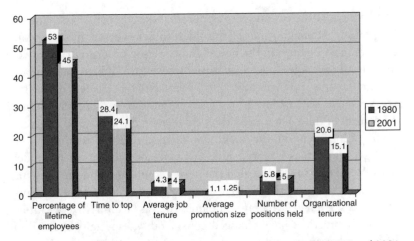

Figure 1.3 Descriptive statistics for top executives: career patterns, 1980 and 2001
Source: Cappelli and Hamori (2005).

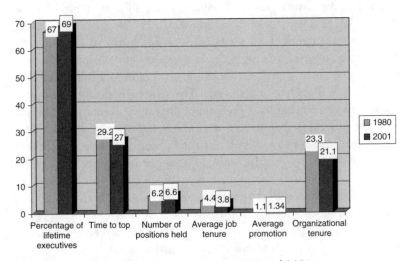

Figure 1.4 Top executives and experiences, 1980 and 2001
Source: Cappelli and Hamori (2005).

are just as likely to be lifers and be with the firm just as long in 2001 as in 1980. Interestingly, these firms also tend to be the "academy" companies, such as General Electric, Exxon, and IBM – the companies that we often look to as models for talent management.

Of course, if the overall pattern across these companies is changing but nothing is changing among the oldest subset of companies, then the changes must be huge in the newer companies in order to drive movement in the average. Indeed, that is what we find. When we compare those companies younger than thirty years with those older than thirty years, even in the Fortune 100, we see extraordinary differences. Only 17 percent of the top ten executives are lifers in the younger companies versus 52 percent in the older companies. Average tenure in the younger companies is about nine years versus eighteen in the older ones. What this suggests is that the newer companies and the growing companies have experiences that are not at all like those of the academy companies. Even in academy companies such as GE and IBM, we know that their practices have changed considerably, especially the end of lifetime job security and the expansion of outside hiring, even if those practices do not appear to have affected yet the very top executives whose careers began decades earlier (Cappelli and Hamori, 2005).

The fact that employers are finding it more difficult to plan for the internal development of staff means that they rely more on outside hiring to meet the demand for talent. Outside hiring of executives is particularly important because the new leaders often bring with them their own team of managers, blocking succession to all the executive roles that are filled from the outside. This process undercuts the development programs that have the goal of producing executives. The job rotation programs that moved candidates rapidly across functional areas, the high-potential and fast-track programs that gave them opportunities more quickly, were all designed to prepare them to be executives, especially general managers. When executives are brought in from the outside, the entire motivation for those programs collapses. Outside hiring of executives also shifts the attention of managers to networks of potential employers outside the firm as they get the message that the way to get ahead involves outside hiring.

The practice of hiring from the outside also creates retention problems at competing employers. Virtually every lateral hire brought into an organization is pulled from another employer, very likely unexpectedly from the perspective of that employer. Their departure causes retention problems, which means that their current employer has lost their investment in those employees. Moreover, any development or succession planning that includes the employee is disrupted as well.

At entry and lower levels

A study in the late 1990s surveyed recruiters and found a sizable increase in the proportion of employers who now sought experienced workers for entry-level jobs, those positions that traditionally were filled by new entrant, college graduates (Rynes, Orlitzky, and Bretz, 1997). My examination of proprietary surveys of employers found them reporting a greater interest in outside hiring to meet skill needs (Cappelli, 1999).

An important development accelerating this outside hiring development for lower-level and more traditional positions has been the rise of non-degree credentials that certify skills and proficiency in various technical areas. These credentials are typically issued by independent organizations outside the educational community and are most associated with information technology (IT), whereby companies such as Microsoft and Cisco issue certifications for individuals who have completed training and demonstrated proficiency in the use of those systems. Literally millions of these credentials have been issued, and, unlike academic degrees, they are highly focused on actual job tasks (see Adelman, 2000, on the rise of certifications and credentialing in the labor market). The consequence of these credentials is to increase the ease with which individuals can move across organizations by certifying that they can perform tasks central to reasonably standard jobs with a high level of proficiency. Together, these developments have accelerated the movement toward something like professional labor markets for jobs that were previously seen as internal, technical functions (see Leicht and Fennell, 1997).

Outside search has become a permanent feature of some industries, with the rise of a professional class of employees who perform more or less the equivalent work in whatever setting they seem to appear in. The field of IT represents perhaps the archetypal case. IT work is defined by standards that are created by vendors (e.g. "Cisco-certified" technicians) or by other organizations (e.g. Cobol programming) to translate across employers. The workers who perform IT tasks therefore have skill sets that translate across organizations: a Java programmer, for example, can do similar work in reasonably similar ways across companies. When the demand for IT services began to explode in the mid-1990s, companies looked outside to find people who could do this work. Because the demand for these workers was so hot, virtually all of them had jobs already. When they were hired, then, they left vacancies in their previous organization that had to be filled from the outside – what

Harrison White (1970) first described as a "vacancy chain" problem. Even a small number of IT vacancies could generate a huge amount of IT hiring in this manner; and the outside search business expanded enormously to meet that demand. What is important about these developments is that outside search became an option – in many cases the preferred option – for providing the routine and commodity-like skills associated with lower-level, non-management jobs. The rise of outside hiring for lower-level and non-executive positions helped create a new set of labor market institutions to match people with jobs.

Finally, if any question remains about whether outside hiring is a passing phase or a new construct here to stay, one need only look at the growth of outside hiring firms. Revenues from corporate recruiting firms that perform outside searches for companies *tripled* just during the mid-1990s (Cappelli, 1999, p. 215). We now have an "employment services industry" that manages this outside labor market, putting workers and employers together. It includes temporary help, professional employer organizations (which take on the legal obligations of an employer but not their day-to-day management) and employment placement agencies of various kinds.[3] This industry itself employed 3.6 million people in the United States in April 2004, with revenues exceeding $100 billion (Staffing Industry Analysts, 2004). The size of the executive search business within that employment services industry is hard to estimate, because there are many small and privately held companies. The best estimates suggest that revenues are about $11.5 billion worldwide, with more than a half of that generated in the United States (Khurana, 2002). Hunt-Scanlon consultants report, that in 2003,

---

[3] Chris Benner (2003), who describes Silicon Valley intermediaries, provides a good typology of labor market intermediaries. He distinguishes between private-sector, membership-based and public intermediaries. Private-sector intermediaries are of four types: temporary help firms; consultant brokerage firms (that recruit professional contractors for temporary positions); Web-based job sites; and professional employer organizations (that provide HR administrative services to firms and are the legal employer of record for employees working for the client firm.) Membership-based intermediaries, such as guild-like and professional associations, place employees who form their membership. Public-sector intermediaries include (1) the range of institutions that make up the workforce development system and aim to connect disadvantaged workers with jobs; (2) education-based institutions that provide adult education and job-related training to employees and have increasingly become market intermediaries; and (3) community and non-profit organizations that engage in job training and placement services.

the combined revenue of the twenty-five largest US search firms was $1.2 billion. In the United States, 54 percent of companies relied on executive search firms to fill executive-level jobs paying above $150,000 between 2001 and 2003 (results from a 2003 survey carried out by the International Association for Corporate and Professional Recruitment).

Online job search

The newest institutions in job search have the potential to offer the most profound changes in attitudes and behavior. Internet job search began with the explosion of personal, career-related information that is available on the Web, making it easier for employers to find possible candidates who were not necessarily looking for a new job. Many people have their résumés (CVs) posted on their personal web pages, but more important for recruiters are more objective sources of Web-based information, such as industry associations or – better yet – those associated with individual employers that report information about workplace achievements. Some of these search techniques can be reasonably sinister, such as "flipping the URL," which means getting inside a company's internal web pages to look for information such as "employee of the month" awards or other indications of competence. In the search for these passive applicants, internet recruiters during the tight labor market of the late 1990s were aided by a slew of new resources, such as sites that paid participants for confidential leads and references about fellow workers who might be interested in moving. Some companies were very creative in finding ways to get potential applicants to reveal their abilities. Cisco Systems, for example, was well known for techniques such as holding contests online with prizes oriented for internet engineers, in part as a way of identifying creative, potential employees.

This information solved what had been the fundamental problem of outside hiring from the days of the first search firms: the issue of adverse selection. Like the Groucho Marx joke about not wanting to join any club that would have him as a member, recruiters want only the best candidates, and those tend to be ones who have no reason to move – in part because they are loyal and in part because their current employers appreciate how good they are. These are known as "passive" candidates, in contrast to those who are actively looking and applying for jobs and may be problem workers who need to find a new job. In the

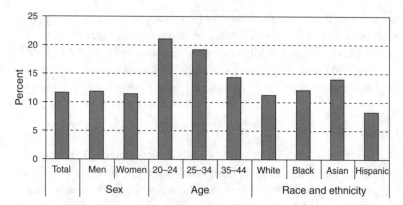

Figure 1.5 Percentage of the civilian non-institutional population who used the internet to search for a job, by selected characteristics, October 2003
Source: Monthly Labor Review (2005b).

past, relying on applicants for outside hires created adverse selection problems because of the risk that applicants were problem workers. Companies could rely on search firms to find passive applicants, but that was such an expensive path that its usefulness was limited to only the highest-paying jobs. Online search, in contrast, made it possible to do what search firms were good at: find good candidates who were not necessarily looking to move, and do so cheaply.

As early as 1998, data from the US Census Bureau found that 15 percent of job seekers were using the internet and that the biggest constraint to its use – one that was rapidly being overcome – was simply gaining access to the internet (Kuhn and Skuterud, 2000). More recently, Census Bureau data found that slightly more than one in every ten individuals aged sixteen and over used the internet between January and October 2003 to search for a job (see figure 1.5).

Further, the growth in internet use as a source for finding jobs has been remarkable, as figure 1.6 suggests.

In 2004 on a typical Monday, the peak time for job searches, Monster.com reported that about 20 million people were searching for jobs on its website, and there were thousands of job boards where résumés and job openings were posted. Research suggests that about two-thirds of the people searching job boards are passive candidates, currently employed and not immediately looking for another job. Some estimates suggest that as much as 10 percent of the time that individuals spend on the internet is spent searching for jobs.

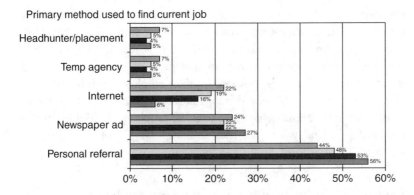

Primary method used to find current job

Started current job:
■ Before Q4 2000 ■ Q4 2000 Q1–Q3 2001 □ Q4 2001–Q1 2002 ▨ Q2–Q3 2002

Figure 1.6 Decreasing importance of personal referrals; macro-conditions could be the driver
Source: Online survey conducted by Forrester Research, November 2002.

More revealing is the finding that the number of executives who say that they have their résumé posted online jumped from 52 percent in 2000 to 75 percent in 2002. A comparison of more than 2,500 users in 2003 and 2004 of BlueSteps, a career management service for senior executives on the Association of Executive Search Consultants (AESC) web page, showed that the salary bracket between $200,000 and $300,000 had the greatest number of executives who had posted their résumés (29 percent). Compared to 2003, this is also the salary bracket that expanded the most rapidly. The $150,000 to $200,000 bracket (28 percent) and the $100,000 to $150,000 bracket (26 percent) are the two next most populous categories. An Execunet Executive Job Market Intelligence 2004 survey concluded that, next to networking with personal and business contacts, searching and responding to internet ads was seen by executives as the most important strategy for advancing their career.

Whether job boards and other online recruiting providers will become important intermediaries between employers and employees, as opposed to simply facilitating the exchange of information between them, is an open question. Sites such as Opus360 and Freeagent.com were working to organize the market for independent contractors, estimated at from 8 to 16 percent of the US workforce. These sites put contractors and customers together and even provide office support for independent contractors. Individuals may also develop some attachment to the job boards and other employment sites, especially those that have helped them find jobs, and may come to trust the information they provide on issues such as career management as more objective and independent than what is provided by their employer. Job boards such as Monster.com are big enough now that they could sell information to large employers about what their average employee is looking for in terms of jobs and where are they looking. They could also provide employees with information about how careers progress.

Evidence of declining attachment between employer and employee

The churning of employees noted above, based on layoffs and outside hiring, has important implications for career issues by shortening the length of time that the employee and employer are together. Shorter tenure makes it much more difficult to do long-term planning and to recoup developmental investments in employees. It may also increase the uncertainty of those attachments, an issue that is harder to measure but just as important.

Trends in tenure

Tenure is driven by layoffs and dismissals but also by quits. The latter procedure accounts for about two-thirds of all job changes – hence the concern about employees being hired away. Most observers are surprised to find that roughly 40 percent of the US workforce have been with their current employer less than two years, a figure that has not changed much in recent decades. This topic has been studied extensively for the United States, and the early studies found reasonable stability in employment when comparing the 1980s with earlier periods (layoffs were higher but quits were lower because jobs were scarce). More recent results, using data from the mid-1990s, have found declines in average tenure, especially for managerial employees but even for the workforce as a whole.[4] They also find large declines in tenure for older, white men in particular, the group historically most protected by internal labor markets. For example, for men approaching

[4] A good survey of the results, at least through the 1990s, is in Neumark (2000).

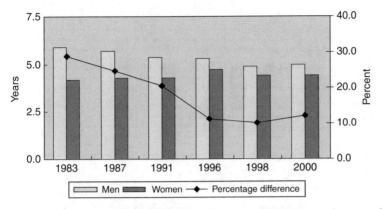

Figure 1.7 Median tenure for employed men and women aged twenty-five and older, selected years 1983–2000
Source: Monthly Labor Review (2000a).

retirement age (fifty-eight to sixty-three) only 29 percent had been with the same employer for ten years or more, as compared to a figure of 47 percent in 1969 (Ruhm, 1995). The percentage of the workforce with long-tenure jobs, ten years or more, declined slightly from the late 1970s through 1993 and then fell sharply through the mid-1990s (Farber, 1997). The rate of dismissals also increased sharply for older workers with more tenure, doubling for workers aged forty-five to fifty-four.[5] The finding that tenure declined for managerial jobs is especially supportive of the arguments for the erosion of internal career systems (Neumark, Polsky, and Hansen, 1999).

Figure 1.7 shows the changes in tenure across the economy as a whole. The figure includes all workers. Managers and corporate employees in general represent only a small part, perhaps less than 10 percent. While tenure for men declined noticeably, tenure for women did not; indeed, it appears to have increased, because women are now less likely to quit their jobs when they have children, in part because of legislated protections (Wellington, 1993).

Changes in tenure for men are more dramatic when one examines the changes within age groups. Because older men quit jobs less frequently,

---

[5] See Polsky (1999) for this result. The other two studies are Bernhardt *et al.* (1999) and Valetta (1996).

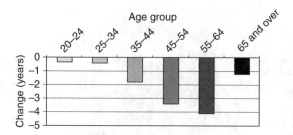

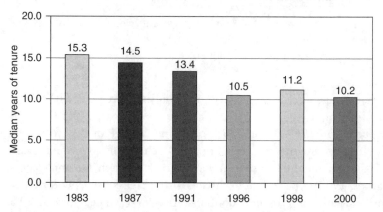

Figure 1.8 Change in median years of tenure, adult men by age, 1983–98
Source: Monthly Labor Review (2000b).

Figure 1.9 Median years of tenure with current employer, men aged fifty-five to sixty-four, 1983–2000
Source: Monthly Labor Review (2000b).

the aging of the workforce over the past decade or so should have worked to *increase* average tenure in the workforce as a whole. Comparing levels within age groups over time controls for that effect. The striking point is that tenure is declining the most precisely among those older age groups that have historically had the highest attachment to their employers, especially the cohort just before retirement.

The most persuasive evidence of a change in the employment relationship comes from studies that follow a cohort of individuals over time. A recent longitudinal study of workers born from 1957 to 1964 indicates how unstable jobs are even for what we think of as the "prime age" workforce. By the 1990s, when these workers were well into middle age, a large percentage of them were still experiencing the type of job insecurity that decades ago we associated with teenage workers. Of those who started a new job in the 1990s, for example, 40 percent saw that job end in less than a year; only 30 percent who started a new job saw it last more than five years.[6]

The most powerful of these studies compares the experience of (initially) young men from 1966 to 1981 to a later group from 1979 through 1994. In the earlier period about 16 percent of workers had stable job histories, as defined by having one or two employers over their career; in the later period it fell to 11 percent. Fifteen percent of the workforce had seven or more employers in the earlier period, a figure that rose to 21 percent in the later period. When comparing equivalent workers, the odds of leaving a job – being dismissed or quitting – after two years was 43 percent greater in the latter cohort (Bernhardt *et al.*, 2001). Another study indicates that the more recent cohort of workers experienced considerably greater changes in their jobs and occupations than did the previous generation even when they remained with the same employer (Hollister, 2006). A third study finds workers in the more recent period changing industries and occupations more frequently than in the previous generation (Kamourov and Manovskii, 2004).[7] We cannot easily tell from these studies whether the changes were instituted by the employer or the employee. Either way, though, they hint at the instability that makes long-term investments in employees and in career planning difficult to achieve. The most recent data from the BLS suggests that tenure increased somewhat from 2000 to 2006, by approximately six months for the average employee.[8] Whether that simply reflects the slowdown in the economy from the red-hot labor market in 2000 or the beginning of a more structural change is difficult to know, however.

The role of compensation and benefits

Evidence of the breakdown of the Organization Man model can also be found in data on compensation. The most important effect is that the

---

[6] US Bureau of Labor Statistics (2004). This study and the others in this section rely on the National Longitudinal Surveys.

[7] This paper uses a different longitudinal survey, the Panel Study of Income Dynamics.

[8] US Bureau of Labor Statistics (2006), table 6, Median years of tenure with current employer for employed wage and salary workers by occupation, selected years, 2000–06 (available at: www.bls.gov/news.release/tenure. t06.htm).

earnings of individuals have become much more variable, and the variation cannot be accounted for by the usual set of individual and job characteristics (Gottschalk and Moffitt, 1994). The instability of unemployment, specifically the growing incidence of job loss, also contributes in important ways to an overall instability of earnings, especially for older workers (Stevens, 2001).

One of the important attributes of the systems of jobs in traditional employment models was the fact that wage levels were set in such a way as to form distinct and clear hierarchies. The technique of "job evalua-tion" described the tools used to fashion wages across jobs so that more senior positions in promotion ladders always paid more than lower positions, encouraging upward mobility. The steady progression of wages based on seniority or tenure was one of the hallmarks of internal systems. By the early 1990s, however, there was no longer any advan-tage to inside moves as compared to those across employers (Wilk and Craig, 1998). The apparent decline in the return to tenure with the same employer is further evidence of the decline of more traditional pay and employment relationships. Researchers studying the semiconduc-tor industry, for example, found a decline in the wage premium paid to more experienced workers. Among the explanations are that new technical skills are becoming more important, and those skills are learned not inside the firm but outside, typically in higher education (Brown, 1997). In aggregate data, the returns to seniority – that is, tenure with the same employer – have collapsed in recent years (Chauvin, 1994). Studies have found a sharp decline in returns to seniority of about $3,000 annually from the 1970s to the 1980s for workers with ten years of seniority.

Another way to describe this effect is that the costs of job changing dropped dramatically. Workers who changed employers every other year saw almost the same earnings rise in the late 1980s as did those who kept the same job for ten years (Marcotte, 1994). Further, the probability that employees who quit would find a job that offers a large pay raise increased by 5 percent over the previous decade while the probability that those who were dismissed will suffer a large decline in their pay rose by 17 percent (Polsky, 1999). These results suggest that a good, lifelong match bet-ween an employee and a single employer is becoming less important in determining an employee's long-term success. By default, what is becoming more important are factors other than the relationship with an individual employer – factors associated with the outside market.

Pension plans have been the aspect of compensation benefit with the most important implications for the employment relationship, as they represent a continuing obligation to employees even if employment ends (at least for vested employees) and, as such, are an indication of a more permanent obligation by employers to employees. While pension coverage has declined over time, more important has been the shift in the nature of pensions from defined benefit plans, through which workers earn the right to predetermined benefit levels according to their years of service, toward defined contribution plans, in which employers make fixed contributions to a retirement fund for each employee, especially 401(K) programs, where employees contribute directly to their retirement fund (Ippolito, 1995). With this shift, the employer no longer bears the risk of guaranteeing a stream of benefits; the employee does. Employees no longer have an incentive to stay with the company long enough to gain access to those pension contributions. The employer's obligations to the employee end with employment, signaling a move away from long-term obligations and relationships. In 1980 84 percent of full-time workers in the United States were covered by a defined benefit pension plan. By 2003, however, the figure was down to 33 percent (Employee Benefit Research Institute, 2005, fig. 10.1).

Finally, it is worth noting that an increasing percentage of the workforce are not employees at all. In 2006 7.4 percent of the workforce consisted of independent contractors, up from 6.4 percent in 2001 (*Monthly Labor Review*, 2005a). It might be reasonable to include contracting out and vendors in this category of independent contracting, at least from the perspective of the original firm, because they represent the movement of work that had been done inside the firm as a fixed cost to work that is now done outside the firm at variable cost.

New models of white-collar work

The arguments above describe the various ways in which the Organization Man model of white-collar careers has eroded. What, though, is taking its place?

The second chapter in this volume, Corporate restructuring and the employment relationship, by John Dencker, tackles the question of what is happening to the traditional managerial jobs and careers in the context of the waves of layoffs and restructuring that continue to reshape corporations. He examines how job security changes and how career paths are altered by looking within a large organization that experienced restructuring. Chapter 3, The up and out in organizations, by Margaret Yap, explores a similar theme, focusing specifically on how promotions have changed over time in a different large corporation.

Call centers have taken over what had been the bulk of lower-level, or entry-level, white-collar jobs. Steffanie Wilk in chapter 4, In the pursuit of quality and quantity: the competing demands in call centers, describes the crucial choices that employers who run call centers make that either help create good jobs or turn them into low-quality, dead-end jobs.

Three's a crowd? Understanding triadic employment relationships, chapter 5, by Matthew Bidwell and Isabel Fernandez-Mateo, explores careers in which individuals are essentially under contract to a third party, an intermediary such as a temp agency, a vendor, or a leased employee organization. These arrangements are increasingly important and are moving further up the hierarchy of skill and responsibility.

The final two chapters consider the career models of a different segment of the workforce, professional service work. The models for managing this work have become more important as more white-collar work gets outsourced to professional service firms. The firms themselves are now seen as offering lessons for corporate organizations, especially for managing ambitious workers using flatter hierarchies with fewer promotions.

Chapter 6, by Peter Sherer, The changed world of large law firms and their lawyers: an opportune context for organizational researchers, describes how the traditional model of law firm careers (internal development, up or out promotion, lifetime engagement) has also changed in much the same way that corporations have experienced. He describes especially the influence of lateral hiring and the different approaches that firms have chosen to manage careers.

Finally, Forrest Briscoe in chapter 7, The upside of bureaucracy: unintended benefits for professional careers describes what is in some ways the opposite development in the more loosely organized world of medical services. He shows how the growth of more corporate models for organizing medical services has helped create careers that look a little more like the corporate model. With the loss of autonomy that comes with the traditional solo or small-group practice, some doctors are gaining flexibility in bureaucratic settings.

Taken together, these accounts drawn from across the economy illustrate the variety of arrangements that are emerging for managing white-collar workers and white-collar careers. There are common threads across them, and they include the rising role of outside hiring and lateral moves in shaping careers and the arrangements for managing them; greater uncertainty about careers and associated arrangements, such as pay; and much greater variety in the arrangements, even within industries and professions, as employers struggle to meet the diverging demands of their product markets.

References

Adelman, C. (2000). A parallel universe. *Change, 32*(3), 20–9.

Allen, J.R. (1966). *Personnel Administration: Changing Scope and Organization.* Studies in Personnel Policy no. 203. New York: National Industrial Conference Board.

American Management Association (1996). *Survey on Downsizing, Job Elimination, and Job Creation.* New York: American Management Association.

Beldt, S.F., and Kewell, D.O. (1980). Where have the promotions gone? *Business, 30*(2), 24.

Belous, R.S. (1989). *The Contingent Economy: The Growth of the Temporary, Part-Time and Subcontracted Workforce.* Washington, D.C.: National Planning Association.

Benner, C. (2003). Labor flexibility and regional development: the role of labor market intermediaries. *Regional Studies, 36*(6/7), 621–33.

Bernhardt, A., Morris, M., Handcock, M.S., and Scott, M.A. (1999). Trends in job instability and wages for young adult men. *Journal of Labor Economics, 17*(4), part 2, S65–S90.

(2001). *Divergent Paths: Economic Mobility in the New American Labor Market.* New York: Russell Sage Foundation.

Brown, C. (ed.) (1997). *The Competitive Semiconductor Manufacturing Human Resources Project.* Berkeley, CA: University of California Press.

Cappelli, P. (1992). Examining managerial displacement. *Academy of Management Journal, 35*(1), 203–17.

(1999). *The New Deal at Work: Managing the Market-Based Employment Relationship.* Boston: Harvard Business School Press.

Cappelli, P., Bassi, L., Katz, H., Knoke, D., Osterman, P., and Useem, M. (1997). *Change at Work.* New York: Oxford University Press.

Cappelli, P., and Hamori, M. (2005). The new road to the top. *Harvard Business Review, 83*(1), 25–32.

Chauvin, K. W. (1994). Firm-specific wage growth and changes in the labor market for managers. *Managerial and Decision Economics, 15*(1), 21–37.

Conference Board (1997). *HR Executive Review: Implementing the New Employment Contract*. New York: Conference Board.

Deloitte Research (2006). *It's 2008: Do You Know Where Your Talent Is? Why Acquisition and Retention Strategies Don't Work*. New York: Deloitte Research. Available at: www.deloitte.com/dtt/research/ 0,1015,sid%3D57843&cid%3D71444,00.html.

Dertouzos, M. L., Lester, R. K., and Solow, R. M. 1989. *Made in America: Regaining the Productive Edge*. Cambridge, MA: MIT Press.

Dill, W. R., Gaver, W. P., and Weber, W. L. (1966). Models and modeling for manpower planning. *Management Science, 13*(4), B142–B167.

Employee Benefit Research Institute (2005). *EBRI Data Book on Employee Benefits*. Available at: www.ebri.org/pdf/publications/books/databook/ DB.Chapter%2010.pdf.

Fallick, B. C., and Fleishman, C. A. (2002). *Employer-to-Employer Flows in the US Labor Market*. Working paper. Washington, DC: Federal Reserve Board.

Farber, H. S. (1997). *The changing face of job loss in the United States, 1981–1995*. Working Paper no. 382. Princeton, NJ: Princeton University, Industrial Relations Section.

(1998). *Has the Rate of Job Loss Increased in the Nineties?* Working Paper no. 394. Princeton, NJ: Princeton University, Industrial Relations Section.

(2003). *Job Loss in the United States 1981–2001*. Working paper no. 9707. Cambridge, MA: National Bureau of Economic Research.

Gottschalk, P., and Moffitt, R. (1994). Welfare dependence: concepts, measures, and trends. *American Economic Review, 84*(2), 38–42.

Hipple, S. (2001). Contingent work. *Monthly Labor Review, 124*(3), 3–27.

Hollister, M. (2006). *Occupational Stability in a Changing Economy*. Working paper. Hanover, NH: Dartmouth College, Department of Sociology.

Ippolito, R. A. (1995). Toward explaining the growth of defined contribution plans. *Industrial Relations, 34*(1), 1–20.

Kamourov, G., and Manovskii, I. (2004). *Rising Occupational and Industry Mobility in the U.S.: 1968–1993*. Working paper. Philadelphia: University of Pennsylvania, Institute for Economic Research.

Khurana, R. (2002). *Searching for a Corporate Savior: The Irrational Quest for Charismatic CEOs*. Princeton, NJ: Princeton University Press.

Kuhn, P., and Skuterud, M. (2000). Job search methods: Internet versus traditional. *Monthly Labor Review, 123*(10), 3–11.

Leicht, K. T., and Fennell, M. L. (1997). The changing organizational context of professional work. *Annual Review of Sociology, 23*, 215–31.

Lucier, C., Kocourek, P., and Habbel, R. (2006). CEO succession 2005: the crest of the wave. *Strategy and Business*, summer, online edition. Available at: www.strategy-business.com/search/archives/?pg =2.

Marcotte, D. (1994). *Evidence of a Fall in the Wage Premium for Job Security*. Working paper. DeKalb, IL: Northern Illinois University, Center for Governmental Studies.

Monthly Labor Review (2000a). Median tenure little changed in recent years. *Monthly Labor Review*, the Editor's Desk, 30 August. Available at: www.bls.gov/opub/ted/2000/aug/wk4/art03.htm.

(2000b) Median tenure declines among older men. *Monthly Labor Review*, the Editor's Desk, 1 September. Available at: www.bls.gov/opub/ted/2000/aug/wk4/art05.htm.

(2004). Displacement rates and occupations. *Monthly Labor Review*, the Editor's Desk, 14 July. Available at: www.bls.gov/opub/ted/2004/jul/wk2/art03.htm.

(2005a). Independent contractors in 2005. *Monthly Labor Review*, the Editor's Desk, 29 July. Available at: www.bls.gov/opub/ted/2005/jul/wk4/art05.htm.

(2005b). Job search via the Internet. *Monthly Labor* Review, the Editor's Desk, 5 August. Available at: www.bls.gov/opub/ted/2005/aug/wk1/art05.htm.

Murphy, K. J., and Zábojník, J. (2004). CEO pay and appointments: a market-based explanation for recent trends. *American Economic Review*, 94(2), 192–6.

Neumark, D. (ed.) (2000). *On the Job: Is Long-Term Employment a Thing of the Past?* New York: Russell Sage Foundation.

Neumark, D., Polsky, D., and Hansen, D. (1999). Has job stability declined yet? New evidence for the 1990s. *Journal of Labor Economics*, 17(4), Part 2, S29–S64.

Ocasio, W. (1999). Institutionalized action and corporate governance: the reliance on rules of CEO succession. *Administrative Science Quarterly*, 44(2), 384–416.

Pearson, A. E. (1966). Sales power through planned careers. *Harvard Business Review*, 44(1), 105–16.

Polsky, D. (1999). Changing consequences of job separation in the United States. *Industrial and Labor Relations Review*, 52(4), 565–80.

Rajan, R., and Wulf, J. (2006). The flattening firm: evidence on the changing nature of firm hierarchies from panel data. *Review of Economics and Statistics*, 88(4), 759–73.

Rowland, K. M., and Sovereign, M. G. (1969). Markov-chain analysis of internal manpower supply. *Industrial Relations*, 9, 88–9.

Ruhm, C. J. (1995). Secular changes in the work and retirement patterns of older men. *Journal of Human Resources*, 30(2), 362–85.

Rynes, S. L., Orlitzky, M. O., and Bretz, R., Jr. (1997). Experienced hiring versus college recruiting: practices and emerging trends. *Personnel Psychology*, 50(2), 309–39.

Staffing Industry Analysts (2004). *Staffing Industry Report 2004*. Los Altos, CA: Staffing Industry Analysts. Available at www.staffingindustry.com/issues/sireport.

Stevens, A. H. (2001). Changes in earnings instability and job loss. *Industrial and Labor Relations Review*, 55(1), 60–78.

US Bureau of Labor Statistics (2004). *Number of Jobs Held, Labor Market Activity, and Earnings Growth among Younger Baby Boomers: Recent Results from a Longitudinal Survey*. Washington, DC: Government Printing Office.

(2006). *Employee Tenure*. News release, 8 September. Washington, DC: US Bureau of Labor Statistics.

Valetta, R. G. (1996). *Has Job Security in the U.S. Declined?* Weekly Letter 96–07. San Francisco: Federal Reserve Bank of San Francisco.

Walker, J. W. (1970). Manpower planning: an integrative approach. *Management of Personnel Quarterly*, 9(1), 38–47.

Wellington, A. J. (1993). Changes in the male/female wage gap 1976–85. *Journal of Human Resources*, 28(2), 383–411.

White, H. C. (1970). *Chains of Opportunity: System Models of Mobility in Organizations*. Cambridge, MA: Harvard University Press.

Wilk, S. L., and Craig, E. A. (1998). *Should I Stay or Should I Go? Occupational Matching and Internal and External Mobility*. Working paper. Philadelphia: University of Pennsylvania, Wharton School, Department of Management.

2 | Corporate restructuring and the employment relationship

JOHN C. DENCKER

Introduction

Widespread corporate restructuring has transformed employment rela-tionships in numerous lasting ways in recent decades, as the process of corporate reduction in force (RIF) ended the careers of many employees and corporate reorganization changed the way managers are evaluated and rewarded (see Cappelli *et al.*, 1997).[1] Scholarly interest in under-standing this transformation process has led to the creation of a wealth of knowledge on employment change from a number of academic disciplines. Economists have analyzed changes in tenure with a firm along age, sex, occupation, and industry lines, showing that – in stark contrast to previous temporary layoffs, which tended to be limited to blue-collar employees – terminations during RIF are now permanent and disproportionately affect previously protected groups such as middle-aged managers in manufacturing firms (Baumol, Blinder, and Wolff, 2003). Psychologists have studied the negative effects of restruc-turing on employees who remain in restructured firms, demonstrating that survivors of RIF often responded with reduced morale and work effort (Brockner *et al.*, 1992). Further, sociologists have examined broad patterns of career mobility, finding that restructuring spurred

I thank Peter Cappelli, Lynn Selhat, and an anonymous reviewer for their valuable comments. This chapter incorporates material from manuscripts derived from my dissertation research (Dencker, 2005, 2006, forthcoming).

[1] I consider corporate restructuring to include (1) planned reductions in force by firms (i.e. large-scale layoffs) and (2) corporate reorganization of a firm's practices, policies, systems, and structures (e.g. performance management transformation). In this chapter I examine these two restructuring components separately, on account of their potentially contrasting effects on the employment relationship. In doing so, I seek to avoid ambiguity stemming from different usages of terms such as "downsizing," which in the 1980s referred largely to layoffs, whereas in recent years it often represents a catch-all term for many types of corporate change.

the movement of employees across organizations and industries (DiPrete, 1993).

Despite the clear effects of restructuring on the employment relationship, our understanding of the upward career mobility patterns of managers in restructured firms is surprisingly limited. Theory in this regard is mixed: organizational demography accounts indicate that restructuring will reduce upward mobility for surviving managers – as RIF limits employment growth and thus lowers promotion rates (see Stewman, 1988) – whereas vacancy chain approaches (see White, 1970) suggest that employment separations during RIF may create promotion opportunities for surviving employees. In both accounts, promotion rates for the survivors of a RIF (i.e. managers remaining in the firm after a RIF) are a function of the employment separation rates in a given job level during that RIF. More specifically, promotion rates for survivors will be reduced if jobs are eliminated during RIF – e.g. by replacing promotion-based incentives with non-recurring bonuses (Baker, 1990) – yet they may be increased if RIFs create job vacancies to be filled by surviving employees.

Due in large part to a lack of information on the effects of job structures on employment outcomes during corporate restructuring, we know little about how employment separation influences the mobility of RIF survivors. For example, studies of employment separation tend to consider jobs in broad terms, such as occupations, and provide little evidence that would distinguish among different hierarchical job levels. Even less evidence is available to understand promotion patterns in restructuring firms, with findings indicating that theory in this regard is incomplete, as managers in a large financial firm who received bonuses were also the most likely to be promoted (Elvira, 2001), thus countering claims of a tradeoff between the two types of rewards. In effect, a complete understanding of the career mobility patterns among survivors of restructuring requires knowledge not only of promotion rates within different job levels in corporate hierarchies but also of separation rates within these levels during restructuring.

My research (Dencker, 2005, 2006, forthcoming) seeks to answer two linked questions about the effect of corporate restructuring on the employment relationship. First, which employees, in which job levels, do firms lay off? Second, what effect does restructuring have on the promotion rates of surviving employees in these job levels? Answers to these questions are important for increasing our understanding of contemporary employment relationships in today's firms, since restructuring continues to be a common feature of large firms. Moreover, these answers can shed light on important issues related to the transition from structured to market-based employment relationships, such as whether this process was efficient (see Cappelli *et al.*, 1997, and Sørensen, 1996).

I seek to answer the research questions that I pose by analyzing employment separations and promotions using longitudinal personnel files of managers in a Fortune 100 US manufacturing firm that engaged in multiple restructurings in the 1980s and early 1990s. Due to the need to assess separation and promotion rates across hierarchical job levels, perhaps the most important source of data is personnel files of firms that restructure. For instance, data from the firm I study allows a unique examination of temporal aspects of careers during periods of restructuring relative to prior periods of stability and growth.

My analyses of separation and promotion rates among managers in the firm show that institutional features of firms such as job structures continue to buffer *certain* managers from market forces, albeit in varying ways over time. Specifically, I find that, during RIF, involuntary departures were restricted to entry-level and middle managers, with upper-level managers departing for reasons of early retirement. In addition, I find that, surprisingly, restructuring increased the promotion rates of surviving upper-level managers substantially – particularly for women managers – while at the same time it reduced significantly the promotion likelihood of entry-level and middle managers. Nevertheless, consistent with much of the literature (Cappelli *et al.*, 1997, and Sørensen, 1996), my findings reveal a trend toward more market-based employment relationships between employees and firms, as previous lifetime employment arrangements have been replaced with employment-at-will contracts. In effect, the "closed" employment systems found in bureaucratic firms after World War II have become more "open" to market forces in a number of ways.

In this chapter, I provide a brief overview of what is known about managerial employment relationships in large firms from the post-WWII period to the present. I then present results from analyses of careers of managers in the manufacturing firm from the 1960s to the 1990s – specifically looking at which managers were laid off, as well as the promotion rates among survivors of restructuring. I conclude by discussing the implications of my findings for twenty-first-century employment models.

The employment relationship in historical context

Employment relationships in large bureaucratic firms in the post-WWII period were highly structured, with institutions such as internal labor markets (ILMs) protecting employees from the vicissitudes of the market (Osterman, 1999). Jobs in ILMs were stable, existing independently of the employees occupying them (White, 1970) and becoming vacant when an incumbent departed the position for a better option or because of retirement. These vacancies were often filled by promoting managers into them from lower-level positions, thus creating a chain of vacancies in hierarchical job ladders. Seniority was an important factor in these promotion decisions, as was a manager's performance relative to other managers.

Managerial careers in the context of corporate restructuring

Norms governing the employment relationship shifted in the early 1980s, due to corporate restructuring. Research on employee tenure patterns using national sample surveys revealed that, in effect, educated, managerial employees who were protected from job displacement in large bureaucratic firms in the post-WWII period experienced an increased likelihood of employment separation from the early 1980s to the early 1990s (Farber, 1998). This was seen, for instance, in work by Cappelli (1992), who finds that managers were disproportionately vulnerable to displacement in the mid-1980s compared to other groups of employees. In addition, Robert Valletta (1998) finds that the probability of dismissal increased over time, particularly for higher-tenure employees, and Kletzer (1998) demonstrates that job displacement rates for employees with college degrees were higher in the 1990s than in the 1980s. Other researchers have used data from firms to document changes in tenure patterns by age groups. Steven Allen, Robert Clark, and Sylvester Schieber (1999) find that mid-career employees were not singled out in RIF decisions as older employees accepted early retirement benefits and younger employees tended to be laid off.

In sum, researchers have generated a wealth of information on the effects of corporate restructuring in terms of RIFs on the employment relationship in respect of length of service and turnover. They have also demonstrated that restructuring in the form of corporate reorganization decentralized decision-making authority and reengineered business processes (Useem and Cappelli, 1997), for example by transforming pay and performance management systems, practices, and policies. Little is known, however, about the effects of these reorganization efforts on the careers of surviving employees.

The study

The firm I have studied was a large, diversified, multidivisional manufacturing firm with global operations. Its corporate office was responsible for strategic planning and corporate activities and its semi-autonomous operating companies were responsible for their own strategic, operating, financial, and human resource decisions and results.

The firm undertook two RIFs, one in the mid-1980s and the other in the early 1990s. The RIF process was decentralized, giving business unit managers some autonomy over who was to be terminated. During the first RIF, broad guidelines about layoff targets were delegated to each division, with decisions about who to terminate being made by senior managers in these divisions. During the second RIF, cutbacks were uniform across the firm, with strategic objectives for all divisions established in committees of senior managers.

Internal documents from the firm identify two main stages. In the first stage, the firm enticed employees to retire or sever voluntarily. In the second stage, the firm undertook layoffs. Early retirement eligibility was fifty years of age and fifteen years of service with the firm. Monetary benefits ranged from nine weeks of pay for employees with one year of tenure in the firm to seventy-one and a half weeks of pay for employees with more than thirty-five years of tenure. Severance benefits were less generous than retirement benefits (e.g. retiring employees obtained pensions). Moreover, severance benefits were withheld if the employee did not sign a termination agreement, which included a provision that prohibited employees from pursuing claims against the corporation.

In the interim between the two RIFs, the firm overhauled its performance management system. Like other large firms, the firm relied on consultants to help transform its performance management system, and sent senior managers to other large firms to assess potential performance management systems. During the process, the firm transitioned from a seniority-based appraisal and reward system to one in which pay was more dependent on a manager's performance relative to other similarly situated managers. As part of this shift, managers were encouraged to become more involved in performance management. The firm required managers to negotiate performance expectations and goals with subordinates early in the performance cycle (year), and to provide feedback to subordinates about their progress in meeting the expectations and goals throughout the cycle, ending with the communication of detailed information on performance ratings to the subordinates. In order to help ensure consistent implementation of the changes, all managers were required to undergo training.

The firm sought to make performance objectives measurable, attainable, and relevant, and also to increase formalization of the new performance management system, and to enforce consistent ratings standards across employees. For instance, supervisors who managed similar groups of subordinates were required to use formal rules to facilitate comparisons.

Data and methods

Data set

The data set analyzed in this chapter comes from a 25 percent random sample of managers in the firm.[2] These records were largely complete, albeit with missing information on education and performance. The final sample size was 7,586 managers in salary grade levels 7 to 24.[3] The grade-level structure in the firm was a system of interrelated jobs hierarchically ranked into grades, each with a specific salary range. Jobs were defined according to the value of the work performed by the employee within them. Naturally, the more valuable jobs were placed into higher grade levels. HR managed the job valuation, with each job's content systematically assessed along the skill, knowledge, and other dimensions that were required to perform the tasks associated with the job. Following this appraisal, the job was formally related to other jobs

---

[2] My research focuses on managers, as much of the available evidence on RIF and promotion relates to them.
[3] Managers such as the CEOs and senior VPs were considered to be above grade.

in the company, and arranged in the grade-level structure based on its value.

Variables

Dependent variables

I examine effects of corporate restructuring on employment relationships using two main dependent variables: (1) employment separation (coded 1 if a manager left the firm in a given year, and 0 otherwise), as well as at a more refined level in terms of (a) retirements, (b) resignations, and (c) layoffs, discharges, and termination for other reasons; and (2) promotion from a lower- to a higher-graded job (coded 1 if a manager was promoted in a given year, and 0 otherwise). Promotions were clearly defined by the firm to involve an increase in a salary grade level.

Independent variables

I examine a number of different independent variables. I consider employment relationships across three broad time periods – 1967 to 1974, 1975 to 1983, and 1984 to 1993 – and control for year dummies for the period 1967 to 1993. The three different historical periods are roughly equal in length, and provide contrasts in employment outcomes in periods of stability, growth, and decline. The year dummies allow me to assess the effects of specific restructuring periods on career outcomes. As I discuss below, I constructed a yearly discrete-time event history data set to analyze the effects of restructuring on careers. Since the multiple restructuring episodes from the firm all occurred within a calendar year, the year dummies provide a sense of whether departure and promotion rates increased or decreased during corporate restructuring. Using broad time frames allows me to assess whether careers during the overall process of restructuring – which occurred in the 1984 to 1993 time frame – were different from those during periods of relative stability (1967–74) and relative growth (1975–83). I expect that employment separation rates will be highest in the restructuring period, and during each RIF year relative to other periods and years. Based on the organizational demography literature (see Stewman, 1988), I expect that promotion rates will be highest during the growth period (1975–83), and lowest during the restructuring period (1984–93). In addition, promotion rates within the restructuring period should be relatively lower during years of RIF and reorganization.

The main job variable is the salary grade level, ranging from levels 7 to 24.[4] I grouped levels that were similar on many dimensions into four categories: entry levels (levels 7, 8, and 9), middle managers in levels 10, 11, and 12, upper middle managers in levels 13, 14, 15, and 16, and senior managers (levels 17 to 24).[5] In terms of employment separations, media and other accounts suggest that middle managers are at the greatest risk of leaving a firm during RIFs, although it is likely that all levels will experience an increased risk of departure during this period. Therefore, in terms of career mobility, I predict that the likelihood of promotion will decrease as grade level increases (see Petersen and Saporta, 2004), and decline for all levels following RIF and reorganization. This decrease will be particular evidence in salary grade levels that had experienced high rates of layoff during corporate restructuring – that is, the higher the employment separation rate in a given level during a RIF the lower the promotion rate of the surviving employees in that level subsequently.

To uncover the effects of job structures on separation and promotion chances during periods of corporate restructuring, I analyze salary grade-level factors such as the duration a manager has spent in a job, and his/her year-end salary as a percentage of the maximum salary of managers in a level.[6] In general, it is expected that separation rates will be a decreasing function of time spent in a job level and salary in range percentile. During a RIF, an efficient (i.e. non-redistributive) layoff policy would involve terminating the lowest-paid and least productive managers, namely those who spent the longest time in a grade level (see Gibbs, 1995).[7] In terms of career mobility, promotion rates in general

---

[4] Career progression through this system involved moving through a number of related jobs. For instance, a manager hired into salary grade level 9 had the job title of economic analyst, and then progressed through the following jobs during his career: senior economic analyst (level 10), staff economic analyst (level 11), senior staff economist (level 12), senior staff financial analyst (level 12), staff director (level 13), senior staff director (level 14), senior staff special economist (level 14), manager of project evaluations (level 15), senior financial manager (level 16), manager financial services and administration (level 16). As this career progression shows, a promotion entailed a change in job title, but a change in job title need not involve a promotion.

[5] The grade level groupings were based on an inspection of the data and discussions with HR managers in the firm.

[6] Wages were converted into 1993 dollars to allow comparison across years.

[7] As part of the change in the performance management system, the firm eliminated managerial performance evaluations. According to the firm, this

should decrease with time spent in a grade level (see Gibbs, 1995), and increase in increasing salary in range percentile (see Elvira, 2001). Following a RIF, promotion rates will be lowest in job levels that experienced the highest separation rates during the RIF, conditional on whether firms eliminated jobs.

I also consider differences in separation and promotion by gender. In terms of RIF, legal considerations may limit any gender differences in employment separations. Expectations with respect to promotion are less clear. Although women have experienced a relative advantage in promotion in increasing job level (see Petersen and Saporta, 2004), scholars have argued that RIF and reorganization have had a negative effect on women's promotion likelihood (see Reskin and Padavic, 1994).

Control variables
Control variables include race, age, tenure, and the division of the firm. The age and tenure variables are time-varying and updated in each year.

Methods

I use discrete-time event history methods (Allison, 1982; Yamaguchi, 1991) to analyze separation and promotion. Discrete-time event history analysis accounts for censoring (i.e. the truncation of an episode due to the ending of the observation period) and changes in independent variables over time (Allison, 1984). These benefits are important, as (1) excluding censored observations can lead to large biases in estimates (Sørensen, 1977), and (2) ad hoc attempts at adding time-varying explanatory variables often make those variables endogenous (Flinn and Heckman, 1980). Each employee's tenure is split into yearly episodes, with managers beginning their career prior to 1967

decision was enacted in order to minimize potential bias, in that supervisors would be precluded from using prior performance when measuring current performance. By eliminating past ratings, the firm sought to remove the problems of labeling employees. In short, "relative performance was not fixed, and an employee's relative position had to be 're-earned' each year." I thus use duration in grade as a proxy for performance, arguing, for instance, that performance is lowest for employees with the most experience in a level due to the disincentives from low promotion prospects (Gibbs, 1995).

contributing only those person-years for which full career information is available. In effect I analyze the entire careers of managers who entered the firm from 1967 to 1993, and evaluate only a portion of the careers in this period for managers who entered the firm in previous periods (see Guo, 1993). If the time of censoring is independent of the hazard for event occurrence, one can define the discrete-time hazard rate as follows (Allison, 1982):

$$P_{it} = Pr\ [T_i = t \mid T_i > / = t, x_{it}] \tag{1}$$

In equation (1), T is the discrete random variable that provides the uncensored time of event occurrence. This hazard rate is the conditional probability that an event occurred at time t, given that it had not yet occurred, and can be estimated using common maximum likelihood methods such as logit models (Allison, 1982, p. 72). Logit coefficients are provided in other forums (Dencker, 2005, 2006, forthcoming). In this chapter, I provide predicted probabilities using the Clarify program (King, Tomz, and Wittenberg, 2000; Tomz, Wittenberg, and King, 2003).

Results

Descriptive statistics

The descriptive statistics in table 2.1 show that the average number of managers in the firm increased throughout the 1970s and early 1980s, before dropping slightly during the restructuring period of the mid-1980s to early 1990s. The slight differences in employment size in the growth period (1975–83) relative to the restructuring period (1984–93) mask large intra-period differences, however. For instance, the size of the workforce varied substantially within the restructuring period, as the firm underwent periods of large-scale layoffs, which were often followed by increased hiring rates.

Table 2.1 also shows that the average tenure and age of managers in periods of restructuring was not significantly lower than in other time periods, with departure rates only two percentage points higher during this period than during the growth period of 1975 to 1983. Nevertheless, other career outcomes changed significantly in the restructuring period. For instance, promotion rates declined substantially in the restructuring period relative to the prior growth period, although they did remain

Table 2.1 *Descriptive statistics, 1967–93*

	1967–93		1967–74		1975–83		1984–93	
Managerial workforce size								
Yearly average	3,038		2,535		3,262		3,239	
Maximum N in a year	3,711		2,720		3,711		3,434	
Minimum N in a year	2,183		2,183		2,821		2,965	
Variable means								
Tenure	14.08	(10.42)	14.84	(10.15)	14.44	(11.15)	13.30	(9.84)
Age	40.39	(10.79)	40.79	(10.38)	40.65	(11.56)	39.91	(10.30)
Duration in grade level	4.81	(4.37)	5.26	(3.83)	4.84	(4.79)	4.51	(4.25)
Employment separation (=1)	0.06	(0.24)	0.03	(0.18)	0.06	(0.24)	0.08	(0.27)
Starting salary grade level	8.33	(1.76)	8.59	(1.86)	8.10	(1.55)	8.47	(1.83)
Promotion (=1)	0.17	(0.38)	0.14	(0.35)	0.20	(0.40)	0.16	(0.37)
Year-end salary	$64,785	($27,259)	$58,837	($23,611)	$64,398	($26,193)	$68,182	($29,320)

Note: Standard deviations are in parentheses. Year-end salary is measured in 1993 constant dollars. Starting salary grade level ranged from level 7 to level 23.

Table 2.2 *Distribution of managers in organizational and demographic groups in selected time periods, 1967–93*

	1967–93	1967–74	1975–83	1984–93
Salary grade levels				
Levels 7–9	43.45	51.42	45.29	36.79
Levels 10–12	38.79	36.10	37.87	41.31
Levels 13–16	15.49	10.44	14.63	19.44
Levels 17–24	2.27	2.04	2.21	2.46
Divisions of the firm				
Corporate office	20.94	7.53	21.01	29.27
Production no. 1	28.67	46.17	26.33	19.82
Production no. 2	29.28	29.14	29.17	28.98
Production no. 3	15.77	10.93	15.70	18.85
Tertiary	5.35	6.23	7.25	3.07
Demographic				
Proportion male	87.09	96.67	89.02	79.34
Proportion white	92.47	96.24	93.41	89.25

above the average for the 1967 to 1993 time frame. In addition, year-end salaries increased throughout the restructuring period.

Table 2.2 reveals extensive changes in the managerial labor force from the 1960s to the 1990s. For instance, there was a strong continuous increase in the proportion of managers in the firm's main corporate office over time, an outcome that goes against the idea that firms were decentralizing in the 1980s and 1990s. In addition, the representation of both women and minorities in management increased over time. Somewhat surprisingly, table 2.2 shows that the proportion of managers in entry salary grade levels decreased substantially during restructuring, whereas the proportion of managers in middle management levels increased over time. This result runs somewhat counter to the conventional wisdom that middle managers bore the brunt of RIF, although it does support Allen and colleagues' (1999) finding that the most junior employees bore the brunt of RIF initiatives. In part, the growth in the proportion of middle managers in the firm during the restructuring period reflects an increase in hiring managers into above-entry-level positions, and a possible decrease in hiring rates in entry-level positions relative to prior periods.

Table 2.3 indicates that the growth in middle management ranks during restructuring may trace to the higher rates of employment separation among entry-level managers relative to managers in middle and upper job levels. Moreover, these entry-level employment separation rates stemmed from two factors: the departure of recently hired employees, and efforts by the firm to lay off managers in positions in which gluts of employees had formed because of barriers to upward mobility, such as for salary grade level 9.[8]

Table 2.3 shows that, as expected, tenure was an increasing function of job level, ranging from ten years in entry-level jobs to nearly twenty-five years in upper management levels. In addition, it suggests that the negative influence of restructuring on tenure was restricted to entry and middle management levels, as upper-level managers experienced little change in tenure during restructuring periods. This finding is somewhat striking, particularly given the use of early retirement policies by the firm and the lack of terminations among these managers during RIF periods. What this pattern indicates is that less senior upper-level managers may have departed the firm at a somewhat higher rate during the restructuring process, perhaps because they sought more stable employment in other firms, and had abilities and skills that were in high demand, whereas employees with mean levels of experience were likely to remain in their jobs.

Finally, the results in table 2.3 indicate that the rate of promotion declined in most salary grade levels during restructuring periods, with the main exception of the upper-level management group. As is shown below, this outcome stems in part from increased rates of promotion during RIFs and reorganization, and of high rates of promotion for female managers in upper levels. Overall, the descriptive statistics reveal that corporate restructuring altered several important career outcomes. They also indicate that the extent of change in the employment relationship depends on the job and demographic group to which a manager belonged.

Employment separation rates

Table 2.4 examines baseline rates of employment separation in different periods. Findings indicate that separation rates for the average

---

[8] Managers in jobs in level 9 normally had to demonstrate an ability to handle tasks required in middle management jobs (levels 10–12). If unable to do so, they would be trapped at that level for the rest of their careers with the firm.

Table 2.3 *Descriptive statistics for salary grade level groups over time, 1967–93*

	1967–93		1967–74		1975–83		1984–93	
Salary grade levels 7 to 9								
Tenure	10.62	(9.85)	12.64	(10.08)	10.53	(10.25)	8.95	(8.81)
Age	36.06	(10.91)	38.11	(10.90)	35.86	(11.45)	34.48	(9.99)
Duration in grade	4.42	(4.31)	4.94	(3.74)	4.43	(4.71)	3.95	(4.25)
Gender (male = 1)	0.79	(0.41)	0.94	(0.24)	0.80	(0.40)	0.64	(0.48)
Race (white = 1)	0.90	(0.30)	0.95	(0.22)	0.91	(0.29)	0.84	(0.37)
Promote	0.17	(0.38)	0.14	(0.35)	0.21	(0.41)	0.16	(0.37)
Employment separation	0.07	(0.26)	0.04	(0.20)	0.07	(0.26)	0.10	(0.29)
Year-end salary	$44,886	($8,786)	$44,432	($8,124)	$45,910	($9,029)	$44,080	($8,862)
Salary grade levels 10 to 12								
Tenure	15.13	(10.07)	16.09	(9.88)	16.11	(10.94)	13.78	(9.22)
Age	42.14	(9.58)	42.50	(9.17)	43.12	(10.25)	41.14	(9.11)
Duration in grade	4.97	(4.36)	5.40	(3.78)	5.05	(4.78)	4.66	(4.36)
Gender (male = 1)	0.92	(0.27)	0.99	(0.09)	0.95	(0.21)	0.85	(0.35)
Race (white = 1)	0.94	(0.24)	0.98	(0.16)	0.95	(0.23)	0.91	(0.28)
Promote	0.18	(0.38)	0.14	(0.35)	0.21	(0.41)	0.17	(0.38)
Employment separation	0.05	(0.23)	0.03	(0.17)	0.05	(0.22)	0.07	(0.26)
Year-end salary	$66,953	($12,124)	$64,068	($11,736)	$67,508	($11,852)	$67,783	($12,323)
Salary grade levels 13 to 16								
Tenure	19.63	(8.96)	19.78	(8.38)	20.49	(9.59)	18.99	(8.64)
Age	46.64	(8.13)	46.44	(7.66)	47.40	(8.74)	46.19	(7.82)

Duration in grade	5.40	(4.37)	0.07	(4.08)	5.39	(4.83)	5.17	(4.10)
Gender (male = 1)	0.96	(0.19)	1.00	(0.05)	0.99	(0.12)	0.94	(0.24)
Race (white = 1)	0.95	(0.21)	0.97	(0.16)	0.97	(0.18)	0.94	(0.24)
Promote	0.16	(0.37)	0.14	(0.35)	0.19	(0.39)	0.16	(0.36)
Employment separation	0.05	(0.21)	0.01	(0.11)	0.05	(0.21)	0.06	(0.23)
Year-end salary	$100,466	($17,933)	$96,119	($16,631)	$99,696	($18,073)	$102,146	($17,946)

Salary grade levels 17 to 24

Tenure	24.82	(8.56)	22.42	(8.18)	25.93	(8.53)	25.18	(8.56)
Age	50.68	(7.09)	48.83	(6.48)	51.77	(7.35)	50.74	(7.00)
Duration in grade	5.83	(4.85)	6.74	(4.06)	6.22	(5.56)	5.03	(4.49)
Gender (male = 1)	0.99	(0.10)	1	(0)	1	(0)	0.98	(0.14)
Race (white = 1)	0.99	(0.12)	0.98	(0.14)	0.99	(0.10)	0.98	(0.12)
Promote	0.16	(0.37)	0.11	(0.32)	0.17	(0.37)	0.18	(0.38)
Employment separation	0.05	(0.23)	0.01	(0.08)	0.06	(0.23)	0.08	(0.27)
Year-end salary	$157,899	($36,977)	$145,964	($39,436)	$155,092	($32,852)	$162,254	($37,481)

Note: Standard deviations are in parentheses. Year-end salary is measured in 1993 constant dollars.

Table 2.4 *Baseline departure rates of managers in a large manufacturing firm for selected variables in selected time periods, 1967–93*

	1967–93	1967–74	1975–83	1984–93	RIF no. 1	RIF no. 2
All managers	6.07	3.37	6.05	7.79	11.87	13.65
Grade levels 7–9	7.10	4.28	7.06	9.62	12.64	14.74
Grade levels 10–12	5.49	2.83	5.34	7.08	11.51	13.09
Grade levels 13–16	4.74	1.32	4.77	5.86	11.44	12.55
Grade levels 17–24	5.43	0.72	5.70	7.66	9.88	16.67
Tenure = 1 year	5.04	2.22	4.52	7.16	10.91	5.33
Tenure = 2 years	7.33	4.06	7.57	8.93	10.88	11.43
Tenure = 3–5 years	8.96	6.11	9.06	10.54	13.40	15.53
Tenure = 6–9 years	6.19	4.26	5.24	7.88	13.23	10.72
Tenure = 10–14 years	3.57	2.66	3.78	3.78	2.48	7.64
Tenure = 15–24 years	2.67	1.07	2.93	3.80	4.67	8.92
Tenure = 25+ years	10.24	4.98	8.78	16.39	28.60	31.66
Age < 25 years	7.41	3.66	7.01	10.58	13.40	17.73
Age = 25–29 years	8.38	6.18	8.12	10.00	14.13	11.78
Age = 30–34 years	5.58	4.43	5.61	6.13	8.65	10.60
Age = 35–39 years	4.11	2.32	4.06	5.01	6.83	7.92
Age = 40–44 years	3.02	1.60	3.09	3.95	5.62	6.90
Age = 45–49 years	2.33	1.10	2.75	3.05	3.70	5.72
Age = 50–54 years	2.54	1.00	1.90	4.49	3.48	14.10
Age = 55–59 years	10.05	2.67	7.34	17.78	33.11	39.15
Age = 60+ years	30.07	21.04	26.99	39.81	52.46	71.43
Duration < 3 years	4.30	2.60	4.80	4.64	7.08	6.42
Duration 3–5 years	7.24	4.48	6.55	9.11	13.73	14.53
Duration 6–9 years	5.55	1.85	5.86	8.94	15.22	16.10
Duration 10–14 years	6.51	3.73	5.71	11.39	13.00	26.81
Duration 15+ years	15.70	23.44	12.92	18.54	27.59	39.37
Salary < 25th percentile	7.12	4.61	7.49	8.36	7.93	15.05
Salary 25th–49th percentile	6.12	4.53	6.16	7.24	11.61	10.03
Salary 50th–74th percentile	5.79	3.49	5.60	7.09	13.30	14.19
Salary > 74th percentile	5.41	1.36	7.24	8.32	13.36	14.60
Gender = female	7.00	2.22	5.93	7.99	9.60	12.68
Gender = male	5.94	3.41	6.06	7.74	12.13	13.97
Race = minority	6.34	3.01	5.84	7.35	5.81	13.94
Race = white	6.05	3.39	6.06	7.85	12.40	13.61

Note: Rates reflect yearly average likelihood of departures of managers for any reason (e.g. retirement, resignation, and termination).

manager were twice as large in each RIF episode as they were in all years of the sample. During the first RIF managers were roughly 50 percent more likely to leave due to retirement than to layoff (with resignation rates similar to layoff rates). During the second RIF managers were twice as likely to retire as they were to resign, and 50 percent more likely to be laid off than to resign. Moreover, the effect of RIF on the employment relationship was extensive, with nearly every managerial group experiencing an increased likelihood of separation in those years, although there was variation in the magnitude of the increase across groups. For instance, whereas managers aged fifty-five to fifty-nine years were four times more likely to depart during RIF than in the 1975 to 1983 period, managers between the ages thirty to forty-nine experienced only a slight increase across the same time frame.

Table 2.4 also shows that employment separation rates during RIF were an increasing function of time spent in a grade level. Moreover, separation rates were an increasing function of salary in a range percentile, the exception being high departure rates in the first salary quartile (< 25th percentile) during the second RIF. In addition, although both men and women experienced a significant increase in separation rates during the restructuring period, men were more likely to depart the firm during RIF than were women.

Table 2.5 provides results from discrete-time event history analyses of employment separation taken from Dencker (2006). Four periods are considered: all years, the restructuring period from 1984 to 1993, and the two RIF episodes in the firm. Results are presented separately for each of three main duration measures – tenure, duration in grade level, and age. Each duration measure was analyzed with all control measures (e.g. division of the firm) included in the models, but with the two other duration measures excluded from the models.[9]

---

[9] As a result of high correlation levels among the duration variables, it is difficult to analyze the effects of one when all three are included in a regression model. Nonetheless, all three variables provide important evidence on the nature of restructuring on employment relationships in terms of which managers depart firms and how. Research on tenure patterns reveals how stable and secure a job is, and research on age patterns reveals the extent to which firms use early retirement programs to overcome limits of legislation, such as the Age Discrimination in Employment Act.

Table 2.5 *Event history analyses predicting employment separation rates by type of separation for tenure, age, and duration categories in selected time periods, 1967–93*

	1967–93				1984–93				RIF no. 1				RIF no. 2			
	(1)	(2)	(3)	(4)	(1)	(2)	(3)	(4)	(1)	(2)	(3)	(4)	(1)	(2)	(3)	(4)
Tenure																
5th percentile	5.58	0.01	4.90	0.25	6.72	0.02	4.74	0.77	10.04	0.25	7.78	1.48	13.07	0.19	5.48	6.51
25th percentile	6.53	0.04	5.13	0.40	7.11	0.05	5.26	1.24	9.80	0.09	4.72	3.17	9.84	0.28	3.84	5.46
50th percentile	3.81	0.20	2.68	0.42	4.44	0.18	2.11	1.29	5.36	0.33	2.50	1.57	7.13	0.84	1.65	3.61
75th percentile	2.62	1.18	0.49	0.17	3.10	1.19	0.58	0.59	3.20	1.45	0.79	0.29	9.19	3.70	0.63	2.25
95th percentile	14.77	12.28	0.13	0.07	20.69	15.61	0.11	0.23	45.25	36.93	0.14	0.48	37.09	36.57	0.15	1.11
Duration in grade																
5th percentile	2.86	0.15	1.69	0.07	3.19	0.18	1.67	0.19	4.37	0.31	2.46	0.21	4.56	0.86	1.15	0.90
25th percentile	4.36	0.31	3.09	0.19	4.75	0.36	2.72	0.56	6.21	0.54	2.99	0.91	7.08	1.23	2.30	2.39
50th percentile	5.77	0.54	4.09	0.36	6.38	0.64	3.43	1.08	8.36	0.89	3.41	2.02	9.99	1.72	2.91	4.28
75th percentile	7.71	1.98	2.28	0.46	10.01	2.12	2.70	1.64	15.32	3.05	3.36	2.03	18.29	4.28	2.42	5.98
95th percentile	8.42	4.92	0.81	0.48	11.50	5.66	0.76	1.22	23.81	13.84	0.30	1.52	29.17	18.50	0.18	6.05
Age																
5th percentile	6.45	0.02	5.12	0.18	7.19	0.04	5.07	0.65	11.38	0.06	6.92	1.16	10.25	0.29	6.07	3.16
25th percentile	5.52	0.01	4.32	0.26	5.30	0.01	3.40	0.87	5.74	0.01	3.41	1.54	7.57	0.03	3.15	4.01
50th percentile	3.13	0.02	2.57	0.35	3.42	0.01	2.26	1.02	3.79	0.01	2.39	1.81	6.42	0.06	1.92	4.29
75th percentile	2.92	0.32	1.12	0.34	4.05	0.30	1.34	1.04	6.75	0.02	1.19	1.36	9.25	1.49	0.92	3.86
90th percentile	7.68	4.39	0.68	0.26	11.23	5.75	0.89	0.91	24.89	12.86	0.68	0.73	22.42	17.27	0.57	1.18
95th percentile	15.41	12.45	0.59	0.22	20.90	16.09	0.74	0.82	42.63	34.62	0.80	0.54	48.34	47.81	0.41	1.67
99th percentile	42.47	36.50	0.53	0.17	54.76	44.05	0.55	0.67	72.62	60.86	2.17	0.36	88.45	74.11	0.28	1.07

Note: Model (1) provides predicted probabilities of all departures, model (2) provides predicted probabilities of resignation, and model (3) provides predicted probabilities of retirement, model (4) provides predicted probabilities of involuntary termination (e.g. layoff). Each model includes only the duration measure of interest, along with controls for salary grade levels, salary in range, gender, race, and the division of the firm. Year dummies were included in non-RIF analyses. Predicted probabilities were generated from logit coefficients reported in Dencker (2006) using the statistical program Clarify (King, Tomz, and Wittenberg, 2000; Tomz, Wittenberg, and King, 2003), with other variables set to mean levels.

Duration measures

Results with respect to the three duration measures indicate that separation rates in all the years of the sample were generally higher in the tails of the age and tenure distributions, and typically an increasing function of duration in a salary grade level. During the restructuring period the pattern of employment separation was similar to other periods, but rates of separation were much higher in this time frame, and were increasing across RIF episodes. In table 2.6 I extend the separation analyses to include age and duration in grade measures in the models (the findings were roughly similar when age was replaced with the tenure measure). The results demonstrate the importance of age in employment separation outcomes, particularly with respect to retirement patterns.

Type of employment separation

In terms of employment separation by type (e.g. layoff, retirement), the results in table 2.5 reveal that, in all years, retirement rates (model 2) were largely an increasing function of duration, and resignation rates (model 3) were a decreasing function of duration. By contrast, layoff rates (model 4) were more varied, and generally much lower than other separation types. In addition, the patterns of retirement and resignation were largely similar across time periods, yet there were noticeable differences in separations resulting from the institution of early retirement programs. For instance, retirement rates for managers of roughly fifty-five years of age (90th age percentile) increased substantially during both RIFs, and increased slightly for managers of roughly fifty years of age (75th age percentile) during the second RIF. Perhaps the biggest change in separation rates in restructuring years relative to other periods was with respect to involuntary separation. Layoff rates during the restructuring era were generally an increasing function of duration in grade percentile, and generally a decreasing albeit non-linear function of age and tenure. Although layoff rates rarely were higher than 5 percent for any duration category during the restructuring period – with all other variables held at mean levels – the change in layoff patterns relative to other periods was substantial. For example, managers of roughly forty years of age (50th age percentile) were ten times more likely to be laid off during the second RIF than they were in an average year. Furthermore, employees with significant amounts of grade-level experience, who were in salary grade levels representing

Table 2.6 *Predicted probabilities of employment separation rates during reduction in force periods*

	RIF no. 1			RIF no. 2		
	Retirement	Resignation	Layoff	Retirement	Resignation	Layoff
Salary grade level						
Levels 7 to 9	0.06	1.33	1.62	0.28	1.31	3.14
Levels 10 to 12	0.10	1.78	0.70	0.34	1.07	2.73
Levels 13 to 16	0.10	1.19	0.22	0.26	1.30	1.44
Levels 17 to 24	0.07	–	–	0.30	2.17	–
Duration in grade						
10th percentile	0.04	1.08	0.17	0.12	0.78	0.79
25th percentile	0.05	1.69	0.77	0.18	1.26	2.16
50th percentile	0.07	2.42	1.80	0.25	1.85	4.00
75th percentile	0.12	3.98	2.22	0.53	3.25	6.30
90th percentile	0.31	0.59	2.48	0.98	0.56	7.76
Salary in range						
10th percentile	0.06	1.48	0.49	0.29	1.75	1.10
25th percentile	0.16	1.75	1.03	0.39	1.13	3.68
50th percentile	0.13	1.70	1.06	0.36	0.99	2.78
75th percentile	0.08	1.44	0.81	0.38	1.03	1.96
90th percentile	0.05	0.97	0.44	0.17	1.40	1.20
Age percentile						
10th percentile	0.11	6.26	1.25	0.73	5.11	3.79
25th percentile	0.02	2.38	1.05	0.03	2.38	3.04
50th percentile	0.01	1.40	0.79	0.04	1.34	2.58
75th percentile	0.19	0.72	0.59	0.81	0.58	2.04
90th percentile	9.09	0.45	0.46	9.67	0.33	1.75
95th percentile	26.10	0.54	0.42	32.47	0.23	1.59
99th percentile	51.58	1.49	0.37	62.16	0.15	1.41

Note: A dash (–) means that the probability could not be estimated. Predicted probabilities were generated from logit coefficients reported in Dencker (2006), using the Clarify statistical program (King, Tomz, and Wittenberg, 2000; Tomz, Wittenberg, and King, 2003), with other variables set to mean levels.

strong barriers to upward mobility (such as level 9 and level 12), experienced a high likelihood of layoff during RIF. This outcome suggests that the firm was not simply easing out managers with early retirements and buyouts.

Job structure

The findings in table 2.6 also reveal clear effects of job structures on employment separation for all separation types. For instance, the rate of layoff decreased within increasing salary grade level, with the upper-level management group experiencing no layoffs in either RIF. As I note in another study (Dencker, 2006), the protection that job structures provided against layoff was strong across the RIFs, but did decline over time. For example, during the first RIF there were zero layoffs above salary grade level 14, with layoff rates declining in increasing level from level 9 to level 14. By contrast, during the second RIF layoffs extended to level 16. Moreover, layoff rates in level 16 were higher than in levels 12 to 15.

In terms of the salary in range variable, table 2.6 suggests that the firm was less restricted from targeting highly paid employees in the first RIF relative to the second RIF. For instance, layoff rates were generally decreasing in the 50th salary percentile and above in the first RIF, and decreasing in the 25th salary percentile and above during the second RIF. Layoff rates for the duration in grade measure suggest that performance was an increasingly important factor in the termination decisions during RIF. This notion can be seen more clearly in figure 2.1, which provides layoff rates during the two RIF episodes for different combinations of the salary in range and duration in grade categories.

Figure 2.1 demonstrates graphically that layoff rates were generally increasing in increasing duration in a grade level in both RIFs, yet with some important differences across the two. During the first RIF layoff rates declined in the upper end of the duration in grade distribution, regardless of salary percentile. By contrast, during the second RIF layoff rates in the upper tail of the duration in grade distribution remained at a roughly constant but high level from the 75th percentile onward for all salary categories. Moreover, whereas the lowest-paid employees had the highest rates of layoff during the second RIF, during the first RIF managers in the 50th salary percentile generally experienced the highest risk of layoff. This outcome may stem in part from changes to the firm's performance management system, in that wages and performance became more tightly linked, thereby providing more information with which to target low-performing and low-paid managers during the second

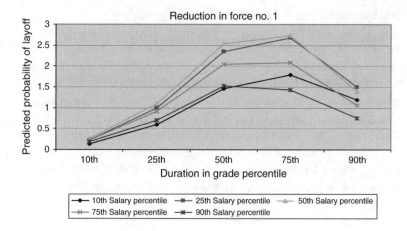

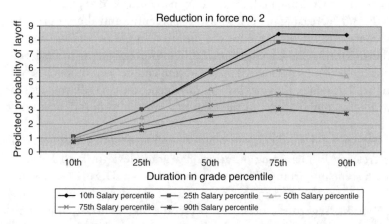

Figure 2.1 Predicted probabilities of layoff for managers by duration in grade and salary in range categories across reduction in force episodes
Note: Probabilities of layoff calculated using the Clarify program (Tomz, Wittenberg, and King, 2003; King, Tomz, and Wittenberg, 2000), based on logit coefficients reported in Dencker (2006).

RIF relative to the first.[10] In addition, differences in layoff patterns across the RIFs may stem from the different contexts within which

---

[10] As part of this change process, the firm sought to increase the variation in ratings by limiting above-average scores, so to make rating more meritocratic.

each RIF occurred. The first RIF occurred prior to anti-takeover legislation, and the second RIF took place after this and other legal changes.

Summary

In sum, the employment separations among managers show the increasing influence of market forces on the employment relationships over time. Layoff rates show that relative performance was critical for a manager's ability to remain with the firm during RIF periods. Over time, RIFs became more like "trimming the fat" layoffs, wherein performance was the key criterion for the termination decision (Baumol, Blinder, and Wolff, 2003), rather than in the first RIF, in which wages seemed to play a bigger, albeit restricted, role. Interviews with managers provided some supportive evidence. An upper-level manager claimed that the firm's strategy of performing "rifle shots" layoffs rather than a single concentrated "shotgun blast" had the unintended consequence of making employees feel they were playing a game of "musical chairs." Nevertheless, managers maintained that there was no dropoff in measurable employee performance, perhaps due to the fears of future job loss that such RIFs may entail (see Katz, 1986). Despite the increased penetration of market forces in the employment relationship, job structures played a key role in layoffs over time, and generated patterns that are somewhat at odds with prevailing wisdom, such as the greater likelihood of termination for entry-level managers relative to middle managers.

Career patterns for managers in restructured firms

My research on the careers of managers in restructured firms focuses primarily on changes in promotion rates over time, and to a lesser extent on the placement of new hires to the firm in different job levels (Dencker, 2005, forthcoming).

Hiring conditions

In terms of hiring conditions, I find that the average starting job level for managers increased from 9.95 in the 1967 to 1974 period, to 10.27

Correlations between wages and performance during the second RIF should thus have been higher than during the first RIF. Given the firm's control over the layoff process during the second RIF relative to the first, the stability of rates for different groups is perhaps not too surprising.

in the 1975 to 1983 period, to 10.67 in the restructuring period of 1984 to 1993. Moreover, the average starting job level increased gradually throughout the restructuring period, reaching 11 by the end of the sample period in 1993. These findings suggest that a common feature of ILMs, namely entry portals, became less important over time, as managers were entering the firm at higher levels than they had in the past.

Promotion rates

Understanding the effect of restructuring on promotion is somewhat complicated due to significant variation in mobility historically. For example, RIF and reorganization had divergent effects on promotion both within and across managerial groups. In order to give an overview of this variation, I provide historical rates of promotion for different managerial groups in table 2.7. These rates indicate that promotion was generally a declining function of job level, and was highest in the employment growth period from 1975 to 1983. A critical exception to this pattern is the upward mobility of upper-level managers. Overall, upper-level managers experienced a gradual but continuous improvement in promotion chances over time. In stark contrast to entry-level and middle managers, however, whose promotion chances declined substantially during restructuring, upper-level managers experienced a strong and significant increase in promotion rates during the restructuring process.

Table 2.8 provides predicted promotion probabilities in selected restructuring years generated from logit coefficients provided in Dencker (2005, forthcoming). For the average manager, promotion rates in most years of restructuring (1984–93) were lower than they were in the entire sample period (1967–93), with the lowest rates of upward mobility occurring during the specific year of a RIF. The promotion patterns in table 2.8 also indicate that job structures modified the influence of restructuring on mobility. For instance, upper-level managers experienced a strong increase in promotion rates in the year following each RIF. By contrast, RIFs had strong negative effects on promotion rates for other managers, with the negative effect typically extending to the following time period. One possible explanation for this important finding is that RIF eliminated both the person and the position in middle management levels, yet eliminated the person but not the position in upper management levels. In part, this variation in promotion is a function of the increasing stability in the number of jobs in a given

Table 2.7 *Baseline promotion rates in selected time periods, 1967–93*

	1967–93	1967–74	1975–83	1984–93
All managers	17.21	13.94	20.31	16.45
Salary grade levels 7–9	22.32	17.06	26.57	21.99
Salary grade levels 10–12	14.14	10.96	15.86	14.48
Salary grade levels 13–16	9.75	8.77	10.88	9.34
Salary grade levels 17–24	10.12	8.23	9.85	11.37
Tenure = 1 year	4.10	7.39	4.99	1.31
Tenure = 2 years	30.49	25.94	41.89	19.03
Tenure = 3–5 years	30.71	24.87	38.64	27.18
Tenure = 6–9 years	24.07	20.48	26.84	24.14
Tenure = 10–14 years	17.53	14.20	18.09	18.45
Tenure = 15–24 years	11.65	9.44	14.21	11.58
Tenure = 25+ years	7.16	5.33	8.84	6.11
Age < 25 years	25.36	24.03	30.81	17.87
Age = 25–29 years	31.18	26.42	37.73	27.76
Age = 30–34 years	25.12	21.34	28.72	24.25
Age = 35–39 years	18.43	14.73	21.38	18.04
Age = 40–44 years	13.54	10.65	15.47	14.19
Age = 45–49 years	10.42	9.05	12.36	10.03
Age = 50–54 years	8.19	6.47	10.26	7.18
Age = 55–59 years	6.22	4.19	7.78	5.33
Age = 60+ years	4.32	2.37	5.64	3.81
Duration in grade < 3 years	20.84	19.36	26.15	16.47
Duration in grade = 3–5 years	19.06	14.79	19.01	21.49
Duration in grade = 6–9 years	11.19	8.80	13.17	12.03
Duration in grade = 10–14 years	7.98	6.09	9.79	8.02
Duration in grade = 15+ years	7.19	6.50	7.68	6.50
Salary in range < 25th percentile	22.14	22.75	24.88	19.58
Salary in range = 25th–49th percentile	17.42	14.32	21.89	15.16
Salary in range = 50th–74th percentile	16.52	13.58	19.09	15.30
Salary in range > 74th percentile	13.56	5.95	16.55	15.77
Gender = female	23.86	27.11	29.42	20.86
Gender = male	16.22	13.48	19.19	15.30
Race = minority	18.27	22.67	20.78	15.91
Race = white	17.12	13.59	20.28	16.52

Note: Rates reflect yearly average likelihood of promotion for managers.

Table 2.8 *Event history analyses predicting promotion rates in selected time periods, 1967–93*

	1967–93	RIF no. 1	RIF no. 1 + 1 year	HRM Δ	HRM Δ + 1 year	HRM Δ + 2 years	RIF no. 2	RIF no. 2 + 1 year
All managers	15.32	12.15	13.87	13.35	15.12	14.57	10.89	13.08
Salary grade level								
Levels 7 to 9	18.02	15.04	16.84	16.33	18.39	19.25	15.53	18.72
Levels 10 to 12	13.55	10.09	11.80	11.64	14.23	13.07	8.97	11.65
Levels 13 to 16	12.24	10.94	12.05	10.83	10.40	9.95	8.31	7.98
Levels 17 to 24	16.42	21.65	22.86	21.24	25.46	15.32	9.91	22.03
Duration in grade								
10th percentile	14.19	10.62	10.81	10.93	10.90	10.64	8.66	10.81
25th percentile	15.05	11.58	12.17	13.01	10.91	13.07	10.08	12.08
50th percentile	15.81	12.54	13.54	14.98	14.25	13.13	11.51	13.31
75th percentile	17.34	14.11	16.20	18.28	24.17	20.66	14.01	15.43
90th percentile	16.92	15.46	20.31	19.88	28.63	26.24	15.95	17.40
Salary in range								
10th percentile	13.03	8.55	9.20	10.85	11.53	10.24	7.15	8.88
25th percentile	14.06	10.12	11.10	11.92	13.02	11.96	8.71	10.69
50th percentile	15.34	12.18	13.95	13.34	15.27	14.75	11.06	13.26
75th percentile	16.60	14.54	16.89	14.72	17.30	17.32	13.44	15.92
90th percentile	17.82	16.64	19.84	16.13	19.47	20.18	16.12	18.49
Age								
10th percentile	28.65	23.54	31.29	25.39	25.22	30.78	22.44	25.28
25th percentile	25.13	21.11	27.00	23.18	23.51	24.34	18.89	21.45
50th percentile	18.34	14.98	17.82	18.21	19.41	16.72	14.09	15.95
75th percentile	10.04	8.10	8.29	9.22	11.16	8.62	7.00	8.87
90th percentile	5.66	3.79	2.79	3.55	5.67	4.96	3.67	4.93
Gender								
Female	16.63	12.72	13.01	14.21	21.00	14.69	11.21	14.89
Male	15.13	12.06	14.01	13.07	13.66	14.54	10.82	12.51

Note: The predicted probabilities were generated from logit coefficients reported in Dencker (forthcoming) using the statistical program Clarify

upper management job level. As one HR manager explained, promotions in entry and middle management levels were often in lockstep, with supervisors allowed to create positions in order to promote a qualified employee. By contrast, promotions in upper job levels typically required that a job become vacant through the death or retirement of a manager. Thus, although promotion rates for senior managers did not increase during the growth period (1975–83) to the extent that they did for entry-level and middle managers (probably because of restrictions in creating new jobs in upper levels), when upper-level jobs became open due to increased rates of early retirement during RIF the firm filled the vacancies through promotion rather than eliminating the jobs entirely.

Another somewhat surprising finding in table 2.8 is that promotion rates for managers in entry and upper management levels increased in several periods following the change in the firm's performance management system. In other words, if reorganization efforts sought to replace long-term rewards such as promotions with short-term bonus-based rewards, as was the case in many firms in this period, one would expect reorganization to slow promotion rates substantially for all managers. Even though the increased upward mobility for upper-level managers in this time frame is consistent with Marta Elvira's (2001) notion that the power of upper-level managers allowed them to reap proportionately larger rewards than managers at lower levels, it is difficult to explain the increased mobility in entry-level positions with this story. My research (Dencker, forthcoming) shows that key factors in this regard are job levels and gender.

Gender

Figure 2.2 presents predicted gender differences in promotion from logit regression models found in Dencker (forthcoming). Results show few gender differences in promotion rates in an average year, with the main exception being a net advantage for women in grade levels 13 and higher. These findings are similar to those emerging from a study using samples of executives from Fortune 100 firms at different points in historical time (Cappelli and Hamori, 2005). This relative advantage held in many years during the restructuring process, and extended to entry levels in the year following reorganization.[11] In a previous study

[11] The gender differences in figure 2.2 underestimate women's promotion advantage in upper management during restructuring. Due to the small numbers of women in upper management, it was not possible to estimate gender

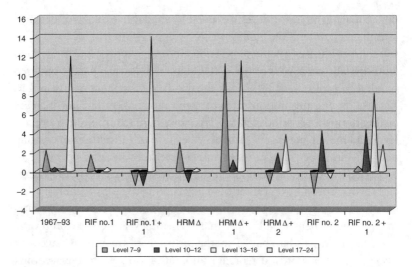

Figure 2.2 Gender differences in predicted probabilities of promotion in selected time periods: women's rates minus men's rates
Note: Probabilities of layoff calculated using the Clarify program (Tomz, Wittenberg, and King, 2003; King, Tomz, and Wittenberg, 2000), from logit coefficients reported in Dencker (forthcoming).

(Dencker, forthcoming) I discuss how the extent to which women's mobility increase in entry levels may have stemmed from a reduction in bias against women resulting from changes to the performance management systems.

The net promotion advantage of women in the upper management levels is somewhat less surprising, as this pattern was observed in large firms in the 1980s (see Petersen and Saporta, 2004). Trond Petersen and Ishak Saporta note that women's progressively higher promotion rates with increasing job levels suggest that the opportunity structure for discrimination is much lower in upper levels than in lower levels – an argument consistent with the findings in my study. In other words, discrimination is arguably more difficult with increasing levels and increasing career length, as (1) the ease with which information on decisions can be obtained increases, (2) the ambiguity of the assembled

differences in the event history analyses. Following reorganization, however, female upper managers were promoted: in the second RIF one out of three women was promoted, and in the year following the second RIF three out of four women were promoted.

information decreases, and (3) the availability of a plaintiff increases. For instance, as more information about an employee's ability is learned, and as an employee's track record is formed, the ability to discriminate becomes more difficult, due in no small part to legal options by employees in higher job levels.

Another rationale for women's somewhat higher promotion rates in upper levels is strong competition (e.g. poaching) for these women, who have already demonstrated an ability to move up the corporate ladder successfully, coupled perhaps with increased pressures to eliminate glass ceilings, such as from the Glass Ceiling Commission (US Department of Labor, 1995). Nevertheless, despite the significant inroads made by women into management in the firm that I have studied – stemming in part from higher rates of employment separation for men – and their increased rate of mobility up the corporate ladder relative to men, few women gained entrance into senior leadership positions in this firm over time. Moreover, women continued to be hired into lower job levels relative to men.

Summary

The findings from my research on the effects of corporate restructuring on employment relationships between managers and a large US manufacturing firm reveal that institutional features of firms such as job structures continue to buffer *certain* managers from market forces, albeit in varying ways over time. Specifically, I find that layoffs were restricted to entry-level and middle managers, with upper-level managers departing for reasons of early retirement. In addition, I find that restructuring increased the promotion rates of surviving upper-level managers substantially – particularly for women managers – while at the same time it reduced significantly the promotion likelihood of entry-level and middle managers.

The findings also indicate that job structures within the firm had non-trivial effects on career outcomes following restructuring, particularly among upper-level managers. For instance, following RIF, the firm typically filled vacancies created in upper levels by promoting surviving managers, rather than eliminating these positions, as they did in entry levels and in middle management levels. Nonetheless, the findings reveal a trend toward more market-based employment contracts. For instance, the increase in average entry job level among all managers from the

1960s to the 1990s suggests that a key feature of ILMs, namely entry into lower job level portals, was eroding over time. In addition, the increased separation rates for low-paid managers with high job level tenure over successive RIFs suggest that wages may have become increasingly a function of performance rather than time in a job, thus increasing the firm's ability to target low-performing managers for layoff over time.

Discussion and conclusions

This chapter provides evidence to enhance our knowledge of the effect of corporate restructuring on upward career mobility – a heretofore little-understood outcome of widespread RIF and reorganization. It does so by answering two linked questions. First, which employees, in which job levels, do firms lay off? Second, what effect does restructuring have on the promotion rates of surviving employees in these job levels? The answers to these questions also help to fill in other gaps in the literature, a key one being a lack of knowledge about the effect of job structures on employment separation and promotion in restructuring firms.

My study of historical managerial career patterns in a large US manufacturing firm shows that corporate restructuring has extensively transformed the careers of many managers in recent decades. During this period the risk of employment separation increased and rates of promotion decreased. These findings are consistent with research on employment separations over time, yet provide additional insights into the nature of restructuring and its effect on career outcomes. For instance, I show that during RIF the likelihood that a manager of a certain age will separate "voluntarily" is a function of factors such as job structures and type of separation, while "involuntary" employment separation appears to be a non-linear function of age and seniority during RIF, and limited to entry-level and middle managers. These results provide additional evidence that shareholder gains from corporate restructuring were largely "efficient" (Jensen, 1993) rather than redistributive (Shleifer and Summers, 1988), with layoffs tending to involve "redundant" rather than highly paid employees (Allen, Clark, and Schieber, 1999; Baumol, Blinder, and Wolff, 2003).

Surprisingly, the research shows that RIF is not bad news to all employees. Indeed, the study shows that the beneficiaries of corporate restructuring were not just shareholders and top management teams (who were "above grade") but also upper management and some mid-

level salary grade level managers. My findings also indicate that restructuring provided an advantage to women in upper job levels, where they
are substantially underrepresented. This is an important issue in contemporary managerial employment models, since the representation of
women in management has grown considerably in recent decades. In
fact, women's representation in management positions increased from
roughly 20 percent in the early 1970s to 45 percent in the early 2000s
(US Bureau of Labor Statistics, 2003). Nevertheless, this research also
reveals that few women were able to transition into upper management
positions in the firm over time, as restructuring slowed promotion rates
for many managers and as women continued to be hired into somewhat
lower job levels than men (Dencker, forthcoming).

Because restructuring has been and continues to be an important
component of the corporate economy, my research has a number of
important implications for the employment relationship between
managers and large firms in a variety of contexts. For instance, the
tremendous growth in merger and acquisition (M&A) activity, both
domestically and cross-border, indicates that, although RIF may be
limited in some non-US contexts, many HR management (HRM)
systems, practices, and policies have been transferred across borders.
Thus, international career patterns may converge to US-based HR
models (see Aguilera and Dencker, 2004). Moreover, although the
continuous restructuring of firms suggests that the influence of market
forces on employment relationships may increase, job structures will
probably continue to play a key role in career outcomes. For example,
even though many large firms have shifted from grade level systems to
job band systems in order to increase flexibility in the provision of
monetary incentives to employees (see Gerhart and Rynes, 2003), these
changes did not eliminate corporate hierarchies. Thus, the transition to
job bands may slow promotion rates, in the sense of true upward
moves, yet it seems that this change simply replaced salary grade level
systems with another, similar structural form.

A final question relates to the implication my findings have for
aspiring and current managers. One basic implication is that it is
good to be at the top of a firm. Indeed, the higher one is in the job
level system, the more rewarding the career outcome. I also find that,
for many managers, the time required to move up the ladder has
increased substantially relative to prior periods. In addition, I show
that, even though wages have increased for many managers, the

historical change in mobility may have had a negative effect on perceptions of career chances for many managers. Ultimately, therefore, what is at issue is "how" one can get to the top quickly. For managers, patience and sustained high levels of performance are necessary, but probably not sufficient, virtues. Rather, in corporations in which upward mobility rates are low, the best way to get a raise and promotion may be to secure an outside offer and threaten to leave the firm.

To conclude, at a broad level of abstraction, my research provides strong evidence in support of a trend toward more market-based contracts, yet an important implication of my research is that many career outcomes seem to be reverting to patterns existing in firms prior to the 1970s. As Max Weber argued, bureaucracy is a stable solution to the uncertainties caused by social relations in organizations that are not governed by formal rules and policies. Given the high uncertainties within restructured organizations, the need for stability may help to explain the continued presence of bureaucratic procedures. In this context, it would seem that jobs and job structures will continue to be fairly stable and important for career mobility. Moreover, pressures to provide longer employment contracts may increase due to demographic forces in society, with people living longer, and with many potential retirees as the baby boomer generation ages. Thus, managers seeking to move up the job ladder in large firms can find useful career advice in classic studies of mobility in bureaucracies, if they mentally replace the man in the grey flannel suit with a more modern version, at least in entry-level and middle management positions.

References

Aguilera, R. V., and Dencker, J. C. (2004). The role of human resource management in cross-border mergers and acquisitions. *International Journal of Human Resource Management*, 8, 1355–70.

Allen, S. G., Clark, R. L., and Schieber, S. (1999). *Has Job Security Vanished in Large Corporations?* Working Paper no. 6966. Cambridge, MA: National Bureau of Economic Research.

Allison, P. (1982). Discrete-time methods for the analysis of event histories. In S. Leinhardt (ed.), *Sociological Methodology 1982* (61–98). San Francisco: Jossey-Bass.

(1984). *Event History Analysis: Regression for Longitudinal Event Data.* Newbury Park, CA: Sage.

Baker, G. P. (1990). Pay-for-performance for middle managers: causes and consequences. *Journal of Applied Corporate Finance*, 3, 50–61.

Baumol, W., Blinder, A., and Wolff, E. (2003). *Downsizing in America: Reality, Causes, and Consequences*. New York: Russell Sage Foundation.

Brockner, J., Grover, S., Reed, T. L., and Dewitt, R. L. (1992). Layoff, job security, and survivors' work effort: evidence of an inverted-U relationship. *Academy of Management Journal*, 35, 413–25.

Cappelli, P. (1992). Examining managerial displacement. *Academy of Management Journal*, 35, 203–17.

Cappelli, P., Bassi, L., Katz, H., Knoke, D., Osterman, P., and Useem, M. (1997). *Change at Work*. New York: Oxford University Press.

Cappelli, P., and Hamori, M. (2005). The new road to the top. *Harvard Business Review*, 83(1), 25–32.

Dencker, J. C. (2005). Corporate restructuring and the intra-organizational mobility response. Mimeo. University of Illinois at Urbana-Champaign, Institute of Labor and Industrial Relations.

(2006). Who do firms lay off and why? Structural accounts of corporate reductions in force. Mimeo. University of Illinois at Urbana-Champaign, Institute of Labor and Industrial Relations.

(forthcoming). Corporate restructuring and sex differences in managerial promotion. *American Sociological Review*.

DiPrete, T. (1993). Industrial restructuring and the mobility response of American workers in the 1980s. *American Sociological Review*, 58, 74–96.

Elvira, M. (2001). Pay me now or pay me later: analyzing the relationship between bonus and promotion incentives. *Work and Occupations*, 28, 346–70.

Farber, H. S. (1998). *Has the Rate of Job Loss Increased in the Nineties?* Working Paper no. 394. Princeton, NJ: Princeton University, Industrial Relations Section.

Flinn, C. J., and Heckman, J. J. (1980). *Models for the Analysis of Labor Force Dynamics*. Discussion Paper 80-3. Chicago: University of Chicago, National Opinion Research Center.

Gerhart, B., and Rynes, S. (2003). *Compensation: Theory, Evidence and Strategic Implications*. Thousand Oaks, CA: Sage.

Gibbs, M. (1995). Incentive compensation in a corporate hierarchy. *Journal of Accounting and Economics*, 19, 247–77.

Guo, G. (1993). Event-history analysis for left-truncated data. In P. V. Marsden (ed.), *Sociological Methodology 1993* (217–43). Washington, DC: American Sociological Association.

Jensen, M. (1993). The modern industrial revolution, exit, and the failure of internal control systems. *Journal of Finance*, 68, 831–80.

Katz, L. F. (1986). *Efficiency Wage Theories: A Partial Evaluation*. Working Paper no. 1906. Cambridge, MA: National Bureau of Economic Research.

King, G., Tomz, M., and Wittenberg, J. (2000). Making the most of statistical analyses: improving interpretation and presentation. *American Journal of Political Science*, 44, 347–61.

Kletzer, L. (1998). Job displacement. *Journal of Economic Perspectives*, 12, 115–36.

Osterman, P. (1999). *Securing Prosperity: The American Labor Market: How It Has Changed and What to Do about It*. Princeton, NJ: Princeton University Press.

Petersen, T., and Saporta, I. (2004). The opportunity structure for discrimination. *American Journal of Sociology*, 109, 852–901.

Reskin, B., and Padavic, I. (1994). *Women and Men at Work*. London: Pine Forge Press.

Shleifer, A., and Summers, L. (1988). Breach of trust in hostile takeovers. In: A. Auerback (ed.), *Corporate Takeovers: Causes and Consequences* (33–56). Chicago: University of Chicago Press.

Sørensen, A. (1977). Estimating rates from retrospective questions. In D. R. Heise (ed.), *Sociological Methodology 1977* (209–23). San Francisco: Jossey-Bass.

(1996). The structural basis of social inequality. *American Journal of Sociology*, 101, 1333–66.

Stewman, S. (1988). Organizational demography. *Annual Review of Sociology*, 14, 173–202.

Tomz, M., Wittenberg, J., and King, G. (2003). *CLARIFY: Software for Interpreting and Presenting Statistical Results*, version 2.1. Stanford University, University of Wisconsin, and Harvard University. Available at http://gking.harvard.edu/.

US Bureau of Labor Statistics (2003). *Employed Persons by Detailed Occupation, Sex, Race and Hispanic or Latino Ethnicity*. Washington, DC: Government Printing Office.

US Department of Labor (1995). *Good for Business: Making Full Use of the Nation's Human Capital*. Fact-Finding Report of the Federal Glass Ceiling Commission. Washington, DC: Government Printing Office.

Useem, M. (1996). *Investor Capitalism*. New York: Basic Books.

Useem, M., and Cappelli, P. (1997). The pressures to restructure employment. In P. Cappelli, L. Bassi, H. Katz, D. Knoke, P. Osterman, and M. Useem (eds.), *Change at Work* (15–65). New York: Oxford University Press.

Valletta, R. G. (1998). *Declining Job Security*. Working Paper 98-02. San Francisco: Federal Reserve Bank of San Francisco.

White, H. (1970). *Chains of Opportunity: System Models of Mobility in Organizations*. Cambridge, MA: Harvard University Press.

Yamaguchi, K. (1991). *Event History Analysis*. Newbury Park, CA: Sage.

3 | The up and out in organizations

MARGARET YAP

Introduction

Social scientists have conducted numerous wage studies in the past few decades, yet promotions and employment separations in organizations remain relatively unexplored areas. In the past decade, as organizations flatten their organizational hierarchies, restructure, merge, and divest to ensure agility, efficiency, and effectiveness, promotions have become less common, whereas separations have become more commonplace. Understanding who gets promoted and exploring the nature of separation have important implications for both the efficiency of organizations and the compensation levels of workers. Using administrative data from between 1996 and 2000 from a large North American high-tech organization with annual employment ranging from 19,000 to 26,000 employees, this chapter explores the trends, the correlates, and the consequences of these two phenomena: promotions, the "up" side of the story, and separations, the "out" side of the story. In particular, the role of race and gender, as well as other factors, in promotions and separations will be explored.

The "up" side of the story

Promotions have a significant positive impact on wage levels: the rate of wage gain is often higher for those who have been promoted than it is for those who have not (Baker, Gibbs, and Holmstrom, 1994a, 1994b; McCue, 1996; Bognanno, 2001). An employee's rank in an organizational hierarchy not only determines the level of financial rewards but also confers other non-pecuniary benefits, such as more autonomy and more opportunities for personal development. It has also been shown that promotions lead to higher levels of job satisfaction (Francesconi, 2001). Promotions therefore, have more than just materialistic and status outcomes.

Why do employers promote their employees? Most organizations, whether their organizational structure is flat or hierarchical, have a number of layers of management. Promotion from within is an efficient way of filling vacancies at senior levels (Doeringer and Piore, 1971). In addition, promotions – or hopes of being promoted – are an effective incentive to elicit effort from workers (Berkowitz and Kotowitz, 1993): not only do they discourage employees from shirking, they can also motivate them to increase their productivity and to acquire new skills and knowledge (Prendergast, 1993). Promotions can also be used as prizes to reward superior performers and can act as a sorting process to differentiate high-potential workers from others (Lazear and Rosen, 1981).

The substantial flattening of organizations in the last two decades has eliminated several layers in most organizations' hierarchies. In this new environment, career achievement through a series of lateral moves works to increase employees' breadth of knowledge and experience, and career achievement has become more common than career advancement through the organization hierarchy. Though these lateral moves may be seen as necessary building blocks for career advancement, it is upward mobility that provides significant monetary and non-monetary returns.

The "out" side of the story

Employment separation is defined as the termination of an employment relationship. There are two parties to every employment relationship: the employer and the employee. The decision to terminate the employment relationship can be either bilateral (agreed to between the parties) or unilateral (initiated either by the employer or the employee). Bilateral decisions to terminate an employment relationship, though less frequent, pose less concern, as they are believed to be both efficient and in the best interests of both parties, as in mutual agreement on early retirement (McLaughlin, 1991). Unilateral decisions, on the other hand, may benefit one party more than the other.

Voluntary separations occur when an employee decides that the benefits of quitting exceed the costs, as when employees quit and move to obtain higher pay or a better job match. Involuntary separations occur when the employer decides that the benefits of separation exceed the costs, as when firms dismiss or lay off workers who are incompetent or who do not share the organization's culture, or whose jobs have become redundant. Both voluntary and involuntary separations may result in private and/or social costs.

Upfront investments by employers – in terms of hiring and training costs – motivate them to reduce employee-initiated terminations. Firms want to retain employees so that the employers can enjoy the return on their investments. Even though some might consider these upfront investments as "sunk" costs, there are still incentives for firms to retain their workers, as they stand to lose knowledge, skills, and expertise when an experienced employee leaves. Employee-initiated separations may, therefore, translate into additional costs in terms of recruiting, hiring, and training a replacement, as well as a decrease in productivity as the replacement climbs the learning curve.

On the other hand, employees do not want to be subject to employer-initiated separations. Employees who are terminated lose not only their pay but also the opportunity to accumulate further firm-specific skills. They also lose all accrued (non-vested) pension and other benefits. Some may even experience difficulty in locating a better or comparable job. Henry Farber (1993) finds that displaced workers – those who lost their jobs as a result of layoffs or plant closings – were less likely to be employed than those who left voluntarily. Even if these displaced workers managed to find alternative employment, they were less likely to find work with the same number of hours, at the same level of compensation, and with the same level of benefits. Employee separation also has costs to society in terms of lost tax revenues, lower retail sales, and possibly higher dependence on income support programs such as employment insurance and other social assistance.

In the new world of work, firms driven by global competition are forced to transform and focus themselves, divesting themselves of both businesses and employees that are not seen as part of their core competencies. Layoffs, mergers, acquisitions, divestitures, downsizing, and outsourcing activities are mechanisms employed by organizations to ensure they have the right number of workers with the right skills at the right place and at the right time. The late 1990s offered many opportunities for workers to better their "job matches."[1] The economic (loss

---

[1] In 1999 the US economy was still expanding, following the trend in the previous eight years. The unemployment rate hit a thirty-year low of less than 4 percent (Martel and Kelter, 2000).

of pay and accrued benefits) and emotional (loss of identity and self-confidence) toll of employer-initiated employment separation on employees can be sizable. On the other hand, employment contracts have become more transactional in their basis (Hall, 1986), moving away from the traditional and long-term relational model.

Approaching the topic

To study these two workplace phenomena, there are several ways information can be collected. One of the ways of assessing advancement opportunities and decisions within the organizational context is by surveying employees. Employees' self-distortions may lead to misconceptions about their career opportunities, however; their perceptions of their career opportunities and promotability may not reflect reality (Rosenbaum, 1984). An alternative method is to research the promotion policies of firms by surveying organizations. Researchers have found that responses provided by company officials are often ambiguous, however, and do not necessarily reflect the firm's actual practices in assigning promotion accurately (Abraham and Medoff, 1985).

Furthermore, as promotion opportunities depend on the firm's technology, product market, rate of organizational growth, and business strategy, national data that omits important characteristics of firms (e.g. demand-side variables) will undoubtedly affect researchers' ability to draw meaningful conclusions. For example, large established firms with progressive and innovative human resource practices may be better able to offer higher rewards, more job security, and better career opportunities (Oi, 1990; Brown and Medoff, 2001).

More importantly, the study of promotions presupposes knowledge of the ordered hierarchy of jobs – organization-level data. Economy-wide studies have tried to overcome this obstacle by looking at wages or changes in job titles that may or may not reflect "true" promotions. The use of firm-level data will not suffer from this measurement problem, as rankings are consistently determined based on the firm's policies. Finally, this approach has the advantages of conventional national data sets with respect to sample size and longitudinal information.

Similarly, the study of separation behaviour, voluntary or otherwise, is best served when information on both the supply side (i.e. the workers) and the demand side (i.e. the employers) is available. Prior research has shown that average quit and layoff rates tend to be lower – all else being equal – in industries in which worker and firm investments in specific training are high (Parsons, 1972).

A focus on race and gender

One may speculate that the labor market experiences of women and racial minorities, in terms of promotions and separations, may differ significantly from the experiences of the traditional workforce. A number of theories can provide insights into the reasons for differential treatment – and, thus, different experiences – for women and racial minorities.[2]

The competitive model and theory of the firm

According to neoclassical economic theory and the theory of the firm, firms strive to maximize profits, and hence the returns to their shareholders. If labor markets are competitive then all employee groups should be paid a wage proportional to their productivity. Considerable empirical evidence, however, suggests that wages for women and racial minorities are lower than those for the traditional white male worker, even after controlling for measurable productive attributes (Benjamin, Gunderson, and Riddell, 2001). Thus, employing more women and racial minorities, especially at higher levels, should lead to higher profitability for the firms. The increase in demand for female and minority employees would then raise their wage levels until they were equal to those of males and whites with the same productivity. Accordingly, the expectation is that women and racial minorities should not experience any disadvantage when it comes to promotion opportunities, once they have been hired into a firm.

Preference and utility

Gary Becker (1957) posits that some employers try to maximize "utility." This "utility" may include profits and a preference for certain gender and racial characteristics of their employees. Such employers are willing to pay a higher wage for traditional white, male labor and accept lower profits, rather than employ equally productive minority or female employees. Put another way, the total cost of hiring women

---

[2] For a comprehensive discussion of theories on discrimination in the labour market, see Benjamin, Gunderson, and Riddell (2001).

and racial minorities carries a certain "invisible" cost that makes their perceived labor costs higher than those of white males.

Similarly, Kenneth Arrow (1973) argues that firms tend to maximize "utility" instead of profits. If employers believe that hiring or promoting women and racial minorities decreases group cohesion or teamwork, they will choose not to promote them and instead keep them at lower levels, where the impact to the "bottom line" is minimized. An implication from Arrow's argument, however, is that firms that decide to employ and promote women or minorities enjoy a competitive advantage in that they can select and promote the best women and members of racial minorities in the labor force, thereby increasing their profits.

Human capital

Human capital theory (Becker, 1964) suggests that people will invest in the accumulation of human capital only when it is believed that the investment will generate a reasonable return in the future. Individuals will acquire skills and experience if they expect those attributes to have positive effects on career advancement. As the gap in educational attainment and labour market experience between white males and women and racial minorities narrows over time, any differential in promotion opportunities between white males and the various race/ gender groups may be expected to decrease.

Internal labour market theory

One of the most common versions of the structural theories is the theory of the internal labor market (Doeringer and Piore, 1971). This theory posits that firms will segment their workforce into two groups: "primary" and "secondary" segments. Employers will invest in training for employees in the primary segment but not those in the secondary segment. Employees in the primary segment receive advancement opportunities but those in the secondary segment do not, even if they invest in their own human capital. Accordingly, if white males are situated in the primary segment and women and racial minorities in the secondary segment, the latter will experience differential treatment with respect to promotion opportunities.

Statistical discrimination

Statistical discrimination takes place when employers utilize information based on the average characteristics of certain groups in their decision-making. This kind of discrimination usually takes place in the hiring process, when employers have only limited information about the applicants' productivity. Analyses of promotion indicate that statistical discrimination may, however, have an indirect effect on promotion probabilities. If, for example, employers believe that women are less mobile because they are trailing their spouses, the women are less likely to receive advancement opportunities. It has also been shown that employers consistently underestimate the performance or productivity of women and racial minorities (Aigner and Cain, 1977). If employers view women as less committed and less productive because they are better suited for – and hence have greater responsibilities for – housework and childrearing, or that racial minorities face limited alternative employment opportunities, employers will not feel the need to provide them with promotions to induce them to stay.

With regard to employment separation, conventional wisdom may lead us to believe that women and racial minorities have lower firm attachment and higher quit rates,[3] and this may have significant consequences for their employment outcomes. Employers tend to hire people with low propensities to quit, especially in "good" jobs, in which there are significant upfront investments in recruiting, hiring, and training. If employers believe that women and racial minorities are more likely to quit than white men then women and racial minorities are less likely to be hired, and, if hired, they may receive less training as employers may be less willing to invest in them. Thus, they will be deprived of potential advancement and learning opportunities (Royalty, 1996).[4] As a result, women and racial minorities may remain stuck in lower-level jobs in which the training requirement (and therefore the employer's investment) is minimal. Finally, the complementary observations that low-level jobs are more likely to become redundant and that low-level job incumbents are more easily replaced imply a higher chance of job loss.

---

[3] There are a number of reasons why women are believed to have a higher quit rate: women quit due to childbearing and childrearing; women generally earn less and thus enjoy a lower opportunity cost for non-market activities; women are believed to be secondary income earners and will be required to move if the spouse finds more attractive employment elsewhere. Racial minorities are also less able than whites to obtain job improvements via mobility.

[4] Anne Royalty (1996), using data on 2,105 women and 2,096 men from the National Longitudinal Survey of Youths (NLSY) 1979–86, finds that predicted turnover probabilities are significantly related to receiving training.

Data

Using administrative data from between 1996 and 2000 from a large North American high-tech organization with annual employment ranging from 19,000 to 26,000 employees, this chapter explores the trends, the correlates, and the consequences of these two phenomena: promotions, the "up" side of the story, and separations, the "out" side of the story. The time period under study is a period of strong economic growth during which skills shortages were widespread and firms struggled to hire and retain their knowledgeable workers by offering high wages and various incentives.

Administrative records from a large firm provide the ideal type of information required for the study of promotions and separation. The advantage of using administrative records is that they offer more accurate measures, with a higher level of integrity, as compared to retrospective analyses of surveys or census data. For example, survey data may contain self-reported errors that are impossible for the researchers to screen and eliminate. An example of a self-reported error is the case in which an employee who was fired by an employer reports a more socially acceptable reason than the actual reason. The use of census data can be inaccurate because, for instance, respondents often have trouble giving an accurate answer to the job tenure question that asks them how many years they have been working for their current employer (Brown and Light, 1992). Administrative records can provide accurate information on employee age, job function, salary, and tenure with the firm,[5] and allow detailed coding of the reasons for separation. They also offer natural controls for, or hold constant, a number of factors that may have a significant impact on termination decisions, including the firm's age, size, industry, business strategy, compensation policy, and career development philosophy, some of which may be difficult to measure or appropriately control for. Within-firm findings, of course, will not reflect any unobserved inter-firm differences.

The data used in the promotion analyses here has been compiled from six consecutive year-end employee files from 1995 to 2000. In this firm there are ten job levels below the chief executive officer level, eight

---

[5] In a study conducted by James Brown and Audrey Light (1992), respondents seem to have had trouble giving an accurate answer to the job tenure question.

of which are included in the analyses in this chapter. The top level represents the presidential-level employees, which accounts for a very small proportion of the sample, and since the strategy and philosophy governing executive compensation and promotion can be quite different it may not be appropriate to include them in the analyses. The ninth level is also excluded from the analyses, because promotions for this group cannot be identified. In addition, as the rules for the promotion of unionized workers may be more seniority-based than those for other salaried workers (Abraham and Medoff, 1985), all unionized employees are also excluded from this part of the analyses. The final data set[6] of over 22,000 employees allows us to consider the impact of variables that are unavailable in cross-sectional data. These include breaks in service and the race/gender composition of the job level/family combination, thus allowing us to determine whether these have differential effects for the race/gender groups with respect to promotion probabilities.

To generate the data set for the separation analyses, four data sources are utilized. The first data source contains the pooled data from archived administrative files on regular full-time employees employed at the end of each year from 1995 to 2000, excluding the level of employees right below the CEO.[7] Each employee is observed only once during his or her career with the firm by selecting the last record of every employee observed in the panel. The final data set yielded over 40,000 employees. Second, data with respect to termination (including information on termination date and termination reason) is merged with this data set. Third, this combined data set is

---

[6] Using the year-end data files for the years 1995 to 2000, and following procedures similar to those of Heidi Hartmann (1987), "matched" files were created by merging pairs of consecutive year-end files. For example, the employee records for year-end 1995 and 1996 were merged into one file and only those employees who existed in both years were kept. Among these observations, those who had received one or more promotions and those who had not were identified. The same process was repeated for the following pairs: 1996/1997, 1997/1998, 1998/1999, and 1999/2000. These procedures generated five different files, with two observations for each of the employees observed. To ensure the independence of the observations, for those employees who received one or more promotions during the time period studied only the first promotions were analyzed. A total of 15,671 promotions took place in the time period observed, of which 12,629, or about 81 percent, reflect first promotions. For those employees who did not receive a promotion, their information as they first entered the data set were used.

[7] As the data files are snapshots at each calendar year end, employees who were hired and terminated during the same calendar year were not included.

merged with a file containing promotion information. To be tagged as having received a promotion, the employee had to be present in any two consecutive year-end files and his or her job level had to be at least one level higher than the previous year. Finally, stock option grant data are merged into the master data set, providing information on grant dates, strike prices, and the number of unvested and "overhang"[8] non-qualified ten-year options.

A recent look at the lie of the land

Promotions

A promotion is defined as a move to a higher job level, by comparing the individual's job level at any two consecutive year-ends of working within the one organization. Evidence of race and gender effects on promotions has produced quite diverse conclusions in previous research. Craig Olson and Brian Becker (1983), using data from the US Quality of Employment Panel and a promotion measure based on self-reported evaluation of job changes by respondents who did not change employer between 1973 and 1977, find that women, in general, were held to higher promotion standards than men, and women received fewer promotions than did men with equal measured abilities. Hartmann (1987), using pooled administrative data from a female-dominated insurance company, finds that being female had a negative but insignificant effect on the probability of promotion, but the effect of race was both negative and significant. Similarly, in the legal profession, Stephen Spurr (1990) finds that women were less likely to be made partners than their male counterparts. On the other hand, others have found "positive" gender effects in promotions. Lea Stewart and William Gudykunst (1982) find that females enjoyed more promotions than men in a financial institution in the north-eastern United States. Barry Gerhart and George Milkovich (1989) find that, at lower levels in the organization hierarchy in a manufacturing firm, women received more promotions than men over a six-year period. Joni Hersch and Kip Viscusi (1996) also find that women were promoted more often than men in their analyses of a sample of employees in a public utility firm.

---

[8] Overhang options refer to the employee stock options that have been granted to employees and that have become vested but not yet exercised by the employees.

Table 3.1 *Percentage of employees promoted by year, 1996–2000*

	Percent promoted					
	1996	1997	1998	1999	2000	1996–2000
White males	19.0	18.5	15.8	17.0	22.0	18.4
White females	19.5	18.3	17.2	16.6	25.2	19.4
Minority males	19.6	17.3	15.9	16.8	20.3	18.0
Minority females	17.2	17.6	17.5	17.5	20.0	17.9
Overall	19.1	18.2	16.2	16.9	22.3	18.5

Still others studies have found that women were promoted at a more rapid rate than men, particularly at higher job levels (Petersen and Saporta, 2004; Spilerman and Petersen, 1999; Barnett, Baron, and Stuart, 2000; Cappelli and Hamori, 2005).

Table 3.1 presents the percentage promoted in each of the various race/gender groups. There is no consistent pattern in the data. For example, minority females were least likely to be promoted in 1996 and 2000, but most likely to be promoted in 1998 and 1999. The likelihood of promotion increased for all four groups in 2000. Throughout the time period under analysis 19.4 percent of white females were promoted, as compared to about 18 percent for other race/gender groups (18.4 percent for white males, 18.0 percent for minority males and 17.9 percent for minority females respectively).

Separations

Separation refers to the ending of the employment relationship, excluding any transfers to other subsidiaries of the companies. Figure 3.1 depicts the overall separation rate. As employment separations vary by cause (Parsons, 1977; Bartel and Borjas, 1981; Mincer, 1986; Ruhm, 1987; McLaughlin, 1991; Keith and McWilliams, 1997), the overall separation rate is also broken down into voluntary separation, involuntary separation, and retirement.[9] The proportion of employees that

---

[9] Retirements can be considered voluntary if the employee decides to retire at his or her own will, and they can be considered involuntary in the case of an employer's mandatory retirement policy or early retirement packages. Separations as a result of retirements have been treated as voluntary (Kidd, 1994) and involuntary

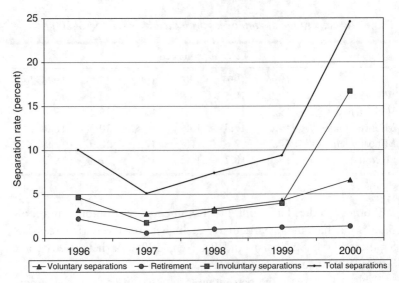

Figure 3.1 Separation rates by year, 1996–2000

severed their employment relationship with the firm decreases slightly from 1996 to 1997 and then rises to a peak in 2000. Similarly, the proportion of employees who retired from the firm drops slightly in 1997 then remains stable at slightly over 1 percent of the employee sample in the next three years. The proportion of voluntary separation tracks fairly closely that of involuntary separation until 1999. The sudden surge in the involuntary separation rate contributes to the significant increase in the total separation rate in 2000.

Over thirty distinct separation reasons were coded in the administrative records, allowing the further disaggregation of voluntary separations into "better prospects" and "personal reasons" and involuntary separations into "divestitures," "layoffs," and "dismissals" (see appendix 3.1). Rates for reason-specific separation were calculated by dividing the number of employees leaving for each reason by the number of active employees at the respective year-ends (see table 3.2). Over the sample period the overall separation rate was a little over 11 percent – voluntary separations (4.0 percent), primarily due to better prospects (2.8 percent),

(Sicherman, 1996). Therefore, retirements are treated as a separate and distinct category (Christofides and McKenna, 1993). In this firm, the retirement age is sixty-five and employees are eligible to retire if they satisfy the rule of eighty-five – i.e. if their age and years of service add up to eighty-five.

Table 3.2 *Separation rates by specific reasons by year, percentages, 1996–2000*

	Voluntary separations			Retirements	Involuntary separations				All separations
	Better prospects	Personal reasons	Total		Divestitures	Layoffs	Dismissals	Total	
1996	2.3	0.9	3.2	2.2	3.1	1.1	0.5	4.6	10.1
1997	2.0	0.8	2.8	0.6	1.2	0.2	0.4	1.8	5.1
1998	1.8	1.5	3.3	1.0	0.8	1.9	0.4	3.1	7.4
1999	2.9	1.3	4.2	1.2	1.0	2.7	0.3	3.9	9.4
2000	4.9	1.7	6.6	1.3	9.7	6.5	0.4	16.7	24.6
Average	2.8	1.2	4.0	1.3	3.1	2.5	0.4	6.0	11.3

and involuntary separations (6.0 percent), mainly due to divestitures (3.1 percent) and layoffs (2.5 percent). Dismissals represented a small proportion of the overall separation rate (0.4 percent).

Correlates of promotions and separations: the usual suspects

Based on the theoretical considerations discussed earlier, this chapter looks at a number of factors that might lead to these outcomes, both on the supply side and on the demand side. In addition to exploring factors that may have an impact on both outcomes, other factors will be discussed that may influence the likelihood of either outcome. Specifically, the chapter deals with work interruption or break in tenure and the race and gender composition of jobs for the promotion analyses, and deals with union status, job track, and incentives to stay in the separation analyses.

Supply-side variables

These comprise a set of conventional human capital and demographic variables, including tenure, age, education attainment, and some measure of performance rating. Breaks in service, whether the employee's tenure with the company is continuous or not, may affect one's promotability and are therefore included in the promotion analyses.

Tenure

Tenure is a proxy for firm-level or specific skill accumulation. In their analyses of promotion for non-union salaried employees in a manufacturing firm in the United States, Katharine Abraham and James Medoff (1985) find evidence that seniority had a substantial negative impact on promotion decisions for 60 percent of the employees, whereas Stewart and Gudykunst (1982) find positive effects of tenure on promotion rates. A logical expectation is that one needs to accumulate enough firm-level skills before being considered ready to be promoted. It is also fair to expect that this effect is not a linear one, however. Studies have found a negative tenure effect on promotions after the initial years – i.e. the effect of tenure on the probability of promotion takes on the shape of an inverted U. Tenure is therefore expected to have a positive effect on the probability of promotion initially, but will demonstrate a negative effect when tenure reaches a certain point in time.

As the accumulation of firm-specific capital (as a result of longer tenure) increases, the probability of quitting decreases (Parsons, 1972). A number of previous studies have found that the probability of job change declines with tenure (Jovanovic, 1979; Blau and Kahn, 1981; Abraham and Farber, 1987; McLaughlin, 1991). Long tenures signal investments by both parties in firm-specific skills accumulation, and since such specific skills cannot be transferred to other employment (Mincer, 1974) both parties will attempt to maximize utility by avoiding employment separation. In addition, long tenure signals a good job match, and thus suggests a higher probability of a continued relationship.

Jacob Mincer and Boyan Jovanovic (1981) show that the probability of employment separation may initially rise with tenure, but should steadily decrease as the length of tenure increases. In other words, the average rate of job change declines with job tenure as specific human capital accumulates, or as information about the quality of a match with the firm accumulates with time (Topel and Ward, 1992). According to the job-matching literature, workers enter into an employment relationship with available (yet incomplete) information at the time of decision-making. As information accumulates during the initial period of employment, workers become more able to decide whether their expectations are met. At the same time, employers can also assess workers' abilities better in addition to the human capital (e.g. education, past experience, and achievements) stated on their résumés – or they may discover workers' incompetence. Once a match is identified, the employment relationship will become more stable. Accordingly, the job-matching theory posits that workers' probability of quitting will decline as tenure on the job increases. Employees with a few years of firm-specific skills may therefore be more marketable and be more likely to leave for a better job (Topel and Ward, 1992). At the other end of the spectrum, employees who have been with the firm for a number of years may not have kept up with the new technologies and innovations in the workplace and thus will be more prone to being laid off.

It is expected, therefore, that in the first years the effect of tenure on separation will be positive and in subsequent years it will be negative, for both voluntary and involuntary separations. As retirement eligibility rules often require a certain number of years of service, a positive correlation between longer lengths of tenure and separation for retirement is expected.

Age and education

Age and education are used as signals to employers in their screening and matching processes. They are included as proxies for general skill accumulation. Conventional beliefs suggest that the probability of promotion increases as one's general skill increases. Researchers have found that educational attainment influences a person's rate of advancement (Spilerman and Lunde, 1991). James Rosenbaum (1979) suggests that, as with job tenure, the relationship between age and promotion opportunity exhibits a curvilinear relationship, in the shape of an inverted U. Therefore, one's opportunity for advancement is expected to increase as one accumulates more general and specific skills up to a certain point, and then decrease. Other studies have found that the incidence of promotion falls with age, however, while education effects are frequently found to be not significant in explaining the incidence of promotion (Lewis, 1986).

Andrew Weiss (1984) shows that younger workers are more likely to quit. There is a high probability that younger workers are still involved in job shopping with the hope of finding the best "match." Younger people may also be more likely to separate due to their minimal investment in firm-specific capital. As workers' age increases, the probability of quitting decreases (Burdett, 1978; Mincer and Jovanovic, 1981; Topel and

Ward, 1992). Workers who are older are less likely to move, for several reasons. First, they are more likely to have found a good match. Second, they will have accumulated a certain level of firm-specific skills that will provide them the greatest return if they stay with the same firm. Finally, they will have more accrued benefits (pension and others) to lose. Taking these into consideration, age is expected to correlate negatively with separation for better prospects, whereas it has no significant effect on separations for personal reasons, divestitures, layoffs, or dismissals, and a positive effect on the likelihood of separation for retirement.

Educational attainment is a proxy for general skill accumulation. Education is usually found to have no significant effect on separation decisions when all types of separations are grouped into one single category. Some have suggested, however, that those who possess higher education will have more general skills and thus have alternative employment opportunities. As these highly educated workers have more options with respect to where they work, the likelihood of them quitting may be higher. On the other hand, those who have less than high school education will be more prone to be laid off as we move to a knowledge economy. There is thus a higher likelihood of voluntary separation as educational attainment increases and a higher likelihood of involuntary separation at lower educational levels. The model considers five different educational attainment levels: less than high school (HS), high school, after high school or college, bachelor's or undergraduate degrees, and, finally, graduate degrees. A category that includes those whose educational attainment information is not available is also included.

Performance rating

Performance rating is a measure to account for an employee's productivity. Objectives are usually agreed to between the employee and his or her supervisor at the beginning of a performance period, followed by an evaluation at the end of the period. Performance ratings, determined by the supervisor in consultation with the employee, are the outcome of the evaluations. A good performance rating, though subjective, is a signal of the quality of output of the employees. All employees are given one of three ratings that denote whether they have exceeded their objectives, achieved their objectives, or failed to meet their objectives. Two dummy variables are included in the model: one reflects superior performance and one shows that objectives have been met. Previous research studies have shown that good performance ratings usually increase the chances of promotion or career advancement (Gibbs, 1995; Igbaria and Greenhaus, 1992). Therefore, in a meritocracy, employees who perform better than others would stand a better chance of being awarded a promotion.

With regard to separations, employees who received good ratings may be more likely to quit. Although one could argue that good ratings may imply a job match, good ratings are also indicators of employees' competence and employability. Firms usually try to retain these high performers with higher salaries, advancement opportunities, and stock options, instead of laying them off. As these predictions go in different directions, empirical findings will help in deciphering their net effects.

Break(s) in service
As the data contains consecutive end-of-year information on all employees and are directly connected to the firm's payroll system, it is possible to establish a "break in service" variable that identifies whether an employee's tenure with the company was continuous or not during the time period studied. For example, an employee who existed in the data set in 1995, 1996, 1997, 1999, and 2000 would be considered to have a break in his or her tenure with the firm. These breaks can represent the incidence of parental, maternal, or educational leave. The reason for the break cannot be determined by the available data. A return from education leave may signal a higher level of skills, whereas a return from maternity or paternity leave may be seen as a depreciation in skills. This variable is included in the model; the variable may not be statistically significant, however, as any significant positive effect may cancel out any negative effect, depending on the nature of the breaks.

Demand-side variables

To aid our understanding of the nuances of the promotion and separation process from the firm's perspective, a set of demand-side variables that account for how work is structured in this firm is explored. What impacts do the characteristics of the firm have on the likelihood of promotion and separation for employees? These variables include job family, job level, base pay, union status, incentives to stay, and the race/gender composition of each job family/level combination.

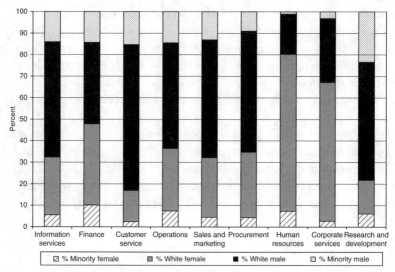

Figure 3.2 Distribution of race/gender groups by job family

Job family

Employees were classified into nine job families based on the functions they perform. Figure 3.2 shows the distribution of the four combinations of race/gender groups in each of the job families. Minorities account for a small percentage of all employees in all job families. The "human resources" function has a high percentage of white females and "customer service" has the highest percentage of white males.

Job level

Employees in each job family (discussed above) can be situated at different job levels in the organization hierarchy based on the complexities and the levels of responsibility of the jobs. Figure 3.3 shows the distribution of the four combinations of race/gender groups by their levels in the organizational hierarchy. There are ten distinct job levels in this firm, of which the tenth level represents the senior management team and was excluded in the analyses. The proportion of white females is higher in the lower job levels, and decreases significantly at the higher levels in the organizational hierarchy. The opposite is true for white males: they are more likely to be situated in the top half of the organization hierarchy. The profiles for racial minorities are quite flat,

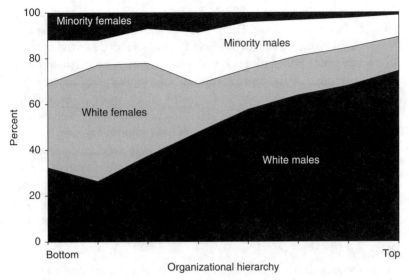

Figure 3.3 Distribution of race/gender groups by job level

with a slight peak at level 5 for minority males, followed by an evident downward trend.

Although the distributional pattern may seem to imply the existence of a sticky floor or a glass ceiling, it can also simply be the consequences of past practices. It is of interest, however, as there may be ramifications affecting the probability of a promotion occurring. For example, conventional wisdom will inform us that it is increasingly difficult to be promoted as one moves up the organizational hierarchy, as the number of positions at the top of the house is smaller than at junior levels. Accordingly, if white males are more often situated at higher job levels, the probability of promotion for white males should be lower than for the other race/gender groups, if promotion decisions are made fairly. For this reason, job level is included as an explanatory variable in the model. For the separation analyses, the nine levels in the organizational hierarchy are categorized into three groups: entry level (levels 1 to 4), feeder group (levels 5 and 6), and management level (levels 7 to 9).

Race/gender composition

The mix of incumbents in jobs may contribute to differential treatment in promotions (Gerhart and Milkovich, 1989; Maume, 1999; Cohen,

Broschak, and Haveman, 1998). There are at least two mechanisms that lead to this outcome. First, as white men are more likely to hold senior level positions than women and minorities, and managers (more often than not) prefer to work with others with similar backgrounds and experiences, women and minorities are less likely (relative to white males) to be promoted into management ranks. Second, research has found that female jobs pay less than jobs predominantly held by men (England, 1992). This finding predicts that white men will be more likely to "admit" fewer women and minorities in order to maintain the value and status of their managerial jobs. To capture the effect of race/gender composition on the probability of promotion, three new variables are created: percentage white female, percentage minority male, and percentage minority female, for each of the job family/level combinations.

Base pay

A firm's wage policy is designed to discourage quits, in order to ensure that the firm can enjoy the return on its investment in its workers. Wage growth has been shown to reduce the likelihood of separations (Munasinghe, 2000). Some firms would also opt to pay efficiency (higher) wages to increase workers' productivity when the monitoring of activities is difficult. Firms may also pay higher wages if they are looking to fill a large number of vacancies in a tight labor market. Finally, the concept of deferred compensation may be part of a firm's policy: firms may choose to pay lower salaries than might be expected at the earlier stages of a worker's career, and somewhat higher levels of compensation than might be expected at a later stage, in order to avoid shirking.

Wages, therefore, can be a key determinant of a decision to change jobs among young workers (Topel and Ward, 1992). The annual salary is included in the model as a proxy for the value of the current job.

A person will change jobs only when the total gain from the change exceeds the costs. As wages increase, the possibility of locating another job with better pay decreases. Studies have show that employees at higher salaries are less likely to terminate the employment relationship voluntarily (Barnes and Jones, 1974; Anderson and Meyer, 1994). Thus, a significant negative relationship between compensation and the propensity to separate voluntarily is expected, while compensation should have no significant effect on retirement or involuntary separation. This is the efficiency wage argument.

Union status

Mechanisms giving workers a stronger voice are associated with lower quit rates (Freeman, 1980). Unions provide a venue for workers to voice their concerns through their grievance process, thus lowering the likelihood of voluntary quits. Studies have shown that union status decreases the likelihood of employment separation (Kidd, 1991; McLaughlin, 1991) and that the effect is much stronger for older workers (Blau and Kahn, 1983).

Conventional wisdom would lead us to believe that unionization will be associated with lower quit rates due to the union/non-union wage premium. Kenneth McLaughlin (1991) finds that the lower separation rate of unionized workers no longer holds when compensation level is controlled for, however. Unionized environments are also more likely to have stringent procedural rules for effecting workforce reduction, thus lowering the likelihood of involuntary separations. Some studies have also found that the negative effect of unionism on separation rates is significant in voluntary quits, while the unionism effect is weak or non-existent in involuntary separations (Freeman, 1980; Swidinsky, 1992).

Unionized workers were excluded from the promotion analyses as the rules for the promotion for unionized workers are often different from those for salaried workers, and may be more seniority-based than the rules for salaried workers (Abraham and Medoff, 1985).

Job track

Employees in this company are also classified into two different job tracks: people managers and individual contributors. Dual career ladders within companies are promotion systems that reward technical personnel with pay, perquisites, and titles similar to those enjoyed by managers, allowing them to do what they do best. Employees in both the individual contributor and management job tracks can attain the same highest job level in the company, though their titles and responsibilities may differ.

Incentives to stay: promotion

As opportunities for advancement, or promotions, may influence the likelihood of separating from the firm, an attempt is made to capture this factor by including a variable that accounts for whether an employee received one or more promotion(s) during the five-year period of this study in the analyses on separations. Since most workers are continually looking for advancement opportunities, any workplace that offers such opportunities should have a lower turnover rate. A promotion usually comes with an increase in total compensation and a higher level of autonomy. More importantly, a promotion offers the employee a higher level of responsibility and the challenges that come with that responsibility. The prediction is that those who have received a promotion are less likely to separate or retire from the firm voluntarily, whereas it is ambiguous as to how promotion would co-vary with the incidence of involuntary separation.

Incentives to stay: employee stock options

With regard to the effectiveness of stock options as a retention tool, the analyses considered (1) whether the employee received one or more stock option grants between 1991 and 2000, and (2) whether the employee had any overhang options (options that had been granted and vested but not yet exercised) or unvested options (options that had been granted but had not become vested).

A stock option is a right given to an employee to purchase a share of the company stock at a certain price at a future date. In addition to being a compensation tool, stock options have become popular as a retention tool. As employees can exercise their options as soon as they become vested, however, the effectiveness of stock options as a retention tool will probably depend on the vesting schedule and stock price appreciation. In this firm, the granting of options is at the firm's discretion, with guidelines provided by the human resources department by job level. Only management employees were eligible for stock option grants until 1999, when the plan became a broad-based scheme. Two variables that capture the likely effect of non-qualified stock options on the employee separation rate are therefore included: (1) overhang options: whether the employee held any options that had become vested but had yet to be exercised; and (2) unvested options: whether the employee had unvested options.

It is unclear what the net effect of stock option grants would be on the probability of turnover.[10] Unvested options are likely to be

---

[10] In separate analyses, the incidence of stock option granting is positively correlated with the incidence of promotion.

negatively correlated with all types of voluntary separation for all race/gender groups. Overhang options will probably have no effect on the rates of voluntary or involuntary separations, as these overhang options can be exercised before the termination date in order to realize any gains.

Finally, several control variables are also included to account for the differences in year of termination and the region where each employee worked.

Empirical results: promotions

Table 3.3 reports the percentage of promotions received by each of the four race/gender groups in the period observed by the data set used in this part of the analyses, not controlling for any differences in characteristics. Overall, a slightly higher percentage of whites (59.4 percent) received one or more promotions than non-whites (55.7 percent), a 3.7 percentage point differential that is statistically significant at the 1 percent level. Differentiating by gender, a higher proportion (57.2 percent) of male employees received one or more promotions, as compared to 54.7 percent of the female employees – a 2.5 percentage point differential that is also statistically significant at the 1 percent level.

Table 3.3 *Comparison of gross promotion rates by race and gender*

	Percentage promoted	Percentage difference from reference group
Overall	56.5	
Whites	59.4	
Non-whites	55.7	−3.7**
Males	57.2	
Females	54.7	−2.6**
White males	60.0	
White females	58.1	−1.9
Minority males	56.7	−3.3**
Minority females	52.6	−7.4**

Notes: Reference categories in italics. **denotes significance at $p < 0.01$.

The gross promotion rates of white males and the other race/gender minority groups are also compared. While the proportion of white females who were promoted was lower than that of white males (58.1 percent versus 60.0 percent), the differential is statistically significant only at the 10 percent level. The promotion gaps between white males and minority males (3.4 percentage points) and between white males and minority females (7.5 percentage points) are both significant at the 1 percent level. Thus, a simple bivariate analysis indicates lower promotion probabilities for both females and minorities, and minority females seem to suffer a "double whammy" in their prospect of career advancement.

Higher proportions of whites were promoted than non-whites and significantly more males were promoted than females. About 60.0 percent of white males in the sample received a promotion during the time period, while only 58.1 percent of white females, 56.7 percent of minority males and 52.6 percent of minority females were promoted. The race/gender promotion gaps are 1.9 percent for white females, 3.3 percent for minority males and 7.4 percent for minority females. Although the gross promotion rates show that all groups were less likely to be promoted than white males, only the minority groups are less likely to be promoted at conventional statistically significant levels.

Table 3.4 presents the descriptive statistics for selected explanatory variables for the various race/gender groups. Over 30 percent of the employees have missing race information and these were reported on as a separate group.[11] White males and white females, on average, are older than the racial minorities and have accumulated a slightly longer average tenure. A higher proportion of racial minorities possess university education than white males and white females. The average job level for white males is 5.5, followed by 5.1 for minority males, and 4.6 for both white and minority females. The pattern in average salaries is almost identical to that in job level: the average salary for white males is highest at $68,000, followed by minority males at $64,000, and both female groups at $54,300.

Although about 14 percent of the full sample received the highest performance rating (i.e. the "exceed" rating), the percentage of whites that received an "exceed" rating was higher than that of the minority groups. Of white males and white females, almost one in five received

---

[11] Employees in this group are somewhat younger and have shorter tenure with the firm, compared to the other race/gender groups.

Table 3.4 *Means and proportions for selected variables by race/ gender groups*

	Overall	White males	White females	Minority males	Minority females	Undisclosed
Proportion promoted	56.5%	60.0%	58.1%	56.7%	52.6%	52.7%
Age (in years)	35.7	37.1	37.3	35.9	34.4	33.7
Tenure (in years)	7.0	9.6	8.6	6.4	5.3	4.1
With university degrees	57.7%	57.1%	41.3%	77.4%	68.5%	57.1%
Job level	5.1	5.5	4.6	5.1	4.6	4.9
Salary (thousand dollars)	61.8	68.4	54.3	64.0	54.3	58.3
With "exceed" rating	13.9%	17.2%	18.7%	13.1%	11.4%	8.9%
With break in service	0.3%	0.4%	0.1%	0.3%	0.3%	0.4%
No. of observations	22,338	7,689	3,388	2,826	901	7,534
	100.0%	34.4%	15.2%	12.7%	4.0%	33.7%

the highest performance rating, whereas the percentages for minority males and minority females who received "exceed" ratings were only 13 percent and 11 percent respectively. This is in line with the observation by Jeffrey Greenhaus, Saroj Parasuraman, and Wayne Wormley (1990) that non-whites received lower job performance ratings that may indirectly affect their promotability. It is unclear to what extent this difference reflects true differences in performance, however, and to what extent it reflects the impact of discrimination. Finally, the percentage of employees with a break in service was very small: 0.4 percent of white males, 0.1 percent of white females, and 0.3 percent of minority groups had a break in service between 1995 and 2000.

Table 3.5 summarizes the a priori expectations for the relationships between each critical variable for promotion and for each termination reason.[12]

---

[12] The effects of most of these variables on promotion are likely to mirror those for "better prospects," apart from salary and job level. Salary would be expected to have a positive correlation with promotability (i.e. the higher one's salary is the more likely one would be to receive a promotion). Job level would be expected to have a negative correlation with promotability, as the number of positions diminishes as one goes up the organizational hierarchy.

Table 3.5. *A priori expectations for key variables on the likelihood of separation (by separation reason) and the likelihood of promotion*

	Voluntary separations		Retirements	Involuntary separations			Promotions
	Better prospects	Personal reasons		Divestitures	Layoffs	Dismissals	
(Relative to white males)							
White females	–	+	+	–	+	No effect	–
Minority males	–	+	–	–	No effect	No effect	–
Minority females	–	+	–	–	No effect	No effect	–
Age	+, –	No effect	+	No effect	No effect	No effect	+
Tenure	–, +, –	No effect	+	No effect	+	No effect	+/–
Education	–, +	+ or –	–	No effect	–	–	+
Performance rating	+	+ or –	No effect	No effect	–	–	+
Union status	–	–	No effect	+	–	–	n/a
Salary	–	–	No effect	No effect	No effect	No effect	+
Job level	+	–	No effect	No effect	–	No effect	–
Promotion	–	No effect	No effect	No effect	–	–	
Stock grants	+	+ or –	No effect	No effect	–	–	n/a
Overhang options	No effect	–	No effect	No effect	No effect	No effect	n/a
Unvested options	–	–	No effect	No effect	–	–	n/a

Table 3.6 reports the marginal effects on the incidence of promotion. Most of the independent variables included in the model exhibited the expected patterns of influence. For example, employees with higher levels of educational attainment are significantly more likely to be promoted. Tenure had a significant inverted U-shaped relationship with the probability of receiving a promotion: a positive effect initially and declining thereafter. Break in service reduced the probability of promotion by 13 percent. The likelihood of promotion also decreased as one moved up the organization hierarchy, confirming the common belief in the increasing difficulty of climbing the corporate ladder. In line with meritocratic principles, employees who performed well relative to others stood a better chance of promotion. Higher salaries were also positively and significantly related to higher promotion probability. In terms of the effect of race/gender job composition, only "percent minority male" had a significant negative effect on the promotion probability in this overall model. "Percent white female" had an insignificant negative effect whereas "percent minority female" had an insignificant positive effect on the likelihood of receiving a promotion. Finally, employees in almost all other job functions were more likely to be promoted than those in research and development. This may reflect the fact that, in this firm, in order to attract employees with specific technical skills, employees here were placed in relatively high levels in the organizational hierarchy at earlier stages of their career.

The only variable that carries a sign other than expected is the age variable. Older employees seem to be significantly less likely to be promoted, and the probability decreases further the older one gets. Although a positive effect is expected, as both age and education are proxies for general skills, a negative effect of age on the probability of promotion is reasonable as the model also controls for tenure. In summary, all race/gender groups were significantly less likely than white males to be promoted even after controlling for an extensive list of factors that affect the promotion probability in the overall model.

The first column of table 3.6 reports the marginal effects on the probability of promotion for the pooled sample for all job levels estimated from the probit model of promotion. Even after controlling for an extensive list of supply-side, demand-side, and control variables, white females, minority males, and minority females were all less likely to receive promotions than white males. White females were 4.5 percent

Table 3.6 *Determinants of promotions by race and gender group, 1996–2000*

	Overall sample		White males		White females		Minority males		Minority females	
	dF/dx	Std. err.	dF/dx	Std. err.	dF/dx	Std. err.	dF/dx	Std. err.	dF/dx	Std. err.
White males										
White females	−0.0454**	0.0121								
Minority males	−0.0788**	0.0123								
Minority females	−0.1612**	0.0192								
Undisclosed	−0.0974**	0.0096								
High school or less										
Post-HS/college	0.0909**	0.0119	0.0756**	0.0214	0.0649*	0.0263	0.0973	0.0508	0.0781	0.0819
Undergraduate degrees	0.1119**	0.0120	0.0648**	0.0228	0.0847**	0.0298	0.0481	0.0487	0.1694*	0.0731
Graduate degrees	0.0963**	0.0135	0.0688**	0.0254	0.1082**	0.0378	0.0709	0.0501	0.1002	0.0823
Age (in years)	−0.0089*	0.0039	−0.0089	0.0072	−0.0124	0.0095	−0.0015	0.0123	0.0199	0.0227
Tenure (in years)	0.0136**	0.0017	0.0079**	0.0027	0.0045	0.0045	0.0223**	0.0062	0.0493**	0.0149
Break in service	−0.1346*	0.0626	−0.2002*	0.0936	−0.2032	0.2910	−0.3448	0.1516	−0.0193	0.3192
Levels 1 and 2										
Level 3	−0.5527**	0.0133	−0.6016**	0.0228	−0.6397**	0.0368	−0.6412**	0.0148	−0.6950**	0.0284
Level 4	−0.4005**	0.0255	−0.3245**	0.0611	−0.5673**	0.0461	−0.5553**	0.0772	−0.6246**	0.0786
Level 5	−0.7400**	0.0175	−0.6534**	0.0467	−0.7215**	0.0374	−0.8241**	0.0609	−0.9328**	0.0284
Level 6	−0.7516**	0.0110	−0.7433**	0.0351	−0.7105**	0.0263	−0.8168**	0.0361	−0.7326**	0.0302
Level 7	−0.7481**	0.0067	−0.8101**	0.0190	−0.7174**	0.0159	−0.7592**	0.0216	−0.6467**	0.0231
Level 8	−0.6479**	0.0043	−0.7137**	0.0098	−0.6361**	0.0101	−0.6528**	0.0132	−0.5709**	0.0199
Annual salary (thousand dollars)	0.0145**	0.0005	0.0148**	0.0009	0.0089**	0.0015	0.0225**	0.0018	0.0224**	0.0035

	(1)		(2)		(3)		(4)		(5)	
Performance rating										
Exceed	0.2904**	0.0097	0.2631**	0.0166	0.3058**	0.0247	0.2897**	0.0281	0.2157**	0.0693
Achieve	0.1648**	0.0101	0.1370**	0.0185	0.1946**	0.0283	0.1717**	0.0297	0.0907	0.0584
Research and development										
Information technology	0.0627**	0.0185	0.0559	0.0309	0.0926*	0.0427	−0.0746	0.0740	0.0426	0.1128
Finance	0.1438**	0.0261	0.1075*	0.0481	0.1109*	0.0511	−0.0045	0.1190	0.2166	0.1372
Customer service	0.1166**	0.0204	0.2130**	0.0251	0.0625	0.0569	0.1392	0.0685	−0.1964	0.1413
Operations	0.0001	0.0187	0.1145**	0.0272	−0.0992*	0.0439	0.0640	0.0674	−0.2044	0.1107
Sales and marketing	0.1730**	0.0158	0.1436**	0.0265	0.1330**	0.0366	0.0030	0.0712	0.2399*	0.1032
Procurement	0.0828**	0.0264	0.1272**	0.0391	0.0360	0.0585	0.0054	0.1246	−0.0543	0.1633
Human resources	0.2440**	0.0319	−0.0163	0.1150	0.2443**	0.0516	−0.4038	0.2086	0.3285	0.1404
Corporate services	−0.0025	0.0375	−0.1033	0.0833	−0.0072	0.0611	0.0204	0.2010	−0.1143	0.2113
Others	−0.3811*	0.1185	0.2065	0.1883	—		—		—	
Job composition										
Percent white female	−0.0007	0.0009	0.0066**	0.0019	−0.0013	0.0017	0.0087	0.0045	−0.0071	0.0049
Pecent minority male	−0.0055**	0.0015	0.0007	0.0025	−0.0008	0.0035	−0.0147**	0.0056	−0.0194*	0.0090
Percent minority female	0.0035	0.0022	0.0084	0.0043	−0.0034	0.0043	0.0338**	0.0096	−0.0039	0.0116
Observed prob.	0.5654		0.6001		0.5817		0.5666		0.5250	
Predicted prob.	0.5784		0.6227		0.5956		0.5889		0.5233	
No. of observations	22,338		7,689		3,383		2,824		899	
LR Chi-sq	5244.02 (43)		1894.01 (39)		642.23 (38)		789.01 (37)		332.89 (37)	
Log likelihood	−12670.12		−4227.54		−1978.40		−1537.84		−455.57	
Pseudo R-sq	0.1715		0.1830		0.1396		0.2042		0.2676	

Notes: Reference categories in italics. ** denotes significance at p < 0.01. * denotes significance at p < 0.05. Includes controls for squared terms for age and tenure, region and year of promotion.

less likely to be promoted than comparable white males, and minority males 7.9 percent less likely. Minority females were 16 percent less likely than similar white males to receive promotions. The model was also estimated excluding those whose race/gender status could not be identified. The results are substantially the same. Table 3.6 also presents the maximum likelihood estimates from the probit model of promotion by race/gender group. The promotion process indeed operates quite differently for the four groups.

Education is a strong positive predictor of promotion for white males and white females. In general, higher educational attainment increases one's likelihood of being promoted. For the minorities, education is not significantly related to the probability of promotion. Age is not a significant predictor of promotion for any group. The effect of tenure on promotion probability takes on the shape of an inverted U for all race/gender groups but the effect is not significant for white females. Break in service seems to have a negative effect on the probability of promotion but is significant only for white males. On average, a white male employee who had a break in service was 20 percent less likely to be promoted than a white male whose service with the company had been continuous.

The effect of job composition on the likelihood of promotion is also quite different for the four race/gender groups. The workforce percentages of white females, minority males, and minority females all increase the promotion probability for white males, but have negative effects on the promotion probability of white females. The percentages of white females and minority females are positively correlated to the promotability of minority males, but the percentage of minority males has a negative effect on the probability of promotion of minority males. Finally, the percentage of minority race/gender compositions of jobs decreases the likelihood of promotion of minority females.

The workforce percentage of white females has a significant positive effect on the promotion probability for white males. White males are 6.6 percent more likely to receive a promotion with every 10 percent increase in the percentage of white females in the job composition. This may be an indication of a phenomenon that some researchers have called the "glass escalator" effect: men are more likely to be promoted in female-dominated occupations (Williams, 1995). On the other hand, the workforce percentage of white females has a negative, though not significant, effect on the promotability of both white and minority females. Finally, the percentage of white females increases the probability of promotion for minority males, but the effect is not statistically significant at conventional levels.

The percentage of minority males significantly lowers the promotion probability for white females and both minority groups, but is significant only for the minority groups. A 10 percent increase in the percentage of minority males in a job decreases the probability of promotion for minority males and minority females by 15 percent and 19 percent respectively. Its effect on the probability of promotion of white males is positive, however, though not significant.

The percentage of minority females in job composition has a significant positive effect on the probability of promotion for minority males. A 1 percent increase in the percentage of minority females significantly increases the minority males' chances for promotion (by 3 percent).

Empirical results: separations

The multinomial logit results for the four-category outcome model are presented in table 3.7. Comparing voluntary separations to those who stayed, white females were 10.5 percent less likely to quit voluntarily than white males. For minority males, the difference in voluntary turnover rates relative to those for white males was not significant after controlling for personal, job, and incentives characteristics. Minority females were actually 8.6 percent less likely to quit than white males. With respect to involuntary separations, it was 13 percent less likely for this to happen to white females than to white males. Minority males and females were also less likely to separate involuntarily than white males (5 percent and 20 percent respectively).

The results show that white females and minority females were less likely than white males to separate for retirement purposes (2 percent and 5 percent respectively). Holding all personal, job, and incentives characteristics constant, the retirement rates of white males and minority males were no longer significantly different.

Age is negatively correlated with the incidence of voluntary separation. The older an employee the less likely it is that he or she will quit. The oldest age group was more likely to separate involuntarily from the company, but the magnitude is small (2 percent). Those aged forty-five and over were also more likely to retire, reflecting the phenomenon of early and normal retirement.

Table 3.7 *Changes in probabilities in the likelihood of voluntary separations, involuntary separations, and retirements (reference group = the stayers)*

	Voluntary separation	Involuntary separation	Retirement
Overall mean	0.1147	0.1779	0.0347
White males			
White females	−0.1054**	−0.1336**	−0.0206**
	(0.0813)	(0.0648)	(0.1066)
Minority males	0.0051	−0.0544**	−0.0091
	(0.0736)	(0.0794)	(0.1647)
Minority females	−0.0861**	−0.2025**	−0.0509**
	(0.1172)	(0.1296)	(0.2997)
Undisclosed	−0.0343**	−0.0440**	−0.0054
	(0.0576)	(0.0526)	(0.1029)
Less than 25 years of age			
25 years to less than 35 years	−0.0304**	−0.0176	0.0048
	(0.0949)	(0.0885)	(1.0605)
35 years to less than 45 years	−0.0761**	0.0367	0.0036
	(0.1027)	(0.0925)	(1.0459)
45 years to less than 55 years	−0.1687**	0.0432	0.1072**
	(0.1310)	(0.1046)	(1.0325)
55 years and over	−0.4222**	0.0180**	0.1621**
	(0.3361)	(0.1332)	(1.0346)
Tenure less than 1 year			
1 to less then 3 years	0.0320	−0.1476**	−0.0062
	(0.0691)	(0.0704)	(0.5209)
3 to less than 5 years	0.0544**	−0.0841**	0.0288
	(0.0869)	(0.0932)	(0.5540)
5 to less than 8 years	0.0487**	−0.0228	0.0311
	(0.0965)	(0.0984)	(0.5344)
8 to less than 10 years	0.0415*	−0.0133	0.0374*
	(0.1234)	(0.1214)	(0.5573)
10 years and over	−0.0205*	0.0411	0.0810**
	(0.0962)	(0.0796)	(0.4363)
Less than high school			
High school	−0.0021	−0.0703**	−0.0309**
	(0.1492)	(0.0821)	(0.1236)

Table 3.7 (*cont.*)

	Voluntary separation	Involuntary separation	Retirement
Post-HS/college	−0.0150	−0.0843**	−0.0409**
	(0.1447)	(0.0791)	(0.1178)
Undergraduate degrees	0.0318	−0.0881**	−0.0498**
	(0.1462)	(0.0921)	(0.1785)
Graduate degrees	0.0864**	−0.0726*	−0.0651**
	(0.1524)	(0.1084)	(0.2354)
Performance rating			
Exceed	0.1209**	0.2959**	0.0631**
	(0.0889)	(0.0972)	(0.2387)
Achieve	0.1015**	0.3058**	0.0689**
	(0.0676)	(0.0701)	(0.1642)
Union	−0.0034	0.1391**	0.0323**
	(0.1371)	(0.1231)	(0.2637)
Salary ($10,000)	0.0001*	−0.0588**	−0.0102**
	(0.0202)	(0.0214)	(0.0438)
Hierarchical group: entry			
Feeder	0.0524**	0.0922**	0.0307**
	(0.0770)	(0.0767)	(0.1998)
Management	0.0578**	0.2931**	0.0602**
	(0.1248)	(0.1235)	(0.2801)
Job track: individual contributor			
Management	0.0043	0.0507**	0.0209**
	(0.1034)	(0.0993)	(0.1667)
Job family: research and development			
Information technology	−0.0981**	0.1761**	0.0100
	(0.1061)	(0.0905)	(0.2318)
Finance	−0.0944**	−0.0781**	−0.0084
	(0.1397)	(0.1503)	(0.3273)
Customer service	−0.1108**	−0.0594**	−0.0140*
	(0.1221)	(0.1091)	(0.1963)
Operations	−0.0672**	0.0244	0.0060
	(0.0820)	(0.0729)	(0.1510)
Sales and marketing	−0.0666**	−0.0464**	−0.0070

Table 3.7 (*cont.*)

	Voluntary separation	Involuntary separation	Retirement
	(0.0976)	(0.1010)	(0.1986)
Procurement	−0.0262	0.1257**	0.0290**
	(0.1577)	(0.1233)	(0.2073)
Human resources	−0.0947**	0.0868*	−0.0059
	(0.2071)	(0.1793)	(0.4375)
Corporate services	−0.1101**	0.0914*	0.0049
	(0.2096)	(0.1662)	(0.2942)
Others	−0.1244**	−0.1239**	−0.0336**
	(0.1787)	(0.1058)	(0.1939)
One or more grant(s) in last ten years	0.1726**	0.0232	0.0198**
	(0.1738)	(0.1821)	(0.2659)
With overhang options	−0.0079	0.1106**	−0.0075
	(0.0908)	(0.1181)	(0.2665)
Received promotion	−0.0584**	−0.0934**	−0.0410**
	(0.0603)	(0.0644)	(0.1775)
LR chi-sq	39449.13		
Log likelihood	−18286.794		
Pseudo R-sq	0.5189		
No. of observations	40,483		

Notes: Reference categories in italics. **denotes significance at $p < 0.01$. *denotes significance at $p < 0.05$. Standard errors in parentheses. Includes controls for unvested options, region, and year of termination.

The likelihood of voluntarily separating was higher for employees who had accumulated more firm-specific skills through longer tenure. Almost all tenure groups were more likely to separate than those with less than one year of service. The only exception was for those with more than ten years of service, who were 2 percent less likely to separate voluntarily. Employees with one to five years of service were less likely to separate involuntarily than those with less than one year of service. This signals that, once a match is found, the probability of employer-initiated terminations is lower. As expected, employees with eight or more years of service were more likely to retire due to eligibility rules in most retirement plans. Employees who had accumulated three to eight years of service were more likely to separate voluntarily, signalling that employees are deviating from the traditional loyal relationship. This supports the new protean career concept, in which employees leave when they find better job matches.

Employees with graduate degrees were 8 percent more likely to leave voluntarily than those with less than a high school diploma, whereas all higher education attainments were associated with a lower probability of involuntary separations and retirements. Employees with more than a high school education were 7 to 9 percent less likely to experience an involuntary separation, and 3 to 7 percent less likely to separate by retirement.

Good performance ratings had positive effects on the likelihood of voluntary and involuntary separation and retirements. High performers were more likely to separate voluntarily because of their abilities and productivities. The large and statistically significant positive coefficient for good performance in involuntary separations is a bit puzzling, as one would expect employers to try to retain their higher performers instead of initiating terminations for these employees. This thesis may shed more light on this puzzle when the employer-initiated terminations are disaggregated into finer categories in the latter part of this chapter. The positive correlation between good performance and retirement is of a smaller magnitude (at 7 percent).

Unionized employees were less likely to quit, although the effect is not statistically significant at conventional levels. Those belonging to a union, however, were more likely to experience employer-initiated or involuntary separations (14 percent more so) and retirement (3 percent) as compared to the non-unionized employees. Employees with higher salaries were more likely to quit (although the effect is small) but were less likely to separate involuntarily or retire from the company. Employees situated at higher levels in the organizational hierarchy were more likely to separate as a result of voluntary and involuntary separations as well as for retirement purposes. Employees in all other job families were less likely to quit than those in research and development, whereas those in information technology, procurement, human resources and corporate services were more likely to experience involuntary turnover.

The receipt of stock option grants is also positively associated with turnover probability, with the strongest effect for voluntary separations. The receipt of stock option grants signals to other employers that the receiving employees are "good," and this may open up more alternative opportunities for recipients. Overhang options do not have any significant effect on separation probability, except for involuntary separations. Having any overhang options increased the likelihood of involuntary separation by 11 percent. This is another anomaly that will be further explored upon disaggregation of involuntary separations. Possession of unvested options reduced the likelihood of separation. Similarly, promotion significantly reduced the likelihood of separation, with the strongest effect on involuntary separations.

Reason-specific probit models

Past researchers have found that differentiating only between employer- and employee-initiated separations may be insufficient and may mask important trends.[13] For example, heightened activities in outsourcing and M&As have prompted significant levels of layoffs and the transfer of employees from one employer to another. It is important to note that employees whose employment was terminated as a result of these transfers did not actually lose their jobs. Divestitures of operations usually involve all workers at a particular unit, and they often continue to perform the same jobs and receive comparable pay packages from another employer. Previous studies have also found that workers enjoyed a higher level of wage gains when separation occurred for better prospects rather than for personal reasons or being laid off, both for men and women (Mincer, 1986; Abbott and Beach, 1994). Men gained more from quits and lost less from layoffs than women. Therefore, the ability to disaggregate further the termination reasons may allow a closer look at whether there are any gender or racial differences depending on the nature of employment separations.

As discussed earlier, both voluntary and involuntary separations may be disaggregated into finer categories. In order to determine

---

[13] Royalty (1998) shows that analyses that aggregate across destinations to which the worker departs (job-to-job versus job-to-non-employment turnover) and that differentiate only between employer- and employee-initiated separations were insufficient, because job-to-job and job-to-non-employment turnover tend to be negatively correlated and the effect of one may offset the other, thus showing no significance.

whether there were any gender or racial differences in the different reasons for separations, six reason-specific probit models are employed. These models were estimated from data on the employees whose employment was terminated. The categories of reasons for termination are (1) voluntary – better prospects, (2) voluntary – personal reasons, (3) retirement, (4) involuntary – position outsourced, (5) involuntary – layoff, or (6) involuntary – dismissal. The dependent variable in each case indicates the reason for the employee's termination.

Among the terminations observed, 35 percent were voluntary quits (24.3 percent left for better prospects and 10.7 percent left for personal reasons), 10.6 percent were retirements, and 54.4 percent were involuntary separations (28.4 percent for divestitures, 22.5 percent for layoffs, and 3.5 percent for dismissals).

The multinomial logit results for the six-category outcome model, which can now be compared across the various termination reasons, are presented in table 3.8. The results show that white females and minority females were almost 18 percent more likely than white males to separate for personal reasons than to separate for better prospects. Minority males were also more likely than white males to separate for personal reasons than for better prospects, by 4.3 percent.

Controlling for personal and job characteristics and incentives to stay, white females were 12 percent more likely than white males to retire than to leave for better prospects. White females were also 27.6 percent more likely than white males to be laid off than to leave for better prospects. Minority males were 8 percent less likely and minority females 7 percent more likely than white males to be laid off than to leave for better prospects. There do not seem to be any significant race/gender differences in separations due to divestitures and dismissals as compared to separations for better prospects.

Conclusions

This chapter provides empirical evidence on the incidence of promotions and separations in a large North American high-tech firm in the late 1990s, including the impacts of both the supply-side variables (i.e. information on the employees) and the demand-side variables (i.e. information on the employers).

Table 3.8 *Changes in probabilities in the likelihood of separation (reference = leave for better prospects, mean = 0.2435)*

	Personal reasons	Retirement	Divestiture	Layoff	Dismissal
Overall mean	0.1071	0.1061	0.2838	0.2249	0.0346
White males					
White females	0.1762**	0.1183**	0.1152	0.2759**	0.0223
	(0.1286)	(0.1594)	(0.1208)	(0.1180)	(0.1932)
Minority males	0.0428**	−0.0399	−0.0869	−0.0801*	0.0043
	(0.1044)	(0.2003)	(0.1120)	(0.1153)	(0.1720)
Minority females	0.1764**	−0.0356	−0.0341	0.0727**	0.0131
	(0.1585)	(0.3718)	(0.2048)	(0.1936)	(0.2971)
Undisclosed	0.0512**	0.0484**	0.0274	0.1019**	0.0098
	(0.0922)	(0.1312)	(0.0822)	(0.0811)	(0.1380)
Less than 25 years of age					
25 years to less	0.0570*	0.0564	0.1992**	0.0646	0.0261*
than 35 years	(0.1569)	(1.0814)	(0.1585)	(0.1470)	(0.2500)
35 years to less	0.0909	0.1483	0.4595**	0.2852**	0.0689**
than 45 years	(0.1697)	(1.0688)	(0.1672)	(0.1558)	(0.2590)
45 years to less	0.1625**	0.6401**	0.9034**	0.7184**	0.1283**
than 55 years	(0.2188)	(1.0602)	(0.1986)	(0.1879)	(0.3015)
55 years and over	0.3846**	1.2489**	1.7915**	1.6219**	0.2625**
	(0.6577)	(1.1762)	(0.5518)	(0.5421)	(0.6423)
Tenure less than 1 year					
1 to less than	−0.0455	0.0897	−0.0046	−0.0860**	−0.0027
3 years	(0.1152)	(0.5522)	(0.1251)	(0.1161)	(0.1795)
3 to less than	−0.0427	0.1641**	0.0269	−0.0473**	0.0024
5 years	(0.1344)	(0.5824)	(0.1474)	(0.1380)	(0.2197)
5 to less than	−0.0366	0.1561*	0.1643**	−0.0289**	0.0106
8 years	(0.1499)	(0.5757)	(0.1520)	(0.1520)	(0.2319)
8 to less than	−0.0185	0.1745*	0.2606**	0.0012*	−0.0034
10 years	(0.1877)	(0.6041)	(0.1788)	(0.1841)	(0.3158)
10 years and over	0.0123	0.4071**	0.5764**	0.2679**	0.0408
	(0.1640)	(0.4743)	(0.1475)	(0.1413)	(0.2230)
Less than high school					
High school	−0.0275	−0.1530**	−0.2390**	−0.1967**	−0.0144
	(0.2641)	(0.2434)	(0.2084)	(0.2119)	(0.2917)

Table 3.8 (*cont.*)

	Personal reasons	Retirement	Divestiture	Layoff	Dismissal
Post-HS/college	−0.0578	−0.1891**	−0.2960**	−0.2009**	−0.0278
	(0.2575)	(0.2297)	(0.2010)	(0.2030)	(0.2857)
Undergraduate	−0.0616	−0.2854**	−0.4151**	−0.3490**	−0.0480*
degrees	(0.2550)	(0.2712)	(0.2067)	(0.2081)	(0.3019)
Graduate	−0.0766	−0.4256**	−0.6247**	−0.5081**	−0.0723**
degrees					
	(0.2617)	(0.3231)	(0.2255)	(0.2198)	(0.3245)
Undisclosed	−0.0434	−0.2279**	−0.3532**	−0.2736**	−0.0416
	(0.2829)	(0.2828)	(0.2328)	(0.2338)	(0.3531)
Performance rating					
Exceed	0.0189	−0.0493	−0.0006	−0.0544	−0.0305**
	(0.1256)	(0.2843)	(0.1348)	(0.1324)	(0.2751)
Achieve	0.0109	−0.0017	0.0156	0.0352	−0.0032
	(0.1009)	(0.2084)	(0.1066)	(0.1014)	(0.1628)
Union	0.0351	0.0730	0.1836*	0.1743**	−0.0098
	(0.2614)	(0.3567)	(0.2154)	(0.2149)	(0.3805)
Salary ($10,000)	−0.0188*	−0.0218	−0.0826**	−0.0475**	−0.0140**
	(0.0361)	(0.0576)	(0.0365)	(0.0337)	(0.0624)
Hierarchical group: entry					
Feeder	−0.0879**	−0.0418	−0.1853**	−0.0765	−0.0289**
	(0.1184)	(0.2415)	(0.1208)	(0.1195)	(0.1853)
Management	−0.0512**	0.0400	0.0422	0.2028**	0.0146
	(0.2225)	(0.3593)	(0.2077)	(0.2006)	(0.3573)
Job track: individual contributor					
Management	−0.0224	0.0498	0.0941*	−0.0069	0.0131
	(0.1827)	(0.2124)	(0.1494)	(0.1448)	(0.2597)
Job family: research and development					
Information	0.1511**	0.2392**	0.8616**	0.4217**	0.0703**
technology	(0.1557)	(0.2721)	(0.1301)	(0.1376)	(0.2476)
Finance	0.0031	0.0260	0.1463*	0.0121	0.0211
	(0.2186)	(0.4194)	(0.2389)	(0.2202)	(0.3278)
Customer service	0.0394	0.0206	0.3390**	−0.0823**	0.0195
	(0.2039)	(0.2615)	(0.1713)	(0.1938)	(0.3000)
Operations	0.0418	0.1118**	0.4168**	0.0944	0.0393**
	(0.1330)	(0.1888)	(0.1139)	(0.1168)	(0.1806)

Table 3.8 (*cont.*)

	Personal reasons	Retirement	Divestiture	Layoff	Dismissal
Sales and	−0.0085	0.0266	0.1917**	0.0284	0.0128
marketing	(0.1670)	(0.2510)	(0.1592)	(0.1494)	(0.2615)
Procurement	−0.0472*	0.0915	0.3609**	0.0671	0.0269
	(0.2870)	(0.2816)	(0.1883)	(0.2027)	(0.3089)
Human	−0.0099	0.0491	0.0593	0.3079**	0.0504**
resources	(0.3392)	(0.5011)	(0.3753)	(0.2475)	(0.3890)
Corporate	−0.0152	0.1323	0.3759**	0.3416**	0.0416
services	(0.3662)	(0.3668)	(0.2757)	(0.2360)	(0.4282)
Others	0.1202**	0.1282**	0.1386	0.2198**	0.0306
	(0.3359)	(0.3213)	(0.2792)	(0.2544)	(0.4201)
One or more	−0.0787	−0.1371	−0.4581**	−0.4287**	−0.0436
grant(s) in last	(0.2188)	(0.3198)	(0.2295)	(0.2218)	(0.3856)
10 years					
With overhang	0.0397	−0.0171	0.1484*	0.1657**	0.0260
options	(0.1476)	(0.3160)	(0.1652)	(0.1687)	(0.3695)
Received	0.0041	−0.0471*	0.0188	0.0109	−0.0147**
promotion	(0.0855)	(0.2043)	(0.0872)	(0.0874)	(0.1605)
LR chi-sq	15271.03				
Log likelihood	−13973.284				
Pseudo R-sq	0.3534				

Notes: Reference categories in italics. **denotes significance at $p < 0.01$. *denotes significance at $p < 0.05$. Standard errors in parentheses. Includes controls for unvested options, region and year of termination.

As in prior studies on promotions, this study found that employees who were promoted enjoyed annual wage gains that were twice the rate for those who were not promoted. Average wage gain for promoted non-whites was significantly higher than for promoted whites. On the other hand, average wage gain for promoted females was lower than that enjoyed by males. Among those who were promoted, white females had lower wage gains than white males, while minority males enjoyed higher wage gains than white males. The wage gain for minority females was not significantly different from that of white males.

Both race and gender, together with education, age, tenure, break in service, salary level, and performance ratings, are significant determinants of promotion for the overall sample. White females were 4.5 percent less likely, minority males 7.9 percent less likely, and minority females 16.1 percent less likely to receive a promotion than white males with the same attributes.

Age and promotion opportunity are negatively related. Tenure exhibits the predicted inverted U-shaped relationship with promotion, and performance is positively related to the incidence of promotion. A break in service with the firm has a negative impact on the likelihood of promotion. Salary level is positively related to promotability: employees with higher salary levels are more likely to be promoted.

The analyses show that promotion is an effective retention tool, as it reduces the likelihood of voluntary separation for all groups. On the other hand, the effectiveness of stock options as a retention tool is dependent on the status of the options. Stock option grants significantly increase the likelihood of separation only for white and minority males, but not for females. Overhang (vested and unexercised) options have no effect on the likelihood of separation for other groups, but significantly increase the likelihood of minority males separating from the firm. Finally, unvested options continue to have significant negative effects on the probability of separation.

Unionized employees are less likely to quit for better prospects or to be dismissed. Unions are often in a position to bargain for competitive pay and benefit packages and usually have comprehensive grievance processes in place, which help to lower the quit rate. Unions also often have stringent rules that govern how and when a unionized employee can be dismissed, thus contributing to the lower dismissal rate. On the other hand, unions tend to be less amenable to workplace flexibility, thus making unionized employees more prone to be laid off.

In addition to analyzing any gender and racial differences among the various reasons for separation, the data also permitted estimation of the effect of promotion and stock options on retention rates. This is possibly the first empirical study to investigate gender and racial differences and the use of stock options in relation to turnover rates for all employees at different levels of an organizational hierarchy. Table 3.9 recaps the proportions terminated among those who were promoted or received stock option grants.

Although similar proportions of employees in each race/gender group were promoted (ranging from 34 to 39 percent), 24.5 percent of previously promoted white males voluntarily left the firm as compared to

Table 3.9 *Proportions terminated among promotees and grant recipients by race/gender, percentages*

	White males	White females	Minority males	Minority females
Proportion promoted	36.3	34.3	39.0	36.3
Proportion terminated (conditioned on promotion)	24.5	22.1	29.2	23.6
Proportion receiving grant	45.8	29.7	47.4	40.6
Proportion terminated (conditioned on receipt of grant)	16.3	10.8	16.3	12.3

22.1 percent for white females, 29.2 percent for minority males, and 23.6 percent for minority females. The multivariate analyses show that promotion is negatively correlated with the probability of separation by 7.6 percent for white males. The negative effect was even stronger for white females: being promoted reduces the separation probability by over 10 percent. The negative promotion effect on the incidence of separation persisted for minority males and females, at 6.3 percent and 2.8 percent respectively. Promotions seemed to be most effective when given to white females.The analyses show that being promoted reduced the likelihood of voluntary separation by 5.8 percent.

Stock option grants increased the likelihood of overall voluntary separation by 17 percent. Overhang options had no effect on voluntary turnover, while unvested options significantly reduced that likelihood. These findings highlight the importance and effectiveness of granting "key" employees stock options as a retention tool. Table 3.9 shows that almost a half of white and minority males received stock option grants, while only about 30 percent of white females did. Among those who had received one or more stock option grants, 16 percent of white males and minority males had separated from the firm. The corresponding proportions for white and minority females were much lower (10.8 percent and 12.3 percent respectively). Stock option grants significantly increased the likelihood of separation only for white males and minority males, but not for the female groups. Overhang options had no effect on the likelihood of separation for other groups, but significantly increased the likelihood of minority males to separate. Finally, unvested options had significant negative effects on the probability of separation.

Even during a period of strong economic growth and a tight labor market, the minority race/gender groups are less likely to leave their employment for better prospects and less likely to be promoted than white males. Policies are required to address the sources of this disadvantage and to recognize and reduce the barriers faced by women and members of the minority groups. The adoption and formalization by firms and organizations of policies, programs, and practices that will accommodate the needs of women and racial minorities will enhance the labor market outcomes of these disadvantaged groups.

Appendix 3.1 Categorization of separation reasons

Voluntary separation	Retirement	Involuntary separation
Better prospects	Retirement	Divestiture
Better career prospect	Delayed retirement	Office closed/divestiture
Salary reason/more	Early retirement,	Outsourced
money	incl. health	Transfer to joint venture
	Normal retirement	(JV)
Personal reasons	Pre-retirement	
Employee dissatisfied		Layoff
Antipathy with		Discontinuation of
colleagues		function
Antipathy with		Layoff
management		Workforce reduction
Contract expired		
Domestic/personal		Dismissal
Failure to return from		Attendance/punctuality
leave		Discharged
Health		Dishonesty
Lack of confidence in		Expiration of recalls
company		Company-initiated
Marriage		Rules violation/
Physical working		misconduct
conditions		Termination
Refused recall		Unsatisfactory
Relocation/leaving		performance
district		
Resignation		
Return to school		
Travelling too long/		
expensive		

References

Abbott, M., and Beach, C. (1994). Wages changes and job changes of Canadian women. *Journal of Human Resources, 29*(2), 429–60.

Abraham, K. G., and Farber, H. S. (1987). Job duration, seniority and earnings. *American Economic Review, 77*(3), 278–97.

Abraham, K. G., and Medoff, J. L. (1985). Length of service and promotions in union and nonunion work groups. *Industrial and Labor Relations Review, 38*(3), 408–20.

Aigner, D. J., and Cain, G. C. (1977). Statistical theories of discrimination in labor markets. *Industrial and Labor Relations Review, 30,* 175–89.

Anderson, P. M., and Meyer, B. D. (1994). The extent and consequences of job turnover. *Brookings Papers on Economic Activity, Microeconomics, 1,* 177–248.

Arrow, K. (1973). The theory of discrimination. In O. Ashenfelter and A. Rees (eds.), *Discrimination in Labour Markets* (3–33). Princeton, NJ: Princeton University Press.

Baker, G. P., Gibbs, M., and Holmstrom, B. (1994a). The internal economics of the firm: evidence from personnel data. *Quarterly Journal of Economics, 109*(4), 881–919.

(1994b). The wage policy of a firm. *Quarterly Journal of Economics, 109*(4), 921–55.

Barnes, W. F., and Jones, E. (1974). Differences in male and female quitting. *Journal of Human Resources, 9*(4), 439–51.

Barnett, W., Baron, J. N., and Stuart, T. (2000). Avenues of attainment: organizational demography and organizational careers in the California civil service. *American Journal of Sociology, 106,* 88–144.

Bartel, A. P., and Borjas, G. J. (1981). Wage growth and job turnover: an empirical analysis. In S. Rosen (ed.), *Studies in Labor Markets* (65–89). Chicago: University of Chicago Press.

Becker, G. (1957). *The Economics of Discrimination.* Chicago: University of Chicago Press.

(1964). *Human Capital.* Chicago: University of Chicago Press.

Benjamin, D., Gunderson, M., and Riddell, C. (2001). *Labour Market Economics: Theory, Evidence and Policy in Canada.* Toronto: McGraw-Hill Ryerson.

Berkowitz, M. K., and Kotowitz, Y. (1993). Promotions as work incentives. *Economic Inquiry, 31,* 342–53.

Blau, F. D., and Kahn, L. M. (1981). Race and sex differences in quits by young workers. *Industrial and Labor Relations Review, 34*(4), 563–77.

(1983). Unionism, seniority and turnover. *Industrial Relations, 22*(3), 362–73.

Bognanno, M. L. (2001). Corporate tournaments. *Journal of Labor Economics*, 19(2), 290–315.

Brown, C., and Medoff, J. L. (2001). *Firm Age and Wages*. Working Paper no. 8552. Cambridge, MA: National Bureau of Economic Research.

Brown, J. N., and Light, A. (1992). Interpreting panel data on job tenure. *Journal of Labor Economics*, 10(3), 219–57.

Burdett, K. (1978). A theory of employee job search and quit rates. *American Economic Review*, 68(1), 212–20.

Cappelli, P., and Hamori, M. (2005). The new road to the top. *Harvard Business Review*, 83(1), 25–32.

Christofides, L. M., and McKenna, C. J. (1993). Employment flows and job tenure in Canada. *Canadian Public Policy*, 19(2), 145–61.

Cohen, L., Broschak, J. P., and Haveman, H. (1998). And then there were more: the effect of organizational sex composition on the hiring and promotion of managers. *American Sociological Review*, 63, 711–27.

Doeringer, P. B., and Piore, M. J. (1971). *Internal Labor Markets and Manpower Analysis*. Lexington, MA: D.C. Heath.

England, P. (1992). *Comparable Worth: Theories and Evidence*. New York: Aldine de Gruyter.

Farber, H. S. (1993). The incidence and costs of job loss: 1982–91. *Brookings Papers on Economic Activity, Microeconomics*, 1, 73–132.

Francesconi, M. (2001). Determinants and consequences of promotions in Britain. *Oxford Bulletin of Economics and Statistics*, 63(3), 279–310.

Freeman, R. B. (1980). The exit–voice tradeoff in the labor market: unionism, job tenure, quits and separations. *Quarterly Journal of Economics*, 94, 643–73.

Gerhart, B. A., and Milkovich, G. T. (1989). Salaries, salary growth and promotions of men and women in a large private firm. In R. T. Michael, H. I. Hartmann, and B. O'Farrell (eds.), *Pay Equity: Empirical Inquiries* (23–43). Washington, DC: National Academy Press.

Gibbs, M. (1995). Incentive compensation in a corporate hierarchy. *Journal of Accounting and Economics*, 19, 247–77.

Greenhaus, J. H., Parasuraman, S., and Wormley, W. M. (1990). Effects of race on organizational experiences, job performance evaluations and career outcomes. *Academy of Management Journal*, 33(1), 64–86.

Hall, D. T. (1986). *Career Development in Organizations*. San Francisco: Jossey-Bass.

Hartmann, H. I. (1987). Internal labor markets and gender: a case study of promotion. In C. Brown and J. A. Pechman (eds.), *Gender in the Workplace* (59–91). Washington, DC: Brookings Institution.

Hersch, J., and Viscusi, W. K. (1996). Gender differences in promotions and wages. *Industrial Relations*, *35*(4), 461–72.

Igbaria, M., and Greenhaus, J. H. (1992). The career advancement prospects of managers and professionals: are MIS employees unique? *Decision Sciences*, *23*, 478–99.

Jovanovic, B. (1979). Job matching and the theory of turnover. *Journal of Political Economy*, *87*(5), part 1, 972–90.

Keith, K., and McWilliams, A. (1997). Job mobility and gender-based wage growth differentials. *Economic Inquiry*, *35*(2), 320–33.

Kidd, M. P. (1991). An econometric analysis of interfirm labour mobility. *Canadian Journal of Economics*, *24*(3), 517–35.

(1994). Some Canadian evidence on the quit/layoff distinction. *Canadian Journal of Economics*, *27*(3), 709–33.

Lazear, E. P., and Rosen, S. (1981). Rank-order tournaments as optimum labor contracts. *Journal of Political Economy*, *89*(5), 841–64.

Lewis, G. B. (1986). Gender and promotions: promotion chances of white men and women in federal white-collar employment. *Journal of Human Resources*, *21*(3), 406–19.

McCue, K. (1996). Promotions and wage growth. *Journal of Labor Economics*, *14*(2), 175–209.

McLaughlin, K. J. (1991). A theory of quits and layoffs with efficient turnover. *Journal of Political Economy*, *99*(1), 1–29.

Martel, J. L., and Kelter, L. A. (2000). The job market remains strong in 1999. *Monthly Labor Review*, *123*(2), 1–21.

Maume, D. J., Jr. (1999). Glass ceilings and glass escalators. *Work and Occupations*, *26*(4), 483–509.

Mincer, J. (1974). *Schooling, Experience and Learning*. New York: New York University Press, for National Bureau of Economic Research.

(1986). Wage changes in job changes. In R. G. Ehrenberg (ed.), *Research in Labor Economics*, vol. VIII, part A (171–97). Greenwich, CT: JAI Press.

Mincer, J., and Jovanovic, B. (1981). Labor mobility and wages. In S. Rosen (ed.), *Studies in Labor Markets* (21–63). Chicago: University of Chicago Press.

Munasinghe, L. (2000). Wage growth and the theory of turnover. *Journal of Labor Economics*, *18*(2), 204–20.

Oi, W. Y. (1990). Employment relations in dual labor markets. *Journal of Labor Economics*, *8*(1), S124–S149.

Olson, C. A., and Becker, B. E. (1983). Sex discrimination in the promotion process. *Industrial and Labor Relations Review*, *36*(4), 624–41.

Parsons, D. O. (1972). Specific human capital: an application to quit rates and layoff rates. *Journal of Political Economy*, *80*(6), 1120–43.

(1977). Models of labor market economics: a theoretical and empirical survey. *Research in Labor Economics, 1*, 185–223.

Petersen, T., and Saporta, I. (2004). The opportunity structure for discrimination. *American Journal of Sociology, 109*, 852–901.

Prendergast, C. (1993). The role of promotion in inducing specific human capital acquisition. *Quarterly Journal of Economics, 108*(2), 523–34.

Rosenbaum, J. E. (1979). Organizational career mobility: promotion chances in a corporation during periods of growth and contraction. *American Journal of Sociology, 85*(1), 21–48.

(1984). *Career Mobility in a Corporate Hierarchy*. Toronto: Academic Press.

Royalty, A. B. (1996). The effects of job turnover on the training of men and women. *Industrial and Labor Relations Review, 49*(3), 506–21.

(1998). Job-to-job and job-to-nonemployment turnover by gender and education level. *Journal of Labor Economics, 16*(2), 392–443.

Ruhm, C. (1987). The economic consequences of labor mobility. *Industrial and Labor Relations Review, 41*(1), 30–45.

Sicherman, N. (1996). Gender differences in departures from a large firm. *Industrial and Labor Relations Review, 49*(3), 484–505.

Spilerman, S., and Lunde, T. (1991). Features of educational attainment and job promotion prospects. *American Journal of Sociology, 97*(3), 689–720.

Spilerman, S., and Petersen, T. (1999). Organization structure, determinants of promotion, and gender differences in attainment. *Social Science Research, 28*, 203–27.

Spurr, S. J. (1990). Sex discrimination in the legal profession: a study of promotion. *Industrial and Labor Relations Review, 43*(4), 406–17.

Stewart, L. P., and Gudykunst, W. B. (1982). Differential factors influencing the hierarchical level and number of promotions of males and females within an organization. *Academy of Management Journal, 25*(3), 586–97.

Swidinsky, R. (1992). Unionism and the job attachment of Canadian workers. *Relations Industrielles, 47*(4), 729–50.

Topel, R. H., and Ward, M. P. (1992). Job mobility and the careers of young men. *Quarterly Journal of Economics, 107*(2), 439–79.

Weiss, A. M. (1984). Determinants of quit behavior. *Journal of Labor Economics, 2*(3), 371–87.

Williams, C. L. (1995). *Still a Man's World: Men Who Do "Women's Work"*. Berkeley, CA: University of California Press.

4 | *In the pursuit of quality and quantity: the competing demands in call centers*

STEFFANIE L. WILK

Introduction

To some, call centers represent the modern-day "factory floor." With strict controls over the quality and quantity of work, Taylorism seems to be alive and well in the call center. The reality is not that simple, however. Call centers, with virtually constant customer contact and attendant interpersonal demands on workers, will always be stressful for workers to a point. How the organization balances the demands of quantity and quality, by controlling the pace and the content (through the scripting and monitoring) of calls, can have a profound effect on the workplace. It can even influence how stressful the interpersonal demands of the job are for workers. Indeed, the choices employers make about how to manage call centers can be more important than the call center context per se in determining employee outcomes.

This chapter starts by providing a basic overview of the call center, highlighting the different types of calls and callers, and the power of technology to control both the quantity and the quality of the service interactions. Much of the chapter is dedicated to a study of how workers struggle to meet the competing demands of quantity and quality. Then I examine all the parties in the interpersonal context for call center workers and highlight the role that supervisors and co-workers may play in mitigating or exacerbating the stresses of the work with customers. The chapter concludes with some thoughts culled from the literature and some ideas for future research.

Competing demands

Getting your bank balance, making an airline reservation, purchasing birthday gifts, and buying groceries can all be done via the telephone.

I would like to thank Erin Coyne for her research assistance.

112

Indeed more and more interactions between customers[1] and organizations are technology-mediated, for example through telephone, the internet, or facsimile. Even fast food drive-through restaurants in the United States are starting to use call center operators. The person taking your order when you drive up may be hundreds of miles away, sitting in a cubicle (Richtel, 2006). Labor statistics that differentiate face-to-face service interactions from technology-mediated ones are rare. Some estimates, however, put the number of workers employed in call centers at 1.5 million in the United States, representing 3 percent of the workforce (Mandelbaum, 2004). Other estimates even go as high as 6 million. Projections suggest that the numbers are growing worldwide, with countries such as the United States, India, the United Kingdom, Canada, and Ireland at the forefront and Caribbean nations, South Africa, and Brazil entering the market as well (Urso, 2004).

Why all this growth? In a word: efficiency. A single representative in a call center can, depending on the job, handle ten to almost 100 customers per hour consistently over a shift (Batt, Hunter, and Wilk, 2003). This efficiency has value for some.

(1) Organizations see this as a means to increase service and/or sales. Indeed, in the fast food example mentioned above, the organization believed that having one person dedicated to "selling" the products and one person dedicated to filling the order provided more opportunities for the focused selling of target products (e.g. desserts).

(2) Customers like the convenience of service or sales on-demand in a virtual 24/7 marketplace. Call centers represent a large portion of that: worldwide, 70 percent of customer transactions representing some $700 billion went through call centers in 1997, and that number is increasing (Mandelbaum, 2004).

For organizations and customers, this appears to be a "win-win" situation. The effects on the employees who staff call centers are less clear, however.

If efficiency were the only goal, employees could focus exclusively on call quantity. They could reduce average handle time (AHT) and increase calls per hour (CPH), two very common metrics in call centers (Gans, Koole, and Mandelbaum, 2003). Most call centers want

---

[1] The term "customer" will be used throughout this chapter to refer to customers, clients, or the public generally.

efficiencies without sacrificing quality, however. The quality of the interaction, even when the average call length is several minutes long, is important enough to generate elaborate quality monitoring systems. As Peter Bain, Aileen Watson, Gareth Mulvey, Phil Taylor, and Gregor Gall, (2002, p. 172) note:

There are no "pure" call centers in which management policy is dedicated exclusively to either qualitative or quantitative objectives. In even the most quantity-driven operation, the aim is to ensure that the customer receives comprehensible information; conversely, employees in the most quality con-scious centers are monitored ... and are expected to handle a minimum number of calls.

Are call centers the factory floors of the future?

Technology and its role in controlling people is the traditional hall-mark of factories. Because technology is relied upon for both quantity and quality control, through, for example, pacing and monitoring systems that control how and how many calls a call center employee handles, some have suggested that call centers are the factory floors of the future. In other words, that call centers, like the traditional fac-tory, may use technology to limit the autonomy of workers and create work that is rote and undesirable. Making such a sweeping general-ization can be misleading, however, since organizational practices and job characteristics can vary so widely in call centers. For example, in a study of call centers from several organizations, Rosemary Batt, Larry Hunter, and Steffanie Wilk (2003) find that turnover rates varied from the single digits to around 400 percent per year. Batt (Batt, 2000; Appelbaum and Batt, 1994; Batt, Hunter, and Wilk, 2003) has also documented variation in how jobs are designed in call centers. She finds that even within a single organization jobs can be rote, with human resources practices that are designed to maximize the control of workers, or be varied, with "high involvement" HR practices.

Moreover, the suggestion of "factory floor" and the use of Taylorist routines (Zapf *et al.*, 2003) in these settings suggest that the jobs are broken down in such a way that they can be staffed by low-skilled workers. (In traditional Taylorism, tasks are parsed, standardized, and aggregated into a job that is easier for workers with little or no training to complete.) At first glance, call centers, with their use of scripts in an effort to regulate the interactions of employees with customers, may appear to fit this category. In reality, though, the complex nature of calls requires many of these workers to think on their feet and be highly reactive. Indeed, the customer, unlike traditional manufacturing jobs, in which Taylorism has been more commonly thought to apply, is part of the service exchange, and the nature of "interactive service work" (Leidner, 1993, p. 1) suggests that there will always be some variation in the encounter that will require workers to think on their feet. Workers in call centers must possess a complex mix of skill types and skill levels that enable them to manage this variation effectively and quickly. Batt (2000) notes that, even for the "mass market" jobs, the skills are varied and complex: "Employees must be skilled in several software packages and have negotiating skills to deal with tough customers" (p. 547).

How much call centers are like factory floors, therefore, is still open to debate. On the one hand, there is a heavy reliance on technology to control the work; on the other hand, technology can go only so far to control an interpersonal exchange between worker and customer that cannot be fully scripted. What *is* interesting about the debate is that it leads us to look at whether attempts to control the quantity and quality of call center work echoes a key charge leveled against mass production: that the work can be dehumanizing, leading to disaffection on the part of the workers. In this chapter I explore the extent to which these charges are supported by the evidence, and examine in particular those features of the call center setting that promote and mitigate these problems.

In the next section I describe in detail the work done in call centers and discuss similarities/differences with respect to traditional factory work. I focus specifically on technology, because of the dehumanizing effects it can have on workers. Following this, I examine in more detail the pressures on call center workers to meet both the quantity and quality requirements of the work. One place where the pressure is manifested is in the interpersonal requirements or demands of the work. The stress on workers to be pleasant and engage in quality interactions with customers but to complete the interaction quickly and within a specified protocol is a precursor to workplace disaffection, which is manifested in greater absenteeism, higher turnover, and lower performance. Finally, I conclude with some issues to consider for the future.

The context: call centers

Types of calls and callers

There is variation in the types of calls, the types of callers, and even who initiates the encounter, and this variation often exists within a single call center. Thus, it is more difficult to differentiate call centers from one another on these dimensions than it is to differentiate the calls themselves. This section briefly highlights the two major categories for differentiating calls: first, who initiates the calls, or whether the call is inbound or outbound; and, second, the purpose of the call, or whether the call is for sales or service, or a combination. As the discussion below notes, these seemingly simple distinctions mask the complexity in the work of call center workers.

Inbound/outbound

An interaction between a customer and a call center worker can be initiated by either party. Calls that are initiated by the customer are called "inbound" calls while those from the call center worker are called "outbound" calls. There are variations on these two types, however. Outbound calls can range from cold calls to warm calls. Outbound calls are "cold calls" when call center workers are attempting to solicit new customers. Callers may be asked if they are interested in purchasing various products and services. These so-called "telemarketers" have encountered intense legal pressure in the United States, where new laws prohibit telemarketers from calling those who opt out of the telephone databases these companies use as a source of new customers (e.g. the Federal Trade Commission's "Do Not Call" lists). So many households have opted out of the databases that the telemarketing industry has a limited customer pool (many outbound call centers have moved overseas: Krol, 2004). Even before these laws went into effect, the climate for telemarketers in the United States was poor. The frequent rejection encountered, along with the commission-based compensation that is common for telemarketers, translates into high turnover for these jobs. One study that included telemarketing call centers finds that an outbound center's turnover rates were close to 400 percent per year, compared to less than 10 percent for a traditional inbound call center (Batt, Hunter, and Wilk, 2003).

Outbound calls are "warm calls" when a call center worker is calling existing or former customers. In these instances the call may be initiated by the call center worker, but the customer is familiar with the organization. These types of outbound calls may be used to follow up on a previous interaction, solicit the collection of payment for good and services, or persuade a former customer to come back.

Inbound calls, those initiated by the customer, make up the majority of calls that are fielded in call centers. Customers typically call a toll-free number to connect with a call center. The customer will either be routed immediately to a person or wait in a queue until a call center worker is available to take the call.[2] Inbound calls can either be service-related, such as product support, account or billing inquiries, or service problems, or they can be sales-related. Inbound callers tend to be more receptive to the call center workers, even if they are calling with a problem. This makes inbound jobs more desirable than outbound call jobs (Batt, Hunter, and Wilk, 2003).

Sales/service
While some calls are service calls and others are sales calls, still others are "blended." Sales or service calls can be for customer support, help desk services, reservations and sales for retailers, for example, and order-taking functions for catalog and Web-based merchants (Gans, Koole, and Mandelbaum, 2003). The term "blended" is most often used to describe a call center that does both sales and service. The true complexity of mixing sales and service is seen at the call level, however. An example of this is when a customer calls into a call center to deal with a billing issue (a service purpose), but the call center worker is required both to serve this original request and to sell other products to the customer. Both service and sales functions are accomplished within a single call and in a short time period. Average call lengths vary from a low of less than a minute for simple service transactions (e.g. operators providing telephone numbers) to around seven minutes for workers serving and selling to various market segments.

---

[2] Many centers use voice response units (VRUs) to automate all or portions of calls. Automation will not be discussed here (interested readers are referred to Gans, Koole, and Mandelbaum, 2003).

In our field work in a telecommunications firm, we found that some call center workers struggled with the sometimes competing demands in the blended calls. One issue that emerged is that the type of skills needed to *serve* a customer may be different from those needed to *sell* to a customer. The latter required more aggressiveness and persuasion while the former required more flexibility and empathy. Some call center workers simply were more skilled or more comfortable doing one or the other. In a study of measures of "customer service orientation," Richard Frei and Michael McDaniel (1998) find that service orientation and sales orientation correlated only around 0.30. They point out that, for example, extraversion, the personality dimension related to outgoingness, is positively related to sales performance but negatively related to service performance.

From the company's perspective, these are strategic choices. Some organizations may want to separate sales and service. These organizations see value in having dedicated staff focused on only one aspect of the customer relationship at a time (Richtel, 2006). In this way they can maximize sales at one point and maximize service in another. Others see the mixing of sales and service in call centers as a natural outgrowth of traditional retail. For example, when customers walk into a store there are often natural opportunities for cross-selling products and services. The customer-initiated phone call regarding a service issue is the equivalent and represents the company's best, and sometimes only, opportunity to cross-sell.

Technology issues

There are few workplaces in which technology plays such an important role as it does in call centers. While technology can be beneficial in many situations, such as when information is easily accessible from customer accounts to answer queries, it also has a dark side for workers. Technology can put pressure on workers to work at a certain pace and at a certain quality level, through the monitoring of actions and interactions. Technology can also determine the type of callers and calls routed to a call center worker. This section begins with a discussion of market segmentation and skill-based routing, as it applies to the workers in these jobs. (For an overview of the operations issues, see Gans, Koole, and Mandelbaum, 2003; for a discussion of the strategic issues, see Batt, 2000.)

Market segmentation and 'skill-based' routing

Technology can allow call center organizations to segment their customers based on, for example, their value to the firm, market, or brand. One way to do this is to have different types of customers use distinct call-in numbers, which will route them to a group of call center workers dedicated to that market. Technology can also be used to route calls to call center workers based on their skills. Often this identification of customer segment is matched to worker skills so that market segmentation and skill-based routing operate together (e.g. a high-value customer is connected to a specially trained worker; Batt, Hunter, and Wilk, 2003), and other times they operate independently. As an example of the former, high-value customers may call a telephone number that routes them to a separate group of call center workers who have the experience and/or training to address their specific issues or concerns. On the other hand, skill-based routing can be independent of value or market segment, such as when calls are routed based on the language spoken (Gans, Koole, and Mandelbaum, 2003). There are clear strategic reasons for using market segmentation as well as skill-based routing, the customization of services and the potential for improved quality, particularly for the customers whose business is most critical, being the key ones (Batt, Hunter, and Wilk, 2003).

Market segmentation and skill-based routing have direct implications on the types of calls and callers that a call center worker receives. Batt (2000) finds that market segmentation creates opportunities within the same organization for work that is "mass market" or "high end" and for workplaces that are characterized by more or less high-involvement work practices. She suggests that, unlike in manufacturing, which has begun to experiment in broad terms with high-involvement practices such as autonomy, incentive compensation, and teams, services tend to use high-involvement practices for only the higher-end market segments. Work in the lower-end market segments, the "mass market" jobs, are less complex and more controlled (Zapf *et al.*, 2003).

Moreover, market segmentation and skill-based routing are contrary to the idea that call center workers are indistinguishable from one another and are interchangeable. Call center workers become specialists rather than generalists. Specialization is based on the premise that, with repetition on a narrow set of tasks, individuals become more adept at the tasks (Smith, 1776). The faster an individual masters a set of tasks the more productive and efficient he or she will be. In call centers, is it better to be a generalist or specialist? Recent research has suggested that doing related, but not the same, tasks is more beneficial for learning (Schilling *et al.*, 2003). Moreover, job design research suggests that repetitive tasks can lead to poor job satisfaction and performance, and thus some variety of tasks is beneficial (Hackman and Oldham, 1980). While this long-standing debate about which approach is more valuable cannot be resolved here, it is important to note that the influence of specialization on workers in call centers is still not fully understood, either for its effect on the worker or on the customer.

One by-product of specialization and market segmentation is the potential opportunity for mobility within call centers. Because different market segments require different skills, workers can move to other, potentially better, market segments as they acquire the relevant experience and skills (Batt, Hunter, and Wilk, 2003). This is assuming, of course, that the call center provides access to developmental opportunities or training for skill development. If those opportunities are not available to workers, then specialization and market segmentation lead to "dead end" jobs. Thus, specialization and market segmentation may create incentives for call center workers to acquire new skills and knowledge, if the organization provides opportunities to do so.

Pacing

Automatic call distribution (ACD) systems route calls to available agents at a rapid pace and with only seconds between calls. For example, in a large insurance company's call centers, workers were given six seconds between calls. Figure 4.1 shows the volume of calls for different industries and different market segments within the industries. The variation reflects the expectations regarding the length of time it would take to complete a "typical" call. For the insurance workers, the average call length was seven minutes, which translates into fifty-six calls per day. Workers in a similar job in the banking industry, however, may take 160 calls a day, on average, because the call requests can be handled more quickly (e.g. bank balance requests). For telecommunications operators, the average cycle time was around thirty seconds, which translates into around 900 calls per day. Estimates of utilization rates of call center workers, which indicate the amount of their workday during which they are taking or available to take calls, range from 80 percent (Frenkel *et al.*, 1998) to *averages* of around 90 to 95 percent

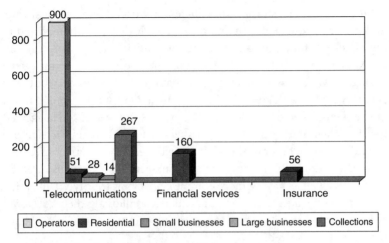

Figure 4.1 Call volume by industry and job type
Source: Modified from Batt, Hunter, and Wilk (2003).

(Gans, Koole, and Mandelbaum, 2003). Thus, they maintain this high pace for the entire workday.

If no agent is available to take calls then the call is placed in queue. Call centers must staff enough workers that the queues do not get too long (long queues increase the likelihood that a customer will hang up, or "abandon"), but not to a level that call center workers are idle.[3] This is made more complex by the peaks and valleys of call volume. For example, call volumes tend to be highest in the morning before work, at midday during lunch breaks, and in the early evening (Gans, Koole, and Mandelbaum, 2003). Waiting in a queue is frustrating for callers. Nira Munichor and Anat Rafaeli (2007) did a study of abandonment rates and call satisfaction under different queue conditions: music only, music plus apologies (e.g. "We are sorry to keep you waiting. Please hold and you will be answered according to your position in line."), and music plus location in the queue (e.g. "You are fourth in line."). They find that providing queue location information gave callers a sense of progress, which resulted in lower abandonment rates and greater satisfaction, especially over the apology condition.

---

[3] A complete discussion of queuing theory or Erlang-C staffing models is beyond the scope of this chapter (for a review of research on these topics, see Gans, Koole, and Mandelbaum, 2003).

Queues create frustration for call center workers as well. Real-time updates of the queue length and average wait time are often posted in the call center for all to see. Implicitly or explicitly, there is pressure on workers to "pick up the pace" and shorten the queue. When the queue is long, however, research has shown that the call length once the caller gets through to an agent is actually longer than when there is not a queue (Gans, Koole, and Mandelbaum, 2003). One reason suggested for this phenomenon is that the callers who remain on the line are typically those who have the most difficult problems (otherwise, they would abandon). By the time they get an agent, they are frustrated by the wait as well as having more complex problems to solve. Time must be spent by the agents calming the callers, or allowing them to "vent" about their long wait, before they can even get to the tricky problems that need to be solved.

Monitoring and scripting

Call centers attempt to control the service interaction itself. One way is through the monitoring of worker interactions with customers. The other is by the use of scripts to control the content of the interaction. Monitoring by supervisors can occur either side by side or remotely. Side-by-side monitoring involves a supervisor sitting with a call center worker and both listening in on a headset to the call while watching over his/her shoulder. Side-by-side monitoring is usually used with novice workers, as it provides real-time feedback to workers. More common is the use of a remote system for monitoring. Remote systems are also used to record a sample of calls for evaluation at a later time. The systems used to monitor workers can tape the audio portion of the interaction and also collect all the screens and keystrokes that go along with the audio. Quality control can evaluate not only the interpersonal aspects of the call (e.g. voice tone, helpfulness) but also if the worker moved through appropriate screens and typed in information correctly. While monitoring per se does not control workers, the knowledge that any call may be monitored to this degree clearly puts pressure on workers to work in an organizationally sanctioned way. As will be discussed later, whether supervisors use monitoring developmentally or punitively can make a difference in the attitudes and behaviors of call center workers. For these latter workers, punitive uses of monitoring can add to the stress level of using technology to control work that is inherently difficult to control.

A more direct method of control is a company's use of scripts. Scripts provide the exact language that a call center worker is expected to use. These may be provided as part of the training and/or be embedded in the technology to allow workers to refer to scripts depending on the content of a call. For example, if a customer calls to ask whether a fee on a bill can be waived, a call center worker may have a script for such a situation. The level of scripting varies widely depending on the company, the industry, and the worker. Industries with more complex regulation, such as banking and insurance, may use scripts more heavily than, for example, retail organizations. Scripting also varies by the worker. Sometimes more novice workers will be required or choose to use scripts more heavily than when they are able to manage the interactions on their own.

While pacing controls throughput, or the quantity of calls taken, monitoring and scripting are attempts to control the quality of the interactions (the "soft" side of the service business: Bain *et al.*, 2002). Like Bain *et al.* (2002) and David Holman, Claire Chissick, and Peter Totterdell (2002), I found in field studies of three organizations' call centers in three separate industries that there are several major categories of quality that are typically judged: conformity to protocols (e.g. openings and closings, "Hello, my name is X, how can I help you?", "Thank you for calling X."); the voice tone (e.g. projecting the right attitude, inflection, pace); professional verbiage (e.g. ticks, the use of "Um," slang); product and service knowledge; and, most critically, appropriate responses to customer (e.g. did the employee focus on the issue quickly and appropriately? Was the issue addressed or the problem solved? Was the customer satisfied?). Little is known about whether all the efforts to control the quality of the interaction translate into noticeable differences for the customer. Control does have some negative consequences for the workers in call centers, however, as is discussed in the next section. The use of technology for both pacing and control epitomizes one of the competing pressures on the workers in these centers: do high-quality customer service and do it quickly.

In sum, within the different call types (e.g. sales or service) lurks wide variance in the nature of the customer interaction. Call center workers must be nimble in their diagnoses of the callers' needs and respond in a way that addresses those needs while also being consistent with the controls in their workplace. Technology in call centers can be used to control the type of customer, the number of calls, and even, to some extent, the content of the customer interaction. The customer often demands customization, while the workplace, through technology, requires standardization. Call center workers must manage this tension. This leads us to a discussion of how call center workers cope with the sometimes competing demands of their employers and their customers.

The call center worker: coping with competing demands

Call center workers juggle the needs of customers with the demands of the firm. This juggling act takes a particular mix and level of skill. Before I discuss the nature of the interpersonal demands of the work, I begin with a brief discussion of the "supply side." What knowledge and skills are required for call center work? Then I focus on the competing demands that these workers face that are inherent to the work and how they affect their attitudes and behaviors. Finally, this section concludes with a discussion of the three groups that comprise the interpersonal context for these workers – customers, supervisors, and co-workers – and their impact on the attitudes and behaviors of call center workers.

The "supply side": knowledge and skills

It is a misnomer to describe center workers as low-skilled (Bain *et al.*, 2002). Even in the most controlled call center environments, the customer–employee exchange hinges on the knowledge and skills of the employee. Moreover, call center workers possess a variety and mix of skills. The main skill categories are: technology, product and service knowledge, and interpersonal (Batt, Hunter, and Wilk, 2003). Technology skills include the ability to find and access information, to maneuver through a myriad of databases and screens, and to operate programs. Product and service knowledge encompasses such things as pricing, the bundling of products or services, and product attributes. Interpersonal skills, such as the ability to calm, persuade, negotiate, and empathize, are an integral part of the exchange in a service or sales encounter.

Indeed, for call center workers, the challenge is to use a single medium – the voice – to convey certain feelings and emotions and sometimes alter the feelings and emotions of the caller. In some call centers workers are given mirrors to keep at their desks, and are encouraged to smile into them while talking to their callers. The act of smiling (simulating positive emotional display) triggers a physiological response that can encourage a positive mood (Zajonc, Murphy, and Inglehart, 1989). Smile and you will feel and sound more positive. While variance exists (e.g. bill collectors: Sutton, 1991), in general customers expect positive emotion from call center workers and rank service quality higher when they get it (Pugh, 2001). Consequently, there is pressure for workers to maintain a positive demeanor at all times. Not only is maintaining a positive demeanor difficult but doing it in a workplace that is attempting to control and manage it is stressful. These interpersonal demands have costs for the employee and, ultimately, for the organization.

Interpersonal demands

The cost of interpersonal demands is most readily seen in call center workers' behaviors. Workers may withdraw from the workplace through tardiness, absenteeism, or, ultimately, turnover in an effort to buffer themselves from the effects of the emotional aspects of the work (e.g. Cote and Morgan, 2002; Pelled and Xin, 1999). Performance may suffer as well (Wright and Cropanzano, 2000; Cropanzano, Rupp, and Byrne, 2003). A critical precursor to these behaviors for service workers is burnout, or increased feelings of emotional exhaustion. Emotional exhaustion occurs when workers' resources are depleted and they "feel they are no longer able to give of themselves" (Maslach and Jackson, 1981, p. 99). Alleviating emotional exhaustion through changes to work characteristics (such as the provision of autonomy), emotional regulation processes (Grandey, 2000), or a more careful selection of workers (e.g. Wilk and Moynihan, 2005) could be important and cost-effective strategies for organizations, as this section suggests.

A common theme in the work characteristics of call center jobs is control. As noted by Alicia Grandey, Glenda Fisk, and Dirk Steiner (2005), control has both internal and external elements. External elements control behavior from outside the person while internal control refers to the self-regulation of behavior. External controls such as pacing, scripting, and monitoring, for example, have been covered in an earlier section. Internal control, or self-regulation, focuses on the affective and emotional aspects of the service exchange process.[4] This

---

[4] Much of the research on the customer–worker exchange has tended to focus on "service workers" more generally. I have used call center samples in particular wherever possible, however.

section focuses specifically on how controls, both from the outside and internal self-regulation, influence workers in call centers as they work to meet the demands of their work. To follow, I look at two specific states in which external and internal controls combine to have a profound effect on call center workers' emotional outlook.

Customization versus conformity

Customers call in to a call center with their own particular issues to be solved and expectations about solving them. As Robin Leidner (1993) points out, organizational attempts to routinize and control work when the customer and employee have to interact to complete the tasks can be difficult. She refers to "routine individuality" to highlight the limits of strict conformity. In light of this, call center organizations' attempts to regulate customer–worker interactions often fall short. Stephen Frenkel, Marek Korczynski, Karen Shire, and May Tam (1998) note that the standardization of the process is often in contrast to the customization of the product in call centers. Said another way, the controls put in place to create conformity around the service interaction are sometimes at odds with the needs of the customer. This can surface as a common frustration for workers in call centers: the inability to do what they know the customer wants or needs. For example, if a customer calls in to a financial services firm and requests that a late fee be waived, the call center worker who takes the call may not have the authorization to do it. He or she may be encouraged to attempt to handle the caller without automatically "escalating" the call to a supervisor, however, who would have the authorization to waive the fee. Only when the customer is sufficiently persistent or demanding (e.g. insisting on speaking with a supervisor, or becoming irate or belligerent) will the call be "escalated" to a person with the authorization.

While this may appear to be illogical on the part of the organization, in fact it may not be. The smaller the number of workers the caller interacts with the less the drain on firm resources. Most call centers have a policy of "one and done" (Gans, Koole, and Mandelbaum, 2003) or "first call resolution," whereby each caller should need to call into the center on only one occasion to have his or her issue resolved and should need to talk to only one person. The customer is believed to benefit, theoretically speaking, from such a system as well. Further, calls such as the one described above can require judgment on the part of the call center worker (e.g. is this a client who is chronically paying late? Is this a value client or does he/she have the potential to be one?). Novice workers, who are often the ones on the front line, may not have the skills and experience to make these judgments. More careful selection and/or longer, more detailed training would be necessary for all new employees to have these skills. Because of the costs involved, many call centers rely on on-the-job training and gradually increase the autonomy of workers to customize the service provided to the customer over time. Neither "first call resolution" policies nor progressive autonomy with experience are inconsistent with customer service when evaluated independently. When they occur together, however, there is potential for the pressures of conformity and customization to clash.

The conflict between workplace controls and customer needs creates frustration for the customer and the worker alike. Customers may learn that getting angry with the person on the phone gets results (e.g. I get angry, but I end up with the person who can waive my late fee.). Thus, we may be training customers to be more aggressive. For call center workers, not only is a lack of control related to stress and lower job satisfaction (de Ruyter, Wetzels, and Feinberg, 2001) but more frustrated and angry customers are an additional stressor. The more negative customers are to workers in call centers the more likely workers will be emotionally exhausted – a significant cause of worker absenteeism (Grandey, Dickter, and Sin, 2004). More aggressive customers will also increase the need for workers to self-regulate their emotions. Grandey, Fisk, and Steiner (2005) find that, when service workers do not have autonomy *and* are required to regulate their emotions (external control and internal self-regulation occur simultaneously), they are more likely to be emotionally exhausted, a component of burnout, than they are in conditions in which one or the other type of control is operating.

Authenticity versus faking

Arlie Hochschild (1979) observes that, in a social exchange between parties, the gestures of one to the other are a function of either surface or deep acting. Surface acting is focused on the outward display of emotion, while deep acting involves the changing of feelings to be consistent with what is displayed. For example, someone who is faking a positive reaction to another would be surface acting, as what is felt and what is displayed are not consistent. For example, the clearly irritated flight attendant who forces a smile and says "It was a pleasure serving you" on your departure from a flight is attempting to surface act. A person who is deep acting may be empathetic or engage in "perspective taking" of others. For example, the bank worker who is sympathetic when a customer complains about a bounced check is engaging in deep acting. Grandey (2000) notes that both surface acting and deep acting involve emotional regulation. She distinguishes these as modification of expression versus modification of feeling respectively.

There is a difference between felt emotion and displayed emotions because of the social norms that govern social exchange in a given context (Hochschild, 1979). If the norms for a given context (e.g. a funeral) suggest an appropriate emotional display (e.g. sadness), we may display the publicly sanctioned emotion even if we do not feel that way (surface act) or try to evoke a sad feeling (deep act) in order to behave in the customary way. In certain work contexts, particularly those that involve contact with the public, organizations create the norms for expected emotional displays (e.g. display rules: Ekman, 1992; Rafaeli and Sutton, 1987). Further, organizations use the emotional displays of their employees as part of the service or sales transaction. This commoditization of emotion (Hochschild, 1983) can be emotionally draining for employees, as they labor to manage their emotions at work through evoking what they do not feel and suppressing what they do. This is the "labor" in emotional labor.

Grandey (2003) tested the effects of surface and deep acting on both worker emotional exhaustion and peer ratings of performance. She finds that surface acting ("faking") was negatively related to performance ratings while deep acting was not. In other words, customers could distinguish when people were faking their emotions rather than expressing what they truly felt. Grandey also finds that engaging in surface acting, but not deep acting, is positively related to emotional exhaustion. Totterdell and Holman (2003) carried out a similar study of surface and deep acting with a sample of call center workers. Their results are consistent with Grandey's: deep acting was positively related to the quality of performance and surface acting was positively related to emotional exhaustion. Totterdell and Holman note, however, that, unlike face-to-face service work, call center workers may find faking easier because they have only one means, the voice, to regulate and find deep acting more difficult. It is more difficult to engage in empathy and perspective taking, actions consistent with deep acting, when you have only the voice of the other party (the customer) as a reference.

Thus, organizations employ external controls (i.e. technological monitoring) and call center workers employ internal controls (i.e. emotional self-regulation) in an effort to manage the interpersonal interactions with customers in an organizationally sanctioned way. Giving the service that a customer expects and doing it day in and day out within the rules of the organization and authentically are the challenges that call center workers face. They are not doing it alone, however. In the next section I examine the research on the kinds of interpersonal contact call center workers have, not only with customers but with co-workers and supervisors. Do these interactions mitigate or exacerbate the tensions inherent in the work?

Interpersonal context in call centers

Customers are an important interpersonal element for workers in all service jobs and for call center workers in particular. Traditional service workers have many more opportunities (e.g. when the store is free of customers) to interact with co-workers or supervisors than call center workers do. Because they are often separated by cubicle walls and wearing headsets and because they are often on the phone 80 to 95 percent of the time (Frenkel *et al.*, 1998; Gans, Koole, and Mandelbaum, 2004), customers are a much more important source of interpersonal contact for call center workers. Supervisors and co-workers can still influence the attitudes and behaviors of workers in call centers, however, as the following discussion highlights.

Customers

The people you work with do not always behave positively towards you (e.g. Glomb, 2002; Glomb *et al.*, 2002), and this includes customers. Generally, the customer's role is typically seen as "demanding" from the point of view of the call center worker. These demands are both cognitive and affective, as call center workers solve problems, answer questions, and sell products or services, and do it all with the proper tone and pleasantness while, potentially, enduring unpleasantness from the customer.

Customer contacts can be demanding simply by virtue of the number or frequency of them (Cordes and Dougherty, 1993). The content of the interaction with customers is where the interpersonal demands are seen most clearly, however. Aggressive or negative customers have, anecdotally at least, always been seen as creating the most negative effects in workers. Call center workers must take the aggression and not reciprocate (e.g. "The customer is always right."). In a study of 198 call center workers, Alicia Grandey, David Dickter, and Hock-Peng Sin (2004) focused specifically on aggressive customers' impact on the emotional exhaustion and absences of workers. They find that a greater frequency of customer verbal aggression toward the worker is related to greater emotional exhaustion experienced by the worker. Emotional exhaustion then mediated the relationship between customers' verbal aggression and workers' absences. Workers with few other means of control will withdraw from the workplace to regulate their mood (George, 1989).

Nancy Rothbard and Steffanie Wilk (2006) studied both customer positive and negative mood and its effect on worker mood and performance. Using experience sampling methodology, they asked call center workers to answer questions about their mood and the customers' mood at several points throughout the day over several weeks. Surprisingly, they find that customer positive mood had a direct positive effect on worker mood but customer negative mood did not. Rothbard and Wilk suggest that this may be a function of the fact that workers are trained to buffer themselves against negative callers and they become more skilled at doing so. This study also looked at how a call center worker's mood might influence performance. Workers in positive moods transferred fewer calls; conversely, workers in negative moods handled fewer calls and were less available to take customer calls. Thus, customers influenced the mood of workers, which in turn influenced their performance – even in a work context with elaborate controls over performance quantity.

In another new study, Anat Rafaeli, Ravit Rozilio, Shy Ravid, and Rellie Derfler (2006) examined the cognitive and emotional effects of being the target of others' anger. They find a curvilinear relationship between angry others and the cognitive capacity for memory and problem solving. When exposed only to angry others, subjects were able to disregard the anger and cognitive processing was not affected. When exposed to very few angry others, there was a boost in cognitive processing, which they suggest was a stimulation effect. When individuals were exposed to a moderate number of angry others, however, their cognitive processing was compromised and their emotional exhaustion was higher. This suggests that the pattern or number of angry callers a worker encounters in a call center could affect his or her cognitive processing and subsequent performance.

Supervisors

Much of the research on the influence of supervisors on the attitudes and behaviors of workers in organizations has tended to look at their potential to support workers (Rhoades and Eisenberger, 2002). When the people that workers work with are supportive, they tend to be more committed and productive in the workplace. In the call center context, however, supervisors can be a source of pressure, particularly because of their role in the performance monitoring of subordinates (e.g. Holman, Chissick, and Totterdell, 2002; Wilk and Moynihan, 2005). As the research to date suggests, the impact of supervisors on call center workers is more nuanced. For Bain *et al.* (2002) and Frenkel *et al.* (1998) it is not the pervasiveness of performance monitoring by supervisors per se that is stressful for workers, it is the way supervisors use technology to that end. For example, in several case studies of call centers in Scotland, Bain *et al.* (2002) find that supervisors were involved in the setting and monitoring of targets (both quantitative and qualitative) for call center workers. The targets created the criteria by which workers' performance was judged, becoming the "Holy Grail." Adding to the traditional pressures of pacing and monitoring, supervisors would post the performance data of workers in public spaces to encourage workers to meet their targets.

Frenkel *et al.* (1998) looked specifically at how workers interpreted the performance management systems in their call center. Their survey finds that workers generally had positive attitudes of performance management and of management. They attribute this to the "facilitative role" that supervisors can play. This role is played when supervisors provide technical knowledge, set clear expectations, reinforce performance norms, and provide psychological support. In an empirical study, Holman, Chissick, and Totterdell (2002) find that monitoring the performance of workers in call centers had both benefits and costs for workers. The benefits involved skill development and a better understanding of the performance criteria. Monitoring intensity, on the other hand, was negatively related to the well-being of

workers in call centers. Job control and supervisory support mod-
erated this relationship. Thus, supervisors can either exacerbate or
ameliorate the effects of the pervasive performance monitoring in
call centers by how they use it (i.e. in a developmental or a punitive
way).

The tradeoffs between supervisory support and pressure can be seen
in a study of call center workers by Wilk and Moynihan (2005). They
looked at supervisors as "display rule keepers" – that is, those in
charge of making sure that the norms regarding the types of emotions
that are acceptable to be expressed in the service exchange are met.
They separately surveyed call center workers and their supervisors,
and find that, when supervisors placed higher importance on the
interpersonal aspects of the work, their workers had higher emotional
exhaustion. It was not having a "demanding boss" that caused workers to feel burned out. It was only the emphasis on the *interpersonal*
aspects of the work, not other aspects (e.g. technology, product or
service knowledge), that mattered for subordinate emotional exhaustion. Moreover, they find this effect controlling for the workers'
perceptions of supervisory support. Thus, worker stress regarding
job demands in call centers varies at the supervisor, not the job,
level. Supervisors can simultaneously be a source of support and a
source of stress for workers.

Co-workers
Service workers generally interact least often with their co-workers and
most often with their customers. Moreover, organizational display
rules – the rules about what emotions to display and when (Ekman,
1992) – are explicit, monitored, and enforced for customer interactions, not co-worker interactions (Grandey, 2000). Thus, the effect that
co-worker interactions have on workers' affect and emotional regulation
processes tends to be less than customer interactions (e.g. Totterdell and
Holman, 2003; Grandey, Tam, and Brauburger, 2002). Though their
role may be small, however, co-workers can influence the attitudes and
behaviors of one another. Research has found that the use of self-
managed teams in a call center increased both sales and self-reported
service quality (Batt, 1999).

Emilio Castilla (2005) examined the relationship between co-workers
and call center worker productivity using a social network analysis.
Many call centers use referrals by existing employees as part of their

staffing strategy (Fernández, Castilla, and Moore, 2000; Castilla, 2005). Castilla (2005) finds that 50 percent of the new hires were referred by an existing employee. This number is large partly because of the incentives the company offered to employees for doing so (e.g. $250 if the referred applicant is hired: Fernández, Castilla, and Moore, 2000). Roberto Fernández, Emilio Castilla, and Paul Moore (2000) find that there is an economic benefit to the investment, in part due to the better applicant pool and the reduction in recruiting costs. Castilla (2005) notes that there is a risk in using social networks for staffing in call centers, however. He finds that, while referrals are more productive initially, the economic benefit does not hold over time. Moreover, he finds that if the referrer leaves the firm then his or her referees' performance drops, even if the referee has been with the firm for some time. Thus, the social connections among employees are important for performance, and "breaking the tie" has consequences.

Conclusions and future directions

How you handle customers who are misinformed can have a strong influence on whether or not they become angry. Even if they become angry, you need to take care to ensure they understand the service. How you handle them matters a lot. Working in a call center is demanding, you are always interacting with people, so your attitude is very important. The job has always been stressful. (Denise, service representative in a call center)

Work in call centers is demanding. Workers juggle the competing demands of quality and quantity, all the while using only their voice to relay information and affect. Working in an environment that attempts to control the uncontrollable – interpersonal exchanges – is clearly stressful for workers. Although the interpersonal aspects of the job are constant, there is great variety in the ways that call centers are run. These differences can have a profound effect on whether they are run like "factories" with tight controls.

Technology separates the two parties in the exchange, worker and customer, providing challenges to the interpersonal exchange. This challenge can be exacerbated if technology is used punitively to control the pacing of the calls to workers and, more importantly, the quality of the exchange. Organizations often have a choice and can create a more supportive environment to mitigate the stress. I offer four ideas on this below. These preliminary conclusions are drawn from the research to date, although they also raise questions that need to be addressed in future research.

Job control should be reduced or its effects mitigated in call centers

One theme that has emerged from the literature is that job control or autonomy is an issue for workers in call centers. While the technology exists to control and monitor workers in call centers, the question is: "when is it too much?" The downside, emotional exhaustion of workers, is one with clear economic costs to the firm. The benefits, in terms of customer perceptions of quality, are still largely unknown, however. In one study, Alicia Grandey, Glenda Fisk, Anna Mattila, Karen Jansen, and Lori Sideman (2005) find that emotional authenticity is important to observers only once competency requirements have been met. Thus, customers may prioritize what is more or less valued in the service interaction: competency first, interpersonal aspects second. If this is true, then using monitoring technology for the development of skills and competencies could be a valuable strategy for firms. It could mitigate the negative effects on workers and provide workers with the tools to serve the customers better.

Deep acting is the preferred emotional regulation strategy in call centers

Not only do customers notice the difference between "faking" and deep acting but there is less emotional exhaustion when workers engage in deep acting. Two key questions remain. How do we encourage more deep acting in call center workers? Are there limits to the amount of deep acting for call center workers? The first question raises the issue of training or selecting for emotional regulation capability. Because deep acting is rooted in the dramaturgical perspective (Grandey, 2000), presumably one can be trained to do it (e.g. actors are trained to evoke the feelings of the character for the audience). Whether or not it can be done in a cost-effective way or with the pool of call center workers is open to question, however.

There may be individuals for whom deep acting comes more naturally. It may be that workers who are more empathetic and more inclined toward perspective taking – two methods for deep acting

(Grandey, 2000) – would engage in deep acting more readily. Call centers could screen and select based on such characteristics. Empathy, for example, may have its limits, however. If call center workers are too empathetic with callers they could become more emotionally drained. Moreover, Totterdell and Holman (2003) suggest that, even if call centers workers are capable of deep acting, the single medium of contact with the customer, the voice, makes it difficult to do so. As additional studies on emotional regulation in call centers are completed, we may get some answers to these questions.

Negative customers are not always bad for workers

While the general belief is that workers are better off dealing with positive or neutral customers than with angry ones, and some research supports this (e.g. Grandey, Dickter, and Sin, 2004), recent research suggests that angry customers may not have an impact on call center workers' mood and may, in fact, be beneficial to how they work. If some workers can buffer themselves against negative customers, the mechanism for how this occurs is still largely unknown, however. Rothbard and Wilk (2006) suggest that learning or experience play a role here, but other factors, such as individual characteristics, may also be important. One possibility is that workers learn to disassociate to some extent from the organization and interpret the customer's anger accordingly. In other words, they adopt the attitude that the customer's anger is not really directed at them but at the organization instead. Another possibility may be that certain workers are more "thick-skinned" naturally, and therefore have a higher threshold for absorbing the anger directed at them. Future research can help uncover the mechanisms for buffering and the interactions between them.

Another interesting new study suggests that negative customers can actually be cognitively stimulating to workers (Rafaeli *et al.*, 2006). This effect occurs only when there are few angry customers in a given period of time, however. Workplace controls that encourage the front-line call center worker to resolve a customer's issue but give him/her little flexibility in how to do so are, in effect, training customers to get angry to receive the service they require. Angry customers will not be rare in such cases. Thus, workplace controls have not only a direct effect on call center worker stress but an indirect one as well, through the effect on customers. Much more research into this phenomenon is needed to understand it fully. If it is the case that some level of angry customers can be beneficial for workers, however, there may be ways for call centers to direct angry callers to different call center workers in ways that optimize these positive effects and minimize the negative ones.

Support from supervisors and co-workers may mitigate stress and improve performance

Customers, logically, have been the primary focus of interpersonal exchange for call center workers. Fostering relationships between workers and supervisors and among co-workers in call centers may be beneficial, however. Supervisors can be either a source of support or a source of strain for workers. The research on call centers suggests that, when supervisors focus on being developmental and supportive, improved attitudes and behaviors on the part of workers results. When supervisors are more demanding of workers the pressures of the job are exacerbated for them (Wilk and Moynihan, 2005). This suggests that better training of supervisors to be sensitive to the demands of the job, and to focus more on improving performance through development rather than through pressure, could improve the workplace for the call center worker.

Another aspect of the workplace environment is co-workers. The social network that may be used to get an individual into the applicant pool of a call center continues to operate after the person has been hired (Castilla, 2005). Co-workers can provide useful information and support, even in work environments in which co-worker contact is limited. The relationships one has can influence the productivity and innovativeness of workers in call centers (Dokko, 2006). Turning our attention to those relationships that exist within the call center may help foster better interactions between workers and customers.

Globalization of call centers will complicate call center work further

With the worldwide proliferation of the use of call center for customer–organization contact, the interest in their effects on organizations, customers, and workers will continue. In fact, globalization is having a profound effect on call centers.

For some, having a call center in one country and customers in another is a simple operations issue to be solved by technology. The impact of globalization on the interpersonal demands of the work may be great, however. Moreover, when the globalization of call centers is the result of outsourcing or "offshoring" there are other concerns as well. I start with the first issue, the interpersonal demands. When call center workers in one country interact with customers in another the expectations of service may be different. Some call centers are encouraging and training their workers to take on a persona similar to that of their customers (e.g. Indian call center workers take on an American persona when serving US customers). Call center management reasons that customers are more comfortable speaking to someone "in their own backyard" rather than someone halfway across the globe. The emotional regulation required for workers in these contexts and the toll it could take are unknown. Moreover, the effects on customers are unknown.

Another issue for globalization is the impact of offshoring on the mobility of workers. For some workers, the call center is the first job in their career path. As those jobs move overseas, the career path will be altered in ways that may not be simple to rectify. For workers, this means that the experience and skills that once were accumulated in the lower jobs in a career ladder will need to be gained elsewhere. For organizations, the ready pool of workers within the firm who understood their products, services, and customers will no longer be available. In such cases, an organization may simply look outside the firm for talent. Recent research suggests, however, that hiring workers from outside the firm with similar occupational experiences may not be without costs (Dokko, Wilk, and Rothbard, 2006). Gina Dokko, Steffanie Wilk, and Nancy Rothbard find that the more prior occupational experience a call center worker had before joining a firm the greater the behavioral and cognitive rigidities that limit the transfer of applicable knowledge and skills. Clearly, therefore, there are long-term implications and costs to offshoring for workers and for organizations.

Even the use of other technologies, such as the internet, does not seem to be reducing the demand for person-to-person contact. Indeed, many firms see call centers as one of a range of means for customer contact that they offer – internet, phone, and e-mail operating as complements for one another and not substitutes. Call centers are stressful for workers, particularly the tension between workplace controls and the interpersonal aspects that do not easily lend themselves to controls. This stress is likely to lead to emotional exhaustion and subsequently to withdrawal and performance problems. Steve Hillmer, Barbara Hillmer, and Gale McRoberts (2004) have calculated the approximate cost of turnover for one call center. By their calculations, it will cost one year's salary for every open position. For the center they studied, which had 60 percent turnover a year, this amounts to over $400,000 every year. The costs of absenteeism and turnover, not to mention the costs of "presenteeism," when workers are on the job but are not engaged by the work, undermine the efficiencies that call centers were designed to capture.

Call centers do not have to represent the modern-day "factory floor," however. Depending upon decisions about management and technology, it is possible to design the call center so as to provide variety, challenge, and a supportive work environment, and to minimize the stresses of constant customer contact.

References

Appelbaum, E., and Batt, R. (1994). *The New American Workplace*. Ithaca, NY: ILR Press.

Bain, P., Watson, A., Mulvey, G., Taylor, P., and Gall, G. (2002). Taylorism, targets and the pursuit of quantity and quality by call centre management. *New Technology, Work and Employment*, *17*(3), 170–85.

Batt, R. (1999). Work organization, technology, and performance in customer service and sales. *Industrial and Labor Relations Review*, *52*(4), 539.

(2000). Strategic segmentation in front-line services: matching customers, employees and human resource systems. *International Journal of Human Resource Management*, *11*(3), 540.

Batt, R., Hunter, L., and. Wilk, S. L. (2003). How and when does management matter? Job quality and career opportunities for call center corkers. In E. Appelbaum, A. Bernhardt, and R. J. Murnane (eds.), *Low-wage America: How Employers are Reshaping Opportunity in the Workplace* (270–316). New York: Russell Sage Foundation.

Castilla, E. J. (2005). Social networks and employee performance in a call center. *American Journal of Sociology*, *110*(5), 1243.

Cordes, C. L., and Dougherty, T. W. (1993). A review and integration of research on job burnout. *Academy of Management Review*, *18*(4), 621–56.

Cote, S., and Morgan, L. (2002). A longitudinal analysis of the association between emotional regulation, job satisfaction, and intentions to quit. *Journal of Organizational Behavior, 23*, 947–62.

Cropanzano, R., Rupp, D., and Byrne, Z. (2003). The relationship of emotional exhaustion to work attitudes, job performance, and organizational citizenship behaviors. *Journal of Applied Psychology, 83*, 160–9.

De Ruyter, K., Wetzels, M., and Feinberg, R. (2001). Role stress in call centers: its effects on employee performance and satisfaction. *Journal of Interactive Marketing, 15*(2), 23.

Dokko, G. (2006). *Heterogeneity in Social Networks and Work Experience as Determinants of Individual Job Performance.* Working paper. New York: New York University, Stern School of Business.

Dokko, G., Wilk, S.L., and Rothbard, N.P. (2006). *Unpacking Prior Experience: How Career History Affects Individual Performance.* Working paper. New York: New York University, Stern School of Business.

Ekman, R. (1992). An argument for basic emotions. *Cognition and Emotion, 6*, 169–200.

Fernández, R.M., Castilla, E.J., and Moore, P. (2000). Social capital at work: networks and employment at a phone center. *American Journal of Sociology, 105*, 1288–356.

Frenkel, S.J., Korczynski, M., Shire, K.A., and Tam, M. (1998). Beyond bureaucracy? Work organization in call centres. *International Journal of Human Resource Management, 9*(6), 957–79.

Frei, R.L., and McDaniel, M.A. (1998). Validity of customer service measures in personnel selection: a review of criterion and construct evidence. *Human Performance, 11*, 1–27.

Gans, N., Koole, G., and Mandelbaum, A. (2003). Telephone call centers: tutorial, review, and research prospects. *Manufacturing and Service Operations Management, 5*(2), 79–141.

George, J.M. (1989). Mood and absence. *Journal of Applied Psychology, 74*, 317–24.

Glomb, T.M. (2002). Workplace anger and aggression: informing conceptual models with data from specific encounters. *Journal of Occupational Health Psychology, 7*(1), 20–36.

Glomb, T.M., Piers, D.G., Steel, G., and Arvey, R.D. (2002). Office sneers, snipes and stab wounds: antecedents, consequences, and implications of workplace violence and aggression. In R.G. Lord, R.J. Klimoski and R. Kanfer (eds.), *Emotions in the Workplace* (227–60). San Francisco: Jossey-Bass.

Grandey, A.A. (2000). Emotion regulation in the workplace: a new way to conceptualize emotional labor. *Journal of Occupational Health Psychology, 5*, 95–110.

(2003). When "the show must go on": surface acting and deep acting as determinants of emotional exhaustion and peer-rated service delivery. *Academy of Management Journal*, 46(1), 86–96.

Grandey, A. A., Dickter, D. N., and Sin, H.-P. (2004). The customer is not always right: customer verbal aggression toward service employees. *Journal of Organizational Behavior*, 25(3), 397–418.

Grandey, A. A., Fisk, G. M., Mattila, A. S., Jansen, K., and Sideman, L. A. (2005). Is "service with a smile" enough? Authenticity of positive displays during service encounters. *Organizational Behavior and Human Decision Processes*, 96, 38–55.

Grandey, A. A. Fisk, G. M., and Steiner, D. D. (2005). Must "service with a smile" be stressful? The moderating role of personal control for American and French employees. *Journal of Applied Psychology*, 90(5), 893.

Grandey, A. A., Tam, A. P., and Brauburger, A. L. (2002). Affective states and traits in the workplace: diary and survey data from young workers. *Motivation and Emotion*, 26, 31–55.

Hackman, R. J., and Oldham, G. (1980). *Work Redesign*. Menlo Park, CA: Addison-Wesley.

Hillmer, S., Hillmer, B., and McRoberts, G. (2004). The real costs of turnover: lessons from a call center. *Human Resource Planning*, 27, 34.

Hochschild, A. R. (1979). Emotion work, feeling rules, and social structure. *American Journal of Sociology*, 85, 551–75.

(1983). *The Managed Heart: Commercialization of Human Feeling*. Berkeley, CA: University of California Press.

Holman, D. J., Chissick, C., and Totterdell, P. (2002). The effects of performance monitoring on emotional labor and well being in call centers. *Motivation and Emotion*, 26, 57–81.

Krol, C. (2004). Tough times for telemarketing. *B to B*, 89(10), 13.

Leidner, R. (1993). *Fast Food, Fast Talk: Service Work and the Routinization of Everyday Life*. Berkeley, CA: University of California Press.

Mandelbaum, A. (2004). *Call Centers (Centres): Research Bibliography with Abstracts*, (version 6). Working paper. Available at Haifa: Technion – Israel Institute of Technology, Faculty of Industrial Engineering and Management. http://ie.technion.ac.il/serveng.

Maslach, C., and Jackson, S. E. (1981). The measurement of experienced burnout. *Journal of Occupational Behavior*, 2, 99–113.

Munichor, N., and Rafaeli, A. (2007). Numbers or apologies? Customer reactions to telephone waiting time fillers. *Journal of Applied Psychology*, 92(2), 511–8.

Pelled, L., and Xin, K. (1999). Down and out: an investigation of the relationship between mood and employee withdrawal behavior. *Journal of Management*, 25(6), 875–95.

Pugh, S. D. (2001). Service with a smile: emotional contagion in the service encounter. *Academy of Management Journal, 44*(5), 1018–27.

Rafaeli, A., Rozilio, R., Ravid, S., and Derfler, R. (2006). *Negative Emotions and Cognitive Performance: On the Costs of Being the Target of Others' Anger*. Working paper. Haifa: Technion – Israel Institute of Technology.

Rafaeli, A., and Sutton, R. I. (1987). The expression of emotion as part of the work role. *Academy of Management Review, 12*(1), 23–37.

Rhoades, L., and Eisenberger, R. (2002). Perceived organizational support: a review of the literature. *Journal of Applied Psychology, 87*, 698–714.

Richtel, M. (2006). The long-distance journey of a fast-food order. *New York Times, 11* April, 1.

Rothbard, N. P., and Wilk, S. L. (2006). *Walking in the Door: Sources and Consequences of Employee Mood on Work Performance*. Working paper. Philadelphia: University of Pennsylvania, Wharton School.

Schilling, M. A., Vidal, P., Ployhart, R. E., and Marangoni, A. (2003). Learning by doing something else: variation, relatedness, and the learning curve. *Management Science, 49*(1), 39–56.

Smith, A. (1776). *An Inquiry into the Nature and Causes of the Wealth of Nations*. London: W. Brittain.

Sutton, R. I. (1991). Maintaining norms about expressed emotions: the case of bill collectors. *Administrative Science Quarterly, 36*, 245–68.

Totterdell, P., and Holman, D. (2003). Emotion regulation in customer service roles: testing a model of emotional labor. *Journal of Occupational Health Psychology, 8*, 55–73.

Urso, N. (2004). Pack your headsets – more call centers are movin' out. *Response, 13*(1), 55.

Wilk, S. L., and Moynihan, L. (2005). Display rule "regulators": the relationship between supervisors and worker emotional exhaustion. *Journal of Applied Psychology, 90*(5), 917.

Wright, T., and Cropanzano, R. (2000). Psychological well-being and job satisfaction as predictors of job performance. *Journal of Occupational Health Psychology, 5*, 84–94.

Zajonc, R. B., Murphy, S. T., and Inglehart, M. (1989). Feeling and facial efference: implications of the vascular theory of emotion. *Psychological Review, 96*, 395–416.

Zapf, D., Isic, A., Bechtoldt, M., and Blau, P. (2003). What is typical for call centre jobs? Job characteristics, and service interactions in different call centres. *European Journal of Work and Organizational Psychology, 12*(4), 311.

5 | Three's a crowd? Understanding triadic employment relationships

MATTHEW BIDWELL AND ISABEL
FERNANDEZ-MATEO

Introduction

There are many facets to the typical employment relationship. At its
very simplest, employment involves the exchange of labor for compensation. Nevertheless, employment relationships also involve control of
the worker by the firm, the acquisition of skills through experience and
training, learning about each others' qualities and intentions, and career
progression as the worker moves from role to role within the organization. In addition, employment usually imposes a variety of specific legal
obligations on both employer and employee. Traditionally, these obligations have been combined into a single relationship between worker
and firm.

In recent years, however, we have seen the growth of "triadic" employment arrangements, in which important characteristics of employment
are divided among workers' relationships with two firms: a "client" and
an "intermediary." The intermediary generally acts as the legal employer
of the worker, but the actual work is performed at a client site. Consider,
for example, employment relationships for temporary agency workers.
Legally, the worker is employed by the agency,[1] which also provides the
worker with compensation and any benefits. Career progression for the
worker often results from the worker being assigned by the agency to
roles in different clients. The worker's relationship with the client also
has clear elements of an employment tie, however: the worker provides
labor to the client at its site; the worker often also accepts substantial
control by the client over his or her work. We cannot therefore understand how the worker is employed without examining both these ties.

Many other industries beyond temporary help agencies display "triadic" features. The outsourcing of services often involves individuals

---

[1] We use the terms "agency," "intermediary," and "staffing firm" interchangeably
throughout the chapter.

working closely with a client firm and accepting control by them, while also being employed by an outsourcing vendor. In professional services, the roles of client and employer can become blurred as close relationships with clients become a central determinant of workers' career success. In order to understand the nature of employment fully in many settings, therefore, we need to look beyond traditional employer–worker dyads and examine the nexus of relationships that surround the employment ties in which workers are embedded. This chapter focuses on triadic employment relationships that involve a labor market intermediary, a worker, and a client firm.

We argue that the distinctive feature of triadic arrangements is that they cannot be understood by examining each tie in isolation; the different ties within the triad interact with each other. For all three participants – workers, intermediaries, and clients – relationships with one of these actors become a tool for managing their relationship with the other. As a result, outcomes such as wages, task assignment, and employment security can be understood only by referring to all three relationships. In order to develop a nuanced understanding of these arrangements, we draw on insights from the sociological literature on exchange theory (Cook and Emerson, 1978; Blau, 1964) and our qualitative analysis of three different studies of triadic employment among high-skilled workers. We discuss the implications of this framework for our conceptualization of new employment relationships more generally.

Defining triadic employment arrangements

In triadic employment relationships, the traditional functions of the employer are shared between the client company and the intermediary. In the archetypal case of temporary help services, the agency is the legal employer of record. It manages the screening, hiring, wage setting, discontinuation of employment, and payment of benefits to the worker. It is also responsible for the administrative aspects associated with maintaining employees on payroll, such as retaining taxes, paying wages, etc.

The client company usually has no contractual relationship with the worker. It is closely involved in many aspects of the employment relationship, however. Often the client will participate in the screening and hiring processes, making final decisions on the candidates proposed to them by the agency. In addition, the client will usually be responsible for all functions relating to the work, including task allocation, supervision of the workers, and even provision of specific training when required. The work frequently takes place at the client's site.

The details of triadic employment can vary along a number of related dimensions, however, even within the same industry settings. First, there is widespread variation in the stability of the worker's relationship with the intermediary. Some workers will expect to build long careers with the same intermediary. Other workers' relationships with the intermediary will last only as long as their assignment with a particular client. Second, there is variation in whether the intermediary is expected to play a role in managing the workers. Some intermediaries sell their services to clients on the basis of their expert project management. Other intermediaries provide only the workers. Third, there is variation in whether workers are expected to bring intermediary-specific knowledge to the client, or whether they are being hired solely for general skills.

These variations make it difficult to construct a clear definition of triadic employment relationships for the purposes of collecting statistics on these arrangements. As a result, detailed statistics on the prevalence of triadic employment relationships are hard to come by. In general, there seems to be a consensus that the importance of mediated work arrangements in general – and agency employment in particular – has increased considerably during the last decade (see Davidov, 2004). According to a recent comparative survey, work through temporary help agencies grew between two- and fivefold during the 1990s (Storrie, 2002, cited in Davidov, 2004). Estimates from various sources suggest that this type of employment could account for as much as 2.7 percent of the labor force in France, around 2 percent in the United Kingdom and United States, and some 0.7 percent in Germany (Storrie, 2002). Precise and comparable statistics on this issue are scarce, however.

In part, this absence of good data reflects the difficulty of defining what exactly constitutes an employment relationship. In the United States, for example, rather than having a single clear definition, courts often rely on the answers to a ten- or even twenty-question test to decide who a worker's formal employer is (Muhl, 2002). Furthermore, the legal status of workers involved in triadic employment relationships varies across countries (see Davidov, 2004).

The US Bureau of Labor Statistics has made some attempt to count the number of individuals in alternative employment arrangements through a biennial supplemental survey of workers, the Contingent and Alternative Employment Arrangements Supplement to the Current Population Survey (CPS). According to the 2005 survey, around 0.9 percent of workers are employed by temporary help agencies, and a further 0.6 percent are employed by firms that contract out their services to other companies. These numbers have remained fairly stable over the ten years that the survey has been running. Given the difficulties in cleanly defining these employment arrangements, however, there is good reason to believe that these figures present a low estimate of triadic employment in the US labor force.

Figures collected from industry-level employment data paint a very different picture of the extent and growth of triadic employment. According to figures provided by the BLS (see table 5.1), temporary help firms employed 2.4 million individuals in 2006, representing around 1.8 percent of the labor force. Professional employer organizations, which provide long-term staffing services for businesses, employed a further 700,000. Large numbers of workers were also employed in computer systems design, management and technical consulting services and business support services, all of which often involve employees working very closely with clients over long periods of time such that the client takes on some characteristics of the employer.

Perhaps most strikingly, the BLS figures reveal rapid growth in the industries that make widespread use of triadic employment relationships. Temporary help services grew by 121 percent between 1990 and 2006. Computer systems design services grew by 202 percent. Professional employer organizations, which serve as employers of record for entire company workforces, grew by an impressive 621 percent. Hence, while triadic employment relationships may still be the exception rather than the norm, they are present in a significant and rapidly growing portion of the US labor market.

It is most likely that this growth in triadic employment relationships reflects a growing trend towards more arm's-length, market-mediated ties between firms and workers (Cappelli, 1999; Osterman, 1999). In response to increased competition in product markets, greater pressures from shareholders, and reduced government regulation, firms have sought to increase their flexibility by limiting their obligations to workers (Pfeffer and Baron, 1988; Cappelli, 1995). Much of the growth of intermediaries can be explained by the need to manage functions that employers have abandoned. We review the many

Table 5.1 *Employment growth in industries with triadic employment arrangements, 1990–2006 (thousands of employees)*

Industry	January 2006	January 1990	Percentage change
Employment placement agencies	289	209	38
Temporary help services	2429	1097	121
Professional employer organizations	699	97	621
Computer systems design and related services	1222.6	405.2	202
Management and technical consulting services	856.3	310.6	176
Business support services	752.7	497	51
Total non-farm employment	132328	107532	23

Source: Bureau of Labor Statistics.

functions that intermediaries provide in the next section. Some growth is also likely to be a response to employment law. A variety of different laws within the United States create obligations between employers and employees (Muhl, 2002). Firms must pay a number of employment taxes and withhold taxes from their employees' pay. In addition, the US tax code requires employers to offer benefits to their employees in order for them to receive favorable tax treatment. As a result, employers can be liable to pay benefits to workers who the courts find to be their employees, as happened in the Microsoft vs. Vizcaino case (*Monthly Labor Review*, 1998). Finally, anti-discrimination legislation and other legal innovations have seriously eroded the "employment at will" doctrine within the United States, making the termination of employment a much more difficult prospect for firms (Autor, 2003). Stephen Barley and Gideon Kunda (2004) argue that client firms often hire workers though an intermediary to shield themselves from these legal obligations.[2]

---

[2] Obviously, when intermediaries function as legal employers of these contractors they are the ones shouldering the employment risks. In these cases, however, it is common for the client to pay a premium to hire agency temps, so the "costs" are ultimately born by the clients as well. Nonetheless, the intermediaries are usually

Merely defining workers as independent contractors does not guarantee that courts will not judge a client firm to be their legal employers, but when workers are hired through an intermediary many lawyers believe that client firms are much less likely to be defined as employers.

Toward an understanding of triadic employment arrangements

The increasing importance of alternative employment relationships has motivated a number of studies that examine the different features of these non-standard work arrangements. Many of these studies have focused on understanding when and why firms choose to use external employees such as temporary help agency workers and out-sourced personnel (e.g. Abraham, 1990; Davis-Blake and Uzzi, 1993; Abraham and Taylor, 1996; Houseman, 2001; Gramm and Schnell, 2001; Houseman, Kalleberg, and Erickcek, 2003). Many of these studies find that a key reason for firms to use external workers is to achieve greater "numerical flexibility" to meet seasonal or uncertain demand, or to fill positions left vacant due to sickness or vacations. Temporary employment also allows firms to screen potential full-time hires (see Autor, 2001), as well as to bypass some internal adminis-trative controls on recruiting, such as hiring freezes, rigid pay scales, unionization, or the requirement to pay benefits (Houseman, 2001).

A second stream of research has focused on the consequences of externalized employment for workers and firms. These studies suggest that contingent work, compared to regular employment, is associated with more of the characteristics of "bad jobs," such as low pay and lack of benefits (Kalleberg, Reskin, and Hudson, 2000), that contingent workers have less organizational commitment than regular employees (Van Dyne and Ang, 1998; Ang and Slaughter, 2001), and that the use of external workers can lead regular employees to have poorer relation-ships with peers and supervisors and increase their intentions to quit (Broschak and Davis-Blake, 2006).

Recent research has also begun to explore the actions and role of intermediaries in these markets, such as IT staffing firms (Barley and Kunda, 2004) and executive search firms (Finlay and Coverdill, 2000). This research emphasizes the variety of functions that intermediaries

---

better able to bear these costs, as they usually offer lower benefits as well as offering short-term employment to all their employees.

perform in the labor market, such as matching workers to firms, negotiating pay (Barley and Kunda, 2004), and screening workers for clients (Autor, 2001). Studies have also examined the broader impacts of these intermediaries in helping certain groups of workers to advance their careers (Bielby and Bielby, 1999) and shaping how client firms are able to achieve greater employment flexibility (Davis-Blake and Broschak, 2000).

These studies provide detailed insights into the causes and consequences of these new employment arrangements. They also provide some indication of how various aspects of employment relationships are "taken over" by employment intermediaries. None of them fully explores the consequences of the *triadic* nature of these settings, however. Instead, most studies tend to examine one set of relationships at a time: the relationship between worker and client; the relationship between worker and agency; or the relationship between agency and client. The distinctive feature of triadic employment relationships, however, is that all three ties are intimately involved in shaping how workers are employed. As a consequence, focusing on any one relationship within the triad can deny some of the most important dynamics that shape that relationship.

This point was made long ago by sociological studies on the structure of interactions among actors. The German sociologist Georg Simmel (see Wolff, 1950) was the first to point out, in an article published in 1902, that the underlying social structure of triadic interactions is fundamentally different from that of dyadic ones. He argued that, as one additional actor is involved in a transaction, the quality and the dynamics of how the parties interact with each other change. In particular, ties bound by a third party give each actor less autonomy, less power, and less independence in relating to the other members of the triad (Krackhardt, 1999). The study of social networks has drawn heavily on this insight to suggest that the way that any single relationship behaves depends on the broader network of ties in which it is embedded (Burt, 1992; Gargiulo, 1993). That is, the terms of the exchange depend not only on the characteristics of the specific relation that is the focus of the exchange but also on the ties that each partner has to the other actors (Baron and Hannan, 1994).

One way to conceptualize the distinctive dynamics of triadic employment arrangements is to examine how the actors use the different ties as a resource for strategic action. Any relationship can be understood as the outcome of two parties seeking to minimize the costs and maximize the benefits that they can obtain. In triadic relationships, each of the actors has an additional resource to use in its interactions with a second party: its ties to the third party. Hence, workers might leverage their ties with the intermediary in order to improve the terms of their relationship with the client; they might also leverage their ties with the client in bargaining with the intermediary. The other ties in the triad similarly provide resources to intermediaries and clients in dealing with workers. This idea is consistent with social exchange theory (Cook and Emerson, 1978; Blau, 1964), which argues that the actors involved in a given exchange can draw on their actual or potential ties to other actors as an additional resource. In the remainder of this chapter we present the results of qualitative research that seeks to identify and to understand these interactions among the different relationships within employment triads. We discuss how actors might, at different times, seek to strengthen relationships (which leads to what we call "reinforcement") or to weaken them (which we call "balancing").[3]

Data and methods

Our data comes from three complementary field studies of triadic ties in high-skill contract labor markets. The figures combine depth and breadth, as they include extensive observations from a number of diverse settings as well as intensive interviews and quantitative data collection within each setting. We integrate two in-depth studies of particular institutional actors – a staffing agency and a client firm – with a broad study of all three participants in the market. The fieldwork was implemented in the market for high-skill information technology contractors, broadly defined. The staffing firm ("the agency") we studied is a global company headquartered in the United States that specializes in placing "creative" IT professionals. We also analyzed the use of contractors within the IT department of a large US financial services firm ("the

---

[3] These correspond closely to the concept of network polarity within social exchange theory (Cook and Whitmeyer, 1992), which classifies ties as positively or negatively connected, depending on how they interact. Ties are positively connected when the magnitude of one exchange in which an actor is involved produces or implies an increase in a second exchange. Conversely, ties are negatively connected when an increase in the frequency or magnitude of one exchange produces a decrease in the second exchange (Emerson, 1972).

bank"). These two in-depth studies are complemented by a third set of cross-firm interviews with agencies, consultants, and clients across a range of different settings that focused on understanding the range of different employment relationships in the IT consulting industry. See table 5.2 for a summary of our data collection and methods.

Study 1: *the agency*

The agency is a large, global staffing firm that specializes in placing workers with creative, technical, and Web-based skills. The firm is headquartered in a major US city and has subsidiaries in more than ten countries – although our study focuses on the United States alone.

The agency operates by matching workers to projects in client firms. It holds a database with extensive information both on contractors looking for projects and on companies looking for workers.[4] The matching begins with the agency receiving an order from a client, and searching its database to find someone that fits the assignment description. This results in a simultaneous matching process whereby candidates are offered potential assignments and clients typically are presented with a selection of résumés. At the same time, price negotiations begin between the agency and the client company. Contractors are paid a percentage of the billing rate the agency receives from the client. Generally the workers do not get to know how much the agency is billing the client for its services, and they rarely have a chance to negotiate wages. Moreover, as part of their general agreement to work together, the agency explicitly advises both client and contractor not to discuss billing rates and wages (Barley and Kunda, 2004, provide a detailed discussion of this issue).

Once the three parties have reached an agreement, the contractor starts working at the client firm's site,[5] usually alongside the company's

---

[4] We use the terms "contractors" and "workers" interchangeably throughout the chapter.

[5] The majority of triadic employment relationships that we analyzed at the agency consisted of individuals working as contractors at the client company's site. The study of the agency did not focus on arrangements in which contractors perform a project for the client firm but work off-site in their own office or studio (see Kunda, Barley, and Evans, 2002, for some examples of this type of relationship). We interviewed a few such independent contractors, who usually charge a lump sum for their work, but most of our analysis is limited to the far more common cases in which contractors work alongside the client firm's regular employees.

Table 5.2 *Summary of three studies of triadic relationships*

	The agency	The bank	The market for IT consulting
Study setting	US office of global staffing agency	IT department of large US financial services firm	Variety of clients, consultants and agencies in IT service market
Types of workers	IT-related graphical design services	IT professionals (systems and software developers)	IT professionals (systems and software developers)
Types of agency services	Short-term staffing of workers to clients	Staffing of workers to clients; management of development projects	Short-term staffing of workers to clients; management of development projects
Research methods	Periodic field observation; interviews; analysis of agency records	Periodic field observation; interviews; surveys; analysis of contracts	Interviews
Quantitative data	Job histories of 251 individuals placed by the agency in 457 clients (1480 projects) over 5 years	Survey data on the staffing and management of 57 software development projects	
Informants	Placement agents, contractors, industry experts	Senior managers, sourcing managers, project managers, developers	Convenience and snowball sample of clients, consultants, agency managers, industry experts
Number of interviews	45	62 (plus 57 in-person surveys)	36

regular employees. The staffing firm is the "employer of record," which means that the worker is formally employed by the intermediary and has no contractual relationship with the client. The client firm pays a fee to the agency – usually per hour of work – for the contractor's services, and the agency in turn pays the worker – also hourly. When the worker receives benefits, these are provided by the staffing firm, not by the client. Formally, the staffing firm is also in charge of supervising the contractor's work and solving any problems that may arise in the relationship. In practice, however, project managers usually deal directly with contractors on a day-to-day basis.[6] Most projects have an established duration – usually a few days or months – but sometimes they are open-ended or are regularly renewed. As a norm, contractors do not receive a salary when they are not assigned to a project by the staffing firm, and often workers are registered with several intermediaries at the same time.

Our data collection at the agency focused particularly on understanding the consequences of triadic employment relationships from the perspective of the worker, but it also aimed to study the internal functioning of labor market intermediaries. We studied the agency over the course of fifteen months. During this period we carried out repeat interviews with the agency's placement agents and, around three times a week, we observed their activities for three to four hours a day. As well as observing the agency, we implemented a series of interviews with individuals who had been affiliated with the agency at some point in their careers, and others who had worked as contractors in this sector but never joined this particular agency.[7] This involved interviews with forty-five individuals, some of whom were interviewed several times. The sample includes thirty-seven contractors (twenty-six of whom had been affiliated with the agency at some point, although not necessarily at the time of the interview), four placement agents at the agency, and two industry experts.[8]

---

[6] By actively managing the external worker, the client runs the risk of being found to be the legal employer of the worker. The demands of smoothly coordinating the work, however, generally require that clients become closely involved in external workers' day-to-day activities.

[7] The former were contacted through the agency's managers, while the latter were members of several professional and industry associations in the local area of the agency's headquarters.

[8] Besides this qualitative data, we also collected a wealth of quantitative information on contractors' job histories. We assembled a data set from a variety of sources

Study 2: the bank

The bank is a large financial services institution based in the United States. Our study focused on its IT department, which employed over 10,000 people and was responsible for developing and maintaining all the systems that the bank used to conduct its business. At the time of the study, around one-third of the developers at the bank were external workers employed under a triadic employment relationship. These external workers fell into three broad categories. T&Ms (time and materials consultants) were hired through staffing firms, but were managed exclusively by managers at the bank. Integrators were employees of consulting firms, which took a more direct role in managing projects, contributing significant institutional expertise. These workers were most likely to be engaged by the bank for very highly skilled work, often involving system design and interaction with the business. Finally, offshore workers were employed by foreign organizations and were usually physically located overseas, commonly in India, to carry out basic, lower-skilled development work. We studied how the bank managed these three types of external workers through interviews with sixty-two individuals at all levels of the organization, and a structured survey of fifty-seven project managers that examined how they managed internal and external workers.

Study 3: organizational forms adopted by intermediaries

The third study was a broad exploration of the relationships of all three participants in the market for IT consultants. Where our studies of the bank and the agency focused on gaining in-depth insights into particular organizational actors, this study sought to understand the variety of different kinds of organizations and relationships present in the market for IT consulting. In particular, we were interested in understanding the variety of organizational forms adopted by the intermediaries, and their implications for the relationship with clients and workers. We

provided by the agency (paper résumés, client information, demographic data, project characteristics, prices, etc.), as well as public information on size and industry classification of clients (see Bidwell and Fernandez-Mateo, 2006, for a full description of our quantitative data). We have comprehensive information on 251 individuals who were placed in 457 different companies between 1998 and 2002, making a total of 1,480 assignments.

interviewed thirty-six informants, including eight consultants, twelve managers of intermediaries, twelve clients and three industry analysts drawn from a convenience sample of clients, consultants, and intermediaries, based on personal contacts and referrals. These informants were associated with a wide variety of different kinds of intermediaries, from those firms that focused purely on staffing to organizations that also sought to provide project management and other institutional expertise to their clients. They were mainly located in the north-east of the United States. We also attended three industry conferences for IT staffing firms.

Data collection and analysis

Our qualitative data collection process consisted of both fieldwork observations and the implementation of semi-structured interviews. The interviews ranged from thirty minutes to two hours, with the average being one hour. We asked open-ended questions, which varied depending on the type of interviewee – worker, client, placement agent, etc. – but in all cases we paid special attention to the relationships among the three parties.

We analyzed these interviews by carefully reading and re-reading our transcripts and field notes, and by using a computer-assisted qualitative analysis tool (Atlas.ti). We used an iterative data analysis process (as described in Glaser and Strauss, 1967, and Miles and Huberman, 1994) in order to build a simple inductive framework for analyzing the different interactions among the participants.

Results: the impact of triadic interactions on employment outcomes

In analyzing our interviews, we find that there were many instances of our informants – unprompted – discussing how one tie would shape the way another tie was formed and managed. These interactions varied along three important dimensions: (1) who was involved in managing the relationships; (2) the kind of outcomes that were affected, including pay, task allocation, and job security; and (3) whether the actors were attempting to reinforce their relationships or balance one relationship with another. We focus on the latter dimension in order to organize the discussion of our findings, since we are interested in the dynamic aspect of how triadic ties interact with each other.

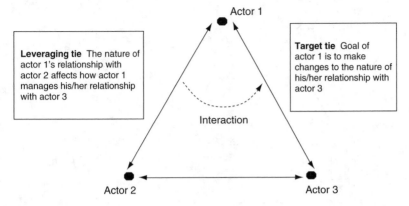

Figure 5.1 Defining interactions within a triad

Reinforcement

The most common pattern of interactions within the triad involved using one tie to strengthen, or "reinforce," another. Quite often actors benefited from strong ties to other actors. In these cases they tried to use this strong tie with one of the parties in order to forge a stronger tie with the other – a process of reinforcement. Such behavior would result in all three ties within the triad becoming stronger, a situation that social exchange theorists describe as "positive polarity" among ties (Cook and Whitmeyer, 1992). In this context, we use the term "strengthening" (and the reverse: "weakening") to mean mostly four things: creating a new tie; increasing the tangible and intangible resource flows that are exchanged through a tie (i.e. information, material resources, reputation); increasing the control that the actor has over the terms of the relationship; or increasing the probability of future transactions. Although each of these outcomes is somewhat different, we felt them to be sufficiently similar that we could collapse them into a single dimension.[9]

[9] To some extent, all these outcomes signal an increase (or decrease) in the tangible and intangible resources that flow through a tie. Establishing a new tie increases the resource flow from zero to some other amount, while increasing the probability of future exchange contributes to a growing flow of resources between the actors at some point in the future. Control could be conceptualized in part as the increased ability of an actor in the relationship to dictate the terms of the exchange, which can be thought of as a consequence of this actor having some resource that the other party values (Emerson, 1976). This conceptualization of relationships as exchange networks closely resembles that of social exchange theorists (Cook and Emerson, 1978; Blau, 1964).

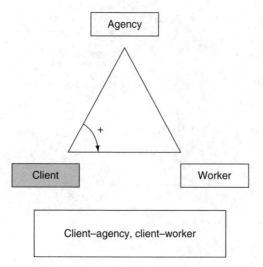

Figure 5.2 Bridging and buffering

Reinforcing behavior was pervasive throughout these triadic systems. We have found examples of it between each of the pairs of ties. We also observe how such reinforcement behaviors contributed to shape a variety of employment terms, including pay, task assignment, and job security. We present examples of these processes below.

Bridging and buffering: reinforcement between client–agency and client–worker ties

All accounts of triadic labor markets begin with the idea that clients leverage their tie with an agency to build a tie with a worker. When clients lack the networks that will help them to recruit workers for short-term assignments they turn instead to agencies, the wider networks of which allow them to propose workers for the position (e.g. Barley and Kunda, 2004). This is the most obvious function of an intermediary: working as a broker by matching workers to firms. Not surprisingly, such brokerage behavior was pervasive throughout the markets we looked at. In most cases, clients would use agencies to find potential contractors, but then do the final selection themselves. In some cases, when the client had a strong enough relationship with an agency, they might instead rely on that agency to perform all the screening for them. For example, managers at the agency we studied mentioned during informal conversations that some clients trusted their judgment on candidates so much that they did not get involved in the selection of candidates at all.

The influence of the agency on the relationships between client and worker extended well beyond its most obvious brokerage function of matching workers to jobs, however. In fact, both workers and clients used agencies to buffer themselves against a variety of risks associated with their ongoing relationship. Agencies facilitated a relationship between client and worker that would otherwise be too risky.

At the most basic level, clients use agencies to buffer them against legal risks. A concern for many clients was that they could be legally classified as the employer of a consultant, and therefore held responsible for withholding taxes from and paying benefits to the worker (see Barley and Kunda, 2004, for a detailed explanation of this issue). As a consequence, clients might insist that workers who approached them be employed by an external agency, even though that agency would have played no role in finding the worker. For example, one consultant told us:

I started working for [the client] as an intern. Then they wanted to bring me on as an employee, but they couldn't get an employee req [requisition form approved]. Instead they called up [the agency] and told them to hire me.

Agencies also protect clients from risks related to workers by guaranteeing their performance. In some cases clients would sign a contract with the agency for the specific work to be performed. If for some reason the worker fails to perform, its relationship with the agency ensures that the work will be completed. In explaining why he preferred to deal with larger agencies that would take responsibility for the work rather than independent contractors, one client said that

larger firms do have extra resources to call on. If you have a small company or individual and they get pneumonia for two weeks, then you are in real trouble. With a larger company, they have back-up project management to make sure that work does get delivered rapidly and on time.

In both these examples, the presence and nature of the agency–client relationship was critical to the formation of a client–worker relationship. Moreover, clients also used agencies to manage their relationship with the workers on an ongoing basis. Perhaps the most extreme example of this was the way that clients used their relationship with agencies to manage wage reductions. As the literature on internal labor

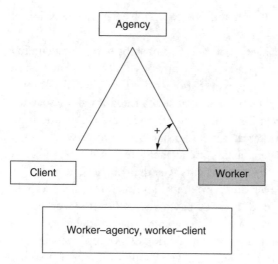

Figure 5.3 Brokering the broker

markets makes clear, it is extremely unusual for firms to reduce the wages of regular employees (Doeringer and Piore, 1971; Baker, Gibbs, and Holmstrom, 1994). During the period 2000–2002, however, demand for IT workers fell sharply in many areas, leading clients to attempt to cut expenditure by reducing consultants' pay. The fact that consultants were formally employed by third-party agencies facilitated these attempts; by positioning the rate cuts as inter-firm transactions, clients were able to reduce the damage to their relationships with the workers. As one client described:

> In fall 2001 we had our first line of reductions. We left it to the vendors as to how to manage it. We just told them: "We want a 10 to 20 percent reduction in your overall bill rate – you figure out how to do it." We told them that 10 percent was the absolute minimum reduction we wanted, and if they got as high as 20 percent they would make us very happy.

Brokering the broker: reinforcement between worker–agency and worker–client ties

Just as clients use agencies for more than simply finding a qualified worker, so workers use agencies for more than simply finding work. Indeed, we find that there were a number of situations in which workers chose to build a relationship through an agency despite having an existing relationship with the client. As we have seen, clients often like to involve agencies in their relationships because of the guarantee this provides about the quality of the work. At times, therefore, workers need to involve an agency in order to maintain and strengthen an existing tie with a client. For example, one manager at an agency explained how workers can act as brokers, introducing an agency to a client in order to shore up their own relationship with the client:

We had a key number two or number three player on a piece of work, where they contracted to us for the first time, as a try-out, if you will. They [the two contract employees] did well. They had access to another client. Tenuous access. But access. It was then much easier to walk in with a portfolio of [the agency's] projects, rather than for John to come back and say I have a ragtag team of folks, and I can assemble a team. Instead he would introduce me. And that's all I had as well. Except I had a body of work, a reference list, and my references were all CFOs [chief financial officers]. So when you pick up a phone, and you get a call in to a CFO, who can then tell you: "I've hired these people three or four times."

Alternatively, workers might choose to work through an agency because of the increased security from ties to a firm that would find them work and provide them with secure pay. When clients wanted to hire these workers, they would have to do so through that agency, even when they had a pre-existing link with them.

Once they started working with the client, workers could exploit their ties with the agency they were using in order to strengthen their relationship with the client. In particular, the agency could be an important source of feedback for the worker about how the job was progressing. For example, one worker described how

I e-mail them [the agency] when I need something, or they e-mail me when they need something, I always ask them to give me [the client] feedback, and they are always like, you know, they love you, everything is great, you know.

We find that there were very tangible ways in which this reinforcement behavior benefited workers. In a separate analysis of wage and billing rates at the agency we studied, we show that workers with long-standing relationships with the agency were able to command higher bill rates from the client, and higher wages overall (Bidwell and Fernandez-Mateo, 2006). Longer relationships with workers allowed the agency to learn about their strengths and weaknesses, and therefore provide a better fit with client needs. This better alignment improved

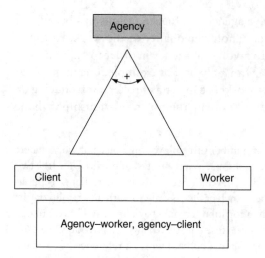

Figure 5.4 A means to an end

the quality of the worker–client relationships, and therefore the amount that clients were willing to pay for a worker.

Reinforcement also occurred when workers leveraged their ties to *clients* to improve their relationships with an *agency*. The most obvious way to achieve this was to ensure that agencies received feedback from the clients when jobs were going well, so that the agencies would be more likely to choose them on future assignments. As one consultant said:

I mean, you make sure that the people you are working for they like what you do and they call up [the agency] and they say: "Oh boy, did he do a good job" – you know, stuff like that.

A means to an end: reinforcement between agency–worker and agency–client ties

While accounts of triadic employment relationships have tended to focus on how the participants – especially intermediaries – achieve the right client–worker match, the three actors are at the same time actively managing their other relationships. Success for agencies depends largely on how they manage their relationships with their clients. When the agency–worker tie is a critical resource in managing client relationships, these ties become reinforcing.

For example, agencies would use workers to build relationships with clients by deciding whom to assign to a particular client. These staffing decisions are not just a case of finding the best fit between worker and job; the nature of the relationship with the client shapes which workers are selected by the agency to work there. For example, if an agency was trying to build a reputation with a new client it would send a worker whom it knew well and trusted to do a good job, in order to make a good impression on the client. As one placement agent told us about new clients:

> I might place the good one there in order to give them a great first impression of [the agency] so they keep doing business with us.

Alternatively, following a failed placement, an agency would try to ensure the next person that it sent was somebody with whom it had an established relationship, and could be trusted to do a good job. As one such worker told us:

> You can always try to send them a good talent to mend things up. I do a lot of that, like I've been sent in to a lot of difficult clients, or I have been sent in to a lot of situations when they want to win a client over.

Close relationships with workers could help agencies to woo clients in other ways. In particular, workers can be a valuable source of information about clients for agencies, helping placement agents to do more deals. This is another reason for agencies to assign workers with whom they have close relationships to key clients. As one placement agent explained:

> We are not in the client, so we need someone to help me understand their structure, the organizational chart. We use for that the talent we place there as well, in order to get a better understanding of the company and see what might be the next step for us to expand.

Such dynamics had important consequences for how ties between clients and workers were built. What kind of job they were matched to was not just a function of workers' skills and the requirements of the job; the nature of agencies' relationships with particular clients also influenced how workers were assigned to jobs.

The need for agencies to build strong client relationships also shaped their ties with workers. To the extent that close relationships with contractors helped agencies to win business, they were more likely to build strong ties to these workers. The need to reinforce client relationships could therefore induce agencies to put workers on a salary. Many of the agencies had arm's-length relationships with their workers, paying them only when they were able to find a job for them. Such an arrangement reduced the agencies' costs, as they did not have to pay the workers for "bench time" when they had not been placed; it also had its disadvantages, however. Without the expectation of a long-term relationship with an agency, workers had less incentive to represent that agency in the best light, and were more likely to seek work elsewhere. As the client's relationship with that agency became more dependent on the skills and performance of the workers it supplied, the agency would be more likely to employ them on a full-time basis. Doing this would also "bind" the workers to some extent, as they would no longer be able to have arrangements with other agencies if they were receiving a full-time salary.

We find that this strengthening of the agency–worker relationship was particularly evident when agencies presented themselves to clients as managing the overall delivery of the services. In these circumstances, agencies wanted to be able to present key workers as possessing the expertise necessary for the project. As it became necessary to draw on this expertise with increasing frequency, it also became necessary to employ these workers full-time. Similarly, when agencies were responsible for the delivery of projects, they might feel that the risks involved in arm's-length relationships with their staff were too great. As one manager in a high-end consulting firm told us:

> People don't feel comfortable going into battle with a lot of mercenaries. When the going gets tough, they are not going to stick around. Similarly, we don't tend to do easy projects. If they were easy, then the clients would do them themselves. We don't want people to run away when the project gets tough, and that is the concern with contractors.

To the extent that workers could directly affect the client relationship, they were more likely to be made employees of an agency. As another manager at the same integrator firm put it:

> Where we use contractors most is where we have the most control of them. This is where [the agency] has been given a job to build a complete system to deliver to the client, and is building it on our own premises. In these cases, if a contractor doesn't shape up then it is pretty easy for us to take corrective action.

> I feel much more nervous about using contractors at the client site. Then they get introduced to the client, get to know people, and we are much more exposed. All of our people have been rigorously screened, but not the contractors. Having them there starts to muddy the water.

Finally, the need to build client relationships could lead the agencies not only to build long-term relationships with the workers but also to train and certify them in new technologies. As the manager of another integrator explained to us:

> Almost everybody is certified. [The agency] will pay for our staff's certification . . . It is an additional feature in your sales. Many of the certification levels in Java and so on are actually pretty rigorous. They give a sense to clients that the people really do know their stuff. The clients don't have to worry about it.

Just as the client–agency tie could provide a motive for agencies to strengthen their ties with their workers, it could also provide a resource for such strengthening. A simple way that agencies achieved this was by providing workers with as much information as possible about the client. This information helped the worker to prepare for the assignment and eased the transition into the new job. As the assignment progressed, regular updates about what was happening at the client company could be useful to the workers. The provision of such information was, therefore, an important service that agencies could offer to the workers, and one that would differentiate them from other agencies (and potentially win over good contract workers). It was also something that contractors often commented on:

> When I worked with [a specific agent], she was amazing, she went to check out everything, she would tell me what they were like, she would tell me what the place is like. She would tell me, you know, how to get there, if there was parking . . . she was very amenable to all the things that would affect me – she was amazing.

On occasion, agencies might also leverage their relationships with clients in more substantial ways to help manage their ties with workers. Given that the client ultimately shaped the conditions of work, agents needed to work with these clients to manage how they improved rewards for workers. An agency's relationship with a client could therefore be used to improve things for the worker. There were examples of such behavior at the bank we studied, where the close relationship between the client and the offshore vendors meant that the bank would be relatively responsive in helping the vendors to manage their relationships with the workers. One of the bank's managers gave us an example of this:

> Now that I have worked with these people [outsourcing vendors] repeatedly, I can guess who the people on the other side will be. I can cut them slack in how they do the work. If they want to fly someone over to do something, I'll let them, even if it is not strictly needed for the project, because it might help to reward and develop the individual. I am happy to do this sort of thing as long as the work comes in under budget.

Balancing

Although strong relationships often benefited the actors within the triad, this was not always the case. Sometimes, strong ties could expose actors to significant costs and risks. For example, relationships with workers might create legal liabilities for clients. This would mostly be due to the risk that contractors – even those hired through agencies – might be classified as employees in the case of a legal dispute. In such a case, agencies would be liable for any benefits awarded to these workers (see *Monthly Labor Review*, 1998). Similarly, the mere existence of a relationship with an intermediary implies that workers and agencies have to pay a price for its services. When these risks and costs become high, actors might seek to use their other relationships to minimize the costs and risks, thereby effectively weakening relationships. We describe these effects as "balancing behavior" (Emerson, 1962; Gargiulo, 1993), in which a stronger relationship with one of the actors actually leads to a weaker relationship with the other one. Once again, such behavior was widespread among all three actors, and had consequences for a variety of employment outcomes.

Disintermediation: balancing between client–worker and agency–worker ties

Many accounts of triadic labor markets paint the intermediary as the *tertius gaudens*, who gains rents from bringing two previously separated parties together (see Wolff, 1950; Burt, 1992; Marsden, 1982). A clear corollary of such a framing is that, once introduced, it is in the interest of the other two parties to remove the broker from the triad. Disintermediating the broker in this way allows the other two parties to

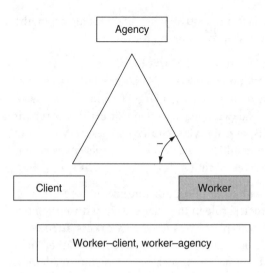

Figure 5.5 Disintermediation

share the rents previously appropriated by the broker – in this case the agency fee.

Attempts at such disintermediation were an important feature of triadic labor markets. In most cases, agencies would write contracts with clients that forbade the client from hiring the worker directly without compensating the agency, or would introduce a non-compete clause that committed the worker and the client to not contracting directly among themselves for a period of time – usually one year – after the intermediary had matched them. In fact, such clauses and provisions are generally part of the business model used by most labor market intermediaries (see also Barley and Kunda, 2004). Furthermore, cases of disintermediation were taken very seriously by agencies, which might even sue workers or clients who broke non-compete agreements. For example, during the course of our research at the agency we studied, one of the agents learned that a contractor had signed a direct agreement with a client the agency had assigned them to a few weeks earlier. Pandemonium ensued. Placement agents shouted at each other, made frantic calls to the agency's lawyers, and threatened client and worker with legal action unless some kind of monetary agreement was reached. Needless to say, ties with both client and contractor were immediately severed.

Even where non-compete clauses are respected by all participants, such legal devices cannot always prevent disintermediation. For example, such contracts are ineffective when individuals from the client firm moved companies. As one contractor told us:

> When a CFO would leave [their current job], having established a personal relationship with one or two players, they understood that the contract house was merely making a large margin, so they were more than happy to deal with me or others directly, because it lowered their cost basis, and we were known entities, so you could walk into an environment and bring a new CFO to this environment up to speed within two weeks' time.

We also saw many instances of partial disintermediation – that is, attempts to minimize agencies' role in the relationship without removing them altogether. An example of this is when workers attempt to negotiate pay and conditions directly with their clients rather than going through agencies. In some cases, such partial disintermediation represents a clear attempt by the two parties to reduce the agencies' rents from the transaction.[10] In other cases, though, partial disintermediation reflects the fact that as the clients and the workers get to know each other they become more likely to resolve issues directly between themselves in a timelier and more efficient manner. These two faces of disintermediation mean that agencies have complex reactions to the phenomenon. For example, one agency manager told us:

> In my firm, more than 90 percent of the consultants are salaried, benefited and have tenure. Because of this, I frown on them going to the client directly to discuss their rate. In previous years, though, they would come back to me and say: "My rate is below the market." This should not be the client's problem. Instead, the agency should continually be in touch with its consultants to ensure that any problems are rapidly resolved.

By contrast, we came across cases in which partial disintermediation directly benefited the agency. According to one contractor:

---

[10] In fact, our quantitative work suggests that workers who are able to establish stronger relationships with clients extract higher rents from the agency (Bidwell and Fernandez-Mateo, 2006). When workers have performed several engagements with the client in the past, retaining their services becomes important for the agency in maintaining its tie with the client. As a result, the agency would pass significantly more of its billings on to the workers.

When I worked for this financial company for almost one year I thought, well, I am becoming very valuable for them, and I think we can up the pay rate, so I spoke to my boss at the client directly, which I guess technically you are not supposed to do, and I said to her: "I really think I should get paid more by the hour," and she agreed. Then I went back to [the placement agent], and said: "I've spoken to the client and we are going to bill more."

Balancing behavior could also happen when workers used the intermediary to distance themselves from their clients. It was usually in the interest of the workers to strengthen their relationship with the clients; after all, this was the source of their pay. Nonetheless, when workers became too dependent on their clients, the agencies could prove a useful resource for reducing this dependence. Perhaps the most obvious example of this behavior was in how agencies protected workers from the risk of non-payment on behalf of the clients. Even when clients did not pay for the work, the contractors would be paid by the agencies – something that would not have happened had the workers been hired directly by the clients as independent contractors.

Workers could also use the agencies to buffer themselves against their clients in other ways. For example, when workers had longer-term relationships with agencies, they might choose to have the agency intercede for them to resolve problems that they encountered with the client company. As one contractor told us:

Well, the people that I see every day, that are my direct managers, I count them as my boss; I'd say they are the people I talk to if I have any [problems] at work, but if I have any question about the way I'm being treated or something like that, I would probably go to [the agency].

In the words of another:

The way you have to do as a contractor for an agency – if you have a problem you have to talk with the agency, call your agent and tell him this is what happens and you are going to have to ... because I am not gonna react.

For particularly valuable workers, the intermediary might even go so far as to provide the worker with the rewards that the client was refusing. One contractor told us:

I managed to negotiate a week off ... [T]hey want to renew the contract, they want to do the same thing for a different client ... I have been able to negotiate that, consequently they were able to negotiate a lower rate with my agent ... "Oh, she is asking for a week off" ... so they are asking for less money ... I get the same rate, I don't pay the difference – I know, because the client told me.

Bargaining and distancing: balancing between client–worker and client–agency ties

Just as the worker could be active in attempting to disintermediate an agency, so could the client. Many of the examples of client-led disintermediation attempts that we came across revolved around information. As Barley and Kunda (2004) note, information about billing rates tends to be jealously guarded by the agencies, on the basis that it helps them to maintain higher margins. In response, many clients attempt to force agencies to practice "open book" pricing, so that all the parties know what the margin is. Such pressures tend to drive down agencies' rent, and may also lead to a deterioration in service in the market. One agency manager told us:

Recently there has been a lot of pressure on margins and clients pushing for greater visibility of their margins. To be honest, we hate this. We are trying to run a business, and this pressure for transparency makes that difficult. We have a $70 million operation in the US, and we are trying to deliver a quality service. The pressure for full disclosure diminishes what they do by just focusing on the labor rate ... People like IBM who pushed for full disclosure said that they do it because they want to make sure that the maximum dollar goes to labor. I am not embarrassed to say that we have shareholders, and so we need to make sure that we are making money for them.

Such partial disintermediation tactics (pushed by the clients) became particularly important when agencies were attempting to present what they did as a service, rather than purely the provision of individuals. By focusing on the individuals that an agency was providing (and thereby downplaying the role of the client–agency relationship in providing the service), clients were able to reduce that agency's rent significantly. One client described the process of negotiating with a high-end consulting firm as follows:

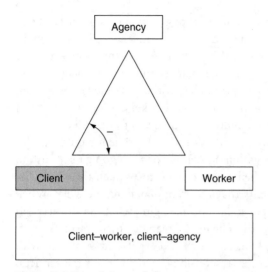

Figure 5.6 Bargaining and distancing

Some of the push back that [the client manager] used was that what looked like very different people had very similar pay levels. Even the terminology is different across these people [for different firms] – so how do you do an apples to apples comparison of the individuals and roles and peg a price on them? You need to come up with a matrix of titles in this company versus those in the other. We kind of did this, but not as formally as we might have ... However, [the client manager] really saved a lot of money on these projects, pushing back on these issues.

While the threat of disintermediation was usually damaging to an agency's interests, sometimes the agency needed to accept it in order to conduct the transaction. Some clients might require the option of direct hiring in order to do business with an agency. For example, when the bank we studied used offshore personnel via a vendor to manage some of its key systems, it became highly dependent on the knowledge of those external workers. This dependence made the bank very vulnerable to "hold-up" behavior by the vendor during contract renegotiations, as the knowledge about the vendors' personnel was effectively irreplaceable. In order to manage this problem, the bank made it a condition of its use of offshore vendors that it had the right to interview and employ the vendors' employees should the relationship between client and vendor be terminated.

It was not always in clients' interest to engage in such partial disintermediation of agencies. Indeed, the reason that clients brought agencies in originally was to balance their relationship with workers. Accordingly, clients would often use their relationships with agencies in order to distance themselves from the workers. For example, when clients were dissatisfied with particular workers, they would often leave the job of releasing the individuals involved to the relevant agencies. There were also many situations in which the client would want to weaken the tie to workers within the context of an ongoing relationship.

The main reason why clients would want to weaken their own ties with workers was to simplify the process of managing the work. When agencies took greater responsbility for managing what the workers did the resources needed by the clients to manage their projects were reduced. Clients achieved this through more detailed contracts with agencies, making the agencies responsible for delivery of the services. This meant that clients could rely on the agencies to do the management. A senior manager at the bank we studied outlined this logic to us as he explained how he was trying to train his subordinates to deal with offshore vendors:

> Anecdotal evidence is no longer acceptable to me in talking about problems with the offshore vendors. My questions would … be, first, should you even be talking to this person? Or is someone else named as the point of contact in the contract? How does this relate to the contract? How has it actually affected your performance on the contract? Are their English skills even relevant to your evaluation of the vendor? [...] We want to focus on "These are the deliverables. Are they acceptable, on time and on price?" Ultimately, you can't control the other issues, and that's supposed to be one of the advantages of outsourcing – you shouldn't be worrying about who they hire.

Building a strong relationship with an agency was therefore critical to the client's ability to reduce its own contact with the workers. There was a clear tension, however, between, on the one hand, the client's desire to minimize the effort devoted to managing the workers and, on the other, its goal of limiting agency margins. Reducing the status of the agency involved to that of a broker enabled the client to lower margins. Limiting the burden of managing the workers required the client to bring the agency back into the relationship as an active participant, however.

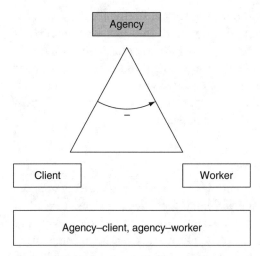

Figure 5.7 Taking themselves out

Taking themselves out: balancing between agency–client and agency–worker ties[11]

As we have seen, disintermediation was generally beneficial to clients and workers, but damaging to agencies. Nevertheless, we did come across instances in which agencies chose to disintermediate themselves – something that it would have been difficult to anticipate from most of the literature on brokerage and intermediation. While intermediating between clients and workers brought returns in the form of fees, it also carried costs. Among the most serious of these costs was the prospect that poor performance on the part of workers would damage agencies' relationships with their clients. In a few cases, agencies perceived these risks to be very high, yet were not able to remove the worker from the client. In those situations, agencies would encourage their clients to hire the worker directly. An agency manager described just such a situation to us:

---

[11] Isabel Fernandez-Mateo (2007) has analyzed a related kind of balancing behavior on the part of agencies, which focuses on price setting. In particular, she finds that intermediaries offer discounts to clients with which they have stronger relationships (those of strategic importance). Instead of this reducing their margins, however, agencies are able to transfer these discounts to workers, who as a result get lower pay rates when assigned to these firms. In a sense, the agencies are using their relationship with the workers to alleviate the price constraint imposed by their ties to powerful clients.

We have had our people do terrible things, like stealing, but had the client not want to do anything about it. This puts me in a difficult position, as ultimately we are liable for what our people do. In one case, we told the client that if they wanted to keep the consultant they would have to convert them, as we were not prepared to deal with the liability of having that person on our payroll. The client then went ahead and converted the person.

Discussion and conclusions

Many new employment relationships are triadic in nature, as opposed to traditional dyadic – employer–employee – relationships. Instead of consisting of a tie between a worker and a firm, these relationships involve three actors in the exchange of employment services: a company, a worker, and an intermediary of some sort (see also Kunda, Barley, and Evans, 2002). As a consequence, understanding new employment arrangements requires the examination of a distinctive feature of triadic relationships: the fact that all three ties within the triad interact with each other. We have used concepts borrowed from social exchange theory (Cook and Emerson, 1978; Blau, 1964) to begin to explore this phenomenon, by arguing that not only do the terms of exchange between two given actors depend on the characteristics of the tie between them, but they are also determined by their ties to other actors. In particular, the "third relationship" can be an additional resource – and sometimes a constraint – that the parties draw on when interacting with the focal actor.

Workers

Our findings on how relationships within a triad interact with each other in high-skilled contract labor markets have important practical implications for workers, intermediaries and clients. Workers involved in mediated arrangements need to understand the existing tie between the client and the intermediary in order to appreciate how their relationship with both actors will evolve. In particular, we have described several ways in which client–agency relationships can significantly affect workers. For example, the strength of the intermediary's tie with the worker – including whether the intermediary employs the worker full-time – depends on whether the intermediary's tie with the client relies on claims of expertise and the provision of guaranteed performance.

Similarly, workers will be more likely to be "managed" by the intermediary rather than the client when the client–agency relationship is stronger. Client–agency relationships also influence job assignment, as agencies' decisions about which workers to allocate to which projects depend in part on how the agencies seek to develop their relationships with different clients. For example, agencies will appoint their most trustworthy contractors to valued current or potential clients, either to protect their relationship with them or to strengthen it for the future. As a result of these processes, workers involved in triadic employment arrangements need to understand how to make full use of their relationship with each party in the triad, and be aware that ties are not just an end in themselves but also a powerful means of shaping other relationships.

Intermediaries and clients

Our findings also have implications for intermediaries and clients. For the former, they are a reminder of the central importance of their relationships with workers in shaping how they deal with clients. For the latter, they illustrate that ties with labor market intermediaries need to become an integral part of their human resources strategy. When using the services of an intermediary, a company is necessarily giving up some control over how workers are managed. Moreover, its relationships with workers are now modified by the activities of another company, which, logically, is pursuing its own agenda. Therefore, companies need to understand that how they deal with intermediaries will affect the terms of their relationships with workers, and ultimately how they behave and perform. One key implication of this argument is that firms (clients) that are heavily invested in the use of externalized work arrangements need to incorporate their strategies for dealing with intermediaries into their companies' general HR strategies. All too often decisions are ad hoc and left to the discretion of individual hiring managers, which might have unintended consequences for the success of flexible staffing arrangements (see Bidwell, 2006).

We should also reconsider the symbiotic relationship between employment intermediaries and the legal institutions surrounding employment (at least in the United States). The basic structure of legislation on topics such as benefit provision and industrial relations is predicated on the fact that workers have a single employer. These assumptions have, in part, helped to spur the growth of triadic employment relationships, as client firms have looked to intermediaries to escape some of the more burdensome obligations attached to employment, such as the provision of benefits. The growth of these triadic arrangements, though, is undermining the policy goals enshrined in the legislation, as clients become increasingly able to pick and choose which obligations and for which workers they will retain responsibility for.

How best to revise the regulatory framework to recognize the reality of modern employment is a tricky question. On the one hand, modifying legal frameworks to make it simpler to identify client firms as co-employers would bring the legal system closer into line with the economic reality. On the other hand, industry responses to the Vizcaino ruling over Microsoft's temporary workers (e.g. Barley and Kunda, 2004) show how increasing employers' obligations to external workers can simply lead to more elaborate schemes to distance clients from workers, quite possibly to the detriment of both parties. Triadic employment arrangements are therefore likely to remain a difficult challenge to public policy for the foreseeable future.

Our qualitative findings also have implications for future research on contingent and intermediated employment. In particular, they argue for the need to examine these work arrangements as systems of ties, in which relationships interact in order to influence outcomes such as wages, task assignment, and employment security. We have offered some examples and patterns of these interactions, which could be used to develop specific hypotheses and test them using quantitative data sets (for a first effort to do this, see Bidwell and Fernandez-Mateo, 2006). In particular, a question that arises from our qualitative fieldwork is this: what are the circumstances under which specific ties will reinforce as opposed to balance each other? We need to extend this research using data from other occupations and types of intermediaries. In particular, we have argued that triadic employment arrangements are becoming more prevalent in the labor market, and that they include not just staffing agencies but also other actors such as outsourcing and even professional services companies. Studying how these interactions play out in other triadic settings should improve understanding of this increasingly important sector of the labor market.

The growth of triadic employment arrangements raises other questions for future research. For example, to what extent does the growth of external employment (employment through intermediaries) affect inequality within the labor market? We might suppose that intermediaries offer client firms the opportunity to cut back on their obligations to some of their most vulnerable workers, such as low-skilled employees, increasing the gaps between the most and least successful. On the other hand, we have seen how intermediaries offer workers new opportunities for action. It is conceivable that some disadvantaged workers may actually find that triadic arrangements allow them to overcome obstacles to their advancement in more traditional relationships. For example, arrangements of this type could work as a stepping stone to permanent employment for workers who are having trouble finding regular jobs. Either way, it is important to gain a deeper understanding of who wins and who loses in triadic employment relationships. William Bielby and Denise Bielby (1999) have made an early attempt to address this question in the context of the film industry, but much more work remains to be done.

A third area that needs to be investigated relates to the sustainability of triadic arrangements. The dynamics of reinforcing and balancing highlight a certain tension in triadic arrangements. Workers are managing important relationships with two separate organizations with interests that sometimes align and sometimes conflict. It is possible that, over time, these dynamics will lead workers to become more clearly identified with one or other employer, effectively breaking up the triad. Examining how and whether workers and firms are able to balance these tensions over time will help us to understand whether triadic employment will continue to be an adjunct to more traditional, dyadic relationships, or whether they will become a precursor to the widespread adoption of network forms of organization.

References

Abraham, K. G. (1990). Restructuring the employment relationship: the growth of market-mediated work arrangements. In K. G. Abraham and R. B. McKersie (eds.), *New Developments in the Labor Market: Toward a New Institutional Paradigm* (85–118). Cambridge, MA: MIT Press.

Abraham, K. G., and Taylor, S. K. (1996). Firms' use of outside contractors: theory and evidence. *Journal of Labor Economics*, 14, 394–434.

Ang, S., and Slaughter, S. A. (2001). Work outcomes and job design for contract versus permanent information systems professionals on software development teams. *MIS Quarterly*, 25(3), 321–50.

Autor, D. H. (2001). Why do temporary help firms provide free general skills training? *Quarterly Journal of Economics, 116*(4), 1409–49.

   (2003). Outsourcing at will: the contribution of unjust dismissal doctrine to the growth of employment outsourcing. *Journal of Labor Economics, 23*(1), 1–42.

Baker, G., Gibbs, M., and Holmstrom, B. (1994). The wage policy of a firm. *Quarterly Journal of Economics, 109*(4), 921–55.

Barley, S. R., and Kunda, G. (2004). *Gurus, Hired Guns and Warm Bodies: Itinerant Experts in a Knowledge Economy*. Princeton, NJ: Princeton University Press.

Baron, J. N., and Hannan, M. T. (1994). The impact of economics on contemporary sociology. *Journal of Economic Literature, 32*(3), 1111–46.

Bidwell, M. 2006. Problems deciding: how the make or buy decision leads to transaction misalignment. Unpublished manuscript. Singapore: INSEAD.

Bidwell, M., and Fernandez-Mateo, I. (2006). Brokerage in the long run: how does relationship duration affect the returns to brokerage? Unpublished manuscript. Singapore: INSEAD.

Bielby, W. T., and Bielby, D. D. (1999). Organizational mediation of project-based labor markets: talent agencies and the careers of screenwriters. *American Sociological Review, 64*(1), 64–85.

Blau, P. M. (1964). *Exchange and Power in Social Life*. New York: Wiley.

Broschak, J. P., and Davis-Blake, A. (2006). Mixing standard work and non-standard deals: the consequences of heterogeneity in employment arrangements. *Academy of Management Journal, 49*(2), 371–93.

Burt, R. S. (1992). *Structural Holes: The Social Structure of Competition*. Cambridge, MA: Harvard University Press.

Cappelli, P. (1995). Rethinking employment. *British Journal of Industrial Relations, 33*(4), 563–602.

   (1999). *The New Deal at Work: Managing the Market-Based Employment Relationship*. Boston: Harvard Business School Press.

Cook, K. S., and Emerson, R. M. (1978). Power, equity and commitment in exchange networks. *American Sociological Review, 43*(5), 721–39.

Cook, K. S., and Whitmeyer, J. M. (1992). Two approaches to social structure: exchange theory and network analysis. *Annual Review of Sociology, 18*, 109–27.

Davidov, G. (2004). Joint employer status in triangular employment relationships. *British Journal of Industrial Relations, 42*(4), 727–46.

Davis-Blake, A., and Broschak, J. P. (2000). Speed bumps of stepping stones: the effects of labor market intermediaries on relational wealth. In C. Leana and D. M. Rousseau (eds.), *Relational Wealth: A New*

Model for Employment in the 21st Century (91–115). Oxford: Oxford University Press.

Davis-Blake, A., and Uzzi, B. (1993). Determinants of employment externalization: a study of temporary workers and independent contractors. *Administrative Science Quarterly, 38*, 195–223.

Doeringer, P. B., and Piore, M. J. (1971). *Internal Labor Markets and Manpower Analysis*. Lexington, MA: D.C. Heath.

Emerson, R. M. (1962). Power-dependence relations. *American Sociological Review, 27*(1), 31–41.

(1972). Exchange theory, part II: exchange relations and networks. In J. Berger, M. Zelditch, and B. Anderson (eds.), *Sociological Theories in Progress*, vol. II (58–87). Boston: Houghton Mifflin.

(1976). Social exchange theory. *Annual Review of Sociology, 2*, 335–62.

Fernandez-Mateo, I. (2007). Who pays the price of brokerage? Transferring constraint through price setting in the staffing sector. *American Sociological Review, 72*(2), 291–317.

Finlay, W., and Coverdill, J. E. (2000). Risk, opportunism and structural holes: how headhunters manage clients and earn fees. *Work and Occupations, 27*(3), 377–405.

Gargiulo, M. (1993). Two-step leverage: managing constraint in organizational politics. *Administrative Science Quarterly, 38*(1), 1–19.

Glaser, B., and Strauss, A. (1967). *The Discovery of Grounded Theory*. Chicago: Aldine de Gruyter.

Gramm, C. L., and Schnell, J. F. (2001). The use of flexible staffing arrangements in core production jobs. *Industrial and Labor Relations Review, 54*(2), 245–58.

Houseman, S. N. (2001). Why employers use flexible staffing arrangements: evidence from an establishment survey. *Industrial and Labor Relations Review, 55*(1), 149–70.

Houseman, S. N., Kalleberg. A. L., and Erickcek, G. A. (2003). The role of temporary agency employment in tight labor markets. *Industrial and Labor Relations Review, 57*(1), 103–27.

Kalleberg, A. L., Reskin, B. F., and Hudson, K. (2000). Bad jobs in America: standard and non-standard employment relations and job quality in the United States. *American Sociological Review, 65*, 256–78.

Krackhardt, D. (1999). The ties that torture: Simmelian tie analysis in organizations. *Research in the Sociology of Organizations, 16*, 183–210.

Kunda, G., Barley, S. R., and Evans, J. (2002). Why do contractors contract? The experience of highly skilled technical professionals in a contingent labor market. *Industrial and Labor Relations Review, 55*(2), 234–61.

Marsden, P. V. (1982). Brokerage behavior in restricted exchange networks. In P. V. Marsden and N. Lin (eds.), *Social Structure and Network Analysis* (201–18). Beverly Hills: Sage.

Miles, M. B., and Huberman, A. M. (1994). *Qualitative Data Analysis* (2nd edn.). Thousand Oaks, CA: Sage.

Monthly Labor Review (1998). The law at work. *121*(10), 32–4.

Muhl, G. (2002). What is an employee? The answer depends on federal law. *Monthly Labor Review, 125*(1), 3–11.

Neumark, D., Polsky, D., & Hansen, D. (1999). Has job stability declined yet? Evidence for the 1990s. *Journal of Labor Economics, 17*(4, 2), S29–S64.

Osterman, P. (1999). *Securing Prosperity: How the American Labor Market has Changed and What to Do about It.* Princeton, NJ: Princeton University Press.

Pfeffer, J., and Baron, J. (1988). Taking the workers back out: recent trends in the structuring of employment. *Research in Organizational Behavior, 10*, 257–303.

Storrie, D. (2002). *Temporary Agency Work in the European Union.* Dublin: European Foundation for the Improvement of Living and Working Conditions.

Van Dyne, L. and Ang, S. (1998). Organizational citizenship behavior of contingent workers in Singapore. *Academy of Management Journal, 41*(6), 692–703.

Wolff, K. H. (ed.) (1950). *The Sociology of Georg Simmel.* Glencoe, IL: Free Press.

6 | The changed world of large law firms and their lawyers: an opportune context for organizational researchers

PETER D. SHERER

He had graduated from Harvard Law School in the early 1970s and had gone to the New York office of a large US law firm, where he had made it up to partner and stayed his entire career. Now he was thinking about retiring. In looking back, he didn't quite know what to think about the firm and how it had changed. Its sheer size, wealth, and geographical expanse had made it different from before even though it had grown gradually and maintained its standing among its rivals. Its lean hierarchy was something of the past as well. While once there had been just partners and associates on the "up to partner or out of the firm" system, now there were a variety of tiers of lawyers, who were managed differently and, as a result, felt differently about the firm. In addition, the firm had gone from developing its own talent with some exceptions to accepting the fact that it had to acquire partners laterally from other firms, a varied lot of real stars, ambitious types from lesser firms, specialists in hot areas, and others who turned out to be just hot air. The firm had varying degrees of success with these talent acquisitions.

The above partner is a microcosm of the changed world of large law firms and their lawyers in the past thirty years.[1] Following what Robert Nelson (1988, p. 7) refers to as the "watershed" that occurred in American law in the 1960s and 1970s, large US law firms have undergone organizational changes since the late 1970s and early 1980s, and the world of lawyers in those firms has changed with it. Those who see the changes as negative (e.g. Asimow, 2001; Glendon, 1994; Linowitz, 1994; Rhode, 2000; Schiltz, 1999) argue that lawyers in large law firms

I appreciate the valuable comments on this chapter that have I received from Peter Cappelli, Laura Empson, Huseyin Leblebici, and an anonymous reviewer.

[1] While the partner is fictitious, a composite of various partners' accounts, the story is very real in capturing what has happened to partners in law firms from the late 1970s to the present.

are more discontented and alienated than ever before. They see the source of the problem as the decline of the traditional professional model of partnership and the rise of a business model that is singularly bent on profits. Others (e.g. Brill, 1989, 1996) who take a positive view of the changes suggest that the large law firm has always operated as a business, only now it does so with market forces, giving partners much more information than they had in the past. They cite, for example, the dramatic rise in the inter-firm or lateral movement of partners as a positive force for lawyers and their firms, in that only those firms that provide the right tangible rewards and intangibles can retain their partners.

The micro-, meso-, and macro-organizational concerns raised by the changes in the world of the large law firm and its lawyers provide organizational researchers with an opportune context in which to build on and extend theoretical arguments and empirical findings in the areas of business strategy, human resource management, organizational behavior, and organizational theory. Since large law firms depend so heavily on their human capital, these four areas all enter into study and, at times, come together almost as one. As these firms share key management practices (e.g. the "up or out" system) with university business schools and other knowledge-based organizations (e.g. consulting firms), organizational researchers can make use of insights that they gain from law firms in understanding these other kinds of organizations.

There are a multitude of issues that might be attractive to organizational researchers in examining the shifts that have taken place in large law firms, yet three topics are of particular relevance: (1) changes in the organizational identity of the large law firm; (2) variations within firms in the management of lawyers; and (3) the acquisition of lateral partners. These topics have particular relevance, for they both capture and raise theoretical debates and fill and create voids in the empirical literature. The topics are described in this chapter in considerable "thickness" in order to convey to organizational researchers their institutional richness. The chapter, therefore, differs from other chapters in this collection in that it focuses on generating theoretical and empirical research rather than presenting theory and findings from a research study.

Before proceeding, let's look at why these three topics are so important and how the changes in large law firms are so opportune for studying them. *Organizational identity* – the central, distinctive, and enduring character of an organization (Albert and Whetten, 1985) – is of great interest to organizational researchers. The majority of the research on organizational identify has looked at instances in which there was a strong and unequivocally negative change, almost a shock, to the organization's extant identity (Dutton and Dukerich, 1992; Elsbach and Kramer, 1996). My research of large law firms suggests, however, that the nature of the change in identity in many of these firms is neither unequivocal nor negative. It involves a gradual yet significant departure from the past along with surprising stability, combining something of the old with something of the new. How such change in identity affects organizational members is not clear a priori and is, thus, important for extending theory and empirical research.

Considerable theoretical interest exists in the field of strategic HRM in studying the *variation in human resource management* that occurs within firms, with emphasis placed almost entirely on a model in which firms have both a core and periphery workforce (Atkinson, 1987). Little in the way of theorizing has been done on alternatives to the core/periphery model, and empirical research on the variation that exists within firms has been limited (Lepak and Snell, 1999). Large law firms experienced changes that led to variation in the management of lawyers within firms. The Cravath model, the standard in firms into the 1980s (Galanter and Palay, 1991; Gilson and Mnookin, 1988; Sherer and Lee, 2002), had two categories of lawyers: partners and associates.[2] Changes that began in the 1980s ultimately did not lead so much to the abandonment of the Cravath model as to additions to it, creating different categories or tiers of lawyers. The multifaceted variation in the large law firm calls into question the almost exclusive emphasis on the core/periphery model and provides the necessary conditions for empirical research to assess the effects of the variation on attitudes and behaviors, resources and capabilities, and firm performance (Becker and Gerhart, 1996; Cappelli and Sherer, 1990; Pearce, 1993; Wernerfelt, 1984).

---

[2] In the large law firm, partnership was built around the Cravath model and had an "up to partner or out of the firm" ("up or out") system (Galanter and Palay, 1991; Gilson and Mnookin, 1988; Sherer and Lee, 2002; Swaine, 1946, 1948).

The *acquisition of lateral partners* is an important theoretical and empirical topic in light of its rise in popularity and sharply contested effects. First, the rise in the popularity of lateral acquisitions is important to institutional theory because it shows how a practice can operate as an exception to a rule and eventually become accepted fact for most firms. It provides an important contrast to the imagery that the adoption of practices is ultimately an all-or-nothing proposition and it helps to delineate the role of agents and the status of their organizations as first movers in the diffusion of practices (DiMaggio and Powell, 1983; Leblebici *et al.*, 1991; Sherer and Lee, 2002). Second, theoretical debate in the business strategy (Barney, 1986; Dierickx and Cool, 1989) and strategic HRM literature (e.g. Boeker, 1997; Lepak and Snell, 1999; Phillips, 2002; Rao and Drazin, 2002; Sherer and Leblebici, 2001) provide sharply contested views on the value of acquiring external assets, mirroring arguments on the merits of acquiring lateral partners. The study of lateral partner acquisitions builds on and adds to the emerging reconciliation of these views in the business strategy literature by showing the importance of firm-internal capabilities for acquiring external assets (Cohen and Levinthal, 1990; Zollo and Singh, 2004).

The chapter will proceed as follows. First, I look at the three topics – changes in the organizational identity of the large law firm, variations within firms in the management of lawyers, and the acquisition of lateral partners – in depth, offering insights into each of them. Within each of these sections I present the relevant theory and research, describe and analyze the context, and conclude with research implications. After this, I offer some conclusions and set out a path for future research.

The changed identity of the large law firm

Stuart Albert and David Whetten (1985, p. 265) argue that an organization, like a person, has an identity that answers such questions as " '[w]ho are we [as an organization]?' 'What kind of business are we in?' or 'What do we want to be?'" They suggest that an organizational identity has to meet three conditions. First, it must capture the central character of an organization, embodying its essence. Second, it must be distinctive in that it distinguishes an organization from other organizations. Third, it must be enduring in that it provides a stable as opposed to fleeting characterization of an organization.

Albert and Whetten suggest that an organizational identity is often taken for granted. They argue that identity comes into question when an organization faces a major character-altering decision or precipitating incident. Under such circumstances, they argue, organizations are forced to think about their identity – what they really stand for and whether they can accept that being altered.

Organizational researchers have linked organizational identity to organizational members' beliefs and actions in two particularly well-known and highly regarded studies (see Bartunek, Rynes, and Ireland, 2006). The first study, by Jane Dutton and Janet Dukerich (1992), examines how employees of the Port Authority of New York and New Jersey were affected by its changed image and how they responded. The Port Authority prided itself on being a highly innovative organization in its role as owner and operator of major structures in the greater New York area, such as the World Trade Center and the George Washington Bridge. In the 1980s, however, problems with homeless people had literally found their way into the facilities of the Port Authority. For example, the 42nd Street bus terminal in New York had become a place where many homeless people had effectively taken residence. Dutton and Dukerich show that the Port Authority was slow to respond to the homelessness crisis because it viewed itself as a technical, not a social welfare, organization. The loss of status in the identity of the Port Authority, say Dutton and Dukerich, demoralized employees.

The second study, by Kimberly Elsbach and Roderick Kramer (1996), examines how organizational members responded to challenges to the identity of their organizations when *Business Week* published its list of the top twenty business schools in 1992. The *Business Week* rankings were relatively novel (started in 1988) at the time of the study, and a number of schools in the top twenty had seen their identities challenged on their core attributes and positional rankings. Elsbach and Kramer show how organizational members responded to the challenges by emphasizing the importance of particular core attributes and by making favorable comparisons of their schools on dimensions neglected by the *Business Week* rankings.

Organizational identity and large law firms

These studies by Dutton and Dukerich and Elsbach and Kramer are very much in line with how Albert and Whetten (1985) see organizational

identity being altered. The changes in organizational identity were quick
to develop, unequivocal in meaning, and negative in nature. How does
this compare to the changes in large law firms? To show what has
happened to large law firms, I examined a balanced panel from *The
American Lawyer's* annual survey of the top 100 revenue-producing US
law firms, the Am Law 100, over the twenty years from 1986 to 2005.[3]
The panel covers the 68 firms that had complete information over the
twenty years.[4] What the data reveals is that most large law firms have
changed significantly over the twenty-year period, although change has
been relatively gradual and, for the most part, not clearly threatening in
nature. The information is presented in a series of figures.[5]

Profits and revenues
Figure 6.1 shows that firm profits per partner for the sixty-eight firms
grew on average from approximately $350,000 in 1986 to over
$1 million in 2005, for an overall growth of over 200 percent. The
average profit per partner for 1986 in 2005 real (as opposed to nom-
inal) dollar values was approximately $650,000, indicating that law
firm profits per partner significantly outgrew the inflation rate.

Figure 6.2 shows that firm revenues were, on average, less than $100
million in 1986; they had grown to over $500 million by 2005, for a
percentage change of over 500 percent. Several firms broke the
$1 billion revenue mark, starting with Skadden and followed by
Baker and McKenzie, and Jones Day.

Size
Figure 6.3 reveals that firms grew from an average size of just under
300 partners and associates in 1986 to an average size of almost 800 in
2005, for an increase of over 150 percent.

---

[3] *The American Lawyer* began to survey firms on their financial data in 1984, but
   the survey was limited to the top fifty in that year and the top seventy-five in
   1985. *The American Lawyer* has continued to survey the top 100 firms ever
   since 1986.
[4] As a result of the censoring, firms that were dissolved or dropped out of the top 100
   are not included in the figures. Thus, the financial figures, while accurate for the
   sixty-eight firms, provide an upward survivor bias to what happened to firms
   during this time.
[5] In calculating mean values across firms, I did not use averages weighted by the size
   of the organizations.

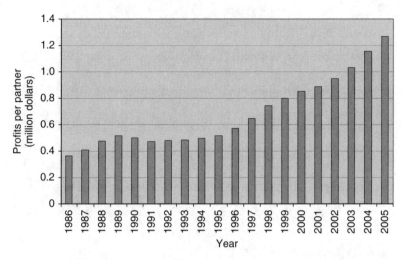

Figure 6.1 Firm profits per partner, 1986–2005

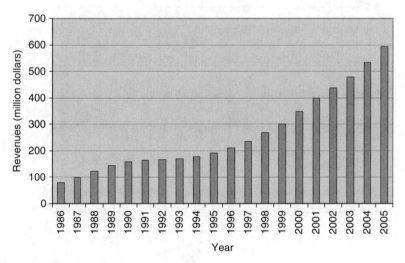

Figure 6.2 Firm revenues, 1986–2005

Leverage ratio

Figure 6.4 shows the leverage ratio (defined as the number of non-equity lawyers divided by the number of equity partners) for firms rose from approximately two in 1986 to three in 2005, for a 50 percent increase.

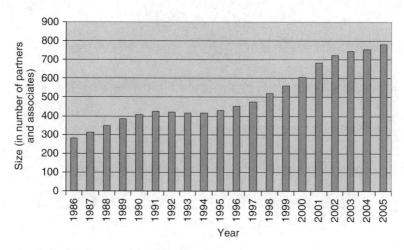

Figure 6.3 Firm size, 1986–2005

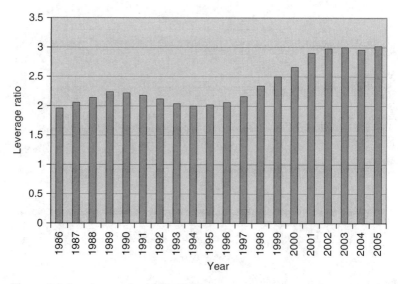

Figure 6.4 Leverage ratio, 1986–2005

Internationalization

Figure 6.5 indicates that the internationalization of firms (defined in terms of the number of lawyers in a firm posted outside the United States) for 1986 was less than 3 percent and by 2005 was approximately 12 percent.

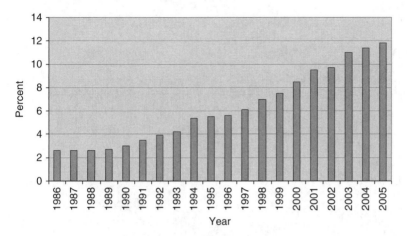

Figure 6.5 Internationalization of large US law firms, 1986–2005

Positional standing

Data on the positional standing of firms over time suggests that, in the midst of the changes, there was also considerable stability. Figure 6.6, updated from Sherer (2004), shows the rankings on profits for partner from 1986 to 2005 for the twenty firms with the highest rankings on profits per partner in 1986. The rankings show considerable stability over time. Only three of the twenty firms significantly lost positional standing, and even they had recovered much of their loss in standing by 2005. Moreover, the temporal correlation for firm profits per partner for the sixty-eight firms from 1986 to 2005 was approximately 0.90, indicating a great deal of continuity over time. This was true too, although not to the same degree, for other measures such as firm revenues and size. It would appear that there are path-dependent processes operating, in that more profitable firms stay more profitable, larger firms stay larger, and so forth.

The relationship of the traditional professional model of partnership versus the business model to profits per partner

Additional data by Steven Brill calls into question the view that the traditional professional model of partnership is associated with lower profitability and the business model is associated with higher profitability. Brill (1990, p. 14) finds that firms with a traditional professional model of partnership, what he calls the pure partnership quotient (PPQ), actually tended to have higher profits than those with a business model: "As we

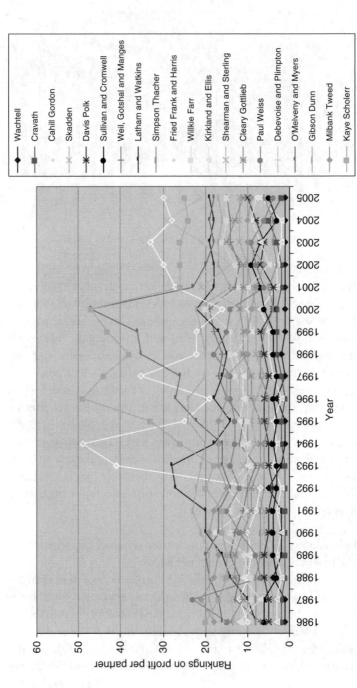

Figure 6.6 Profits per partner rankings for top twenty ranked firms, 1986–2005
Source: Updated from Sherer (2004).

can readily see, low PPQ – running the business like a 'corporation' – doesn't in many instances offer high partner profits; if anything, the correlation works the other way . . ." Even today there is a strategic cluster of highly elite firms (Sherer, 2007), which includes some of the most profitable firms, such as Cravath, that have more of a traditional model of partnership. Furthermore, James Collins and Jerry Porras (1996) argue that corporations can have different identities, as there is no one monolithic corporate model singularly bent on profits. For example, they show how Johnson and Johnson's credo historically placed shareholders second to other key stakeholders (e.g. doctors, nurses, patients) and how this belief guided the company's actions through events such as the Tylenol crisis. Thus, Brill's data on law firms and Collins and Porras's characterizations of the many faces of corporations call into question the wisdom of making generalizations about a singular change in character of the large law firm to that of a corporate business model.[6]

What the context of law firms highlights therefore is that change in identity does not have to be relatively sudden, unequivocal in meaning, nor negative in nature. Many organizations evolve gradually and reach a threshold at which their character has been fundamentally altered. Additionally, the vast majority of the twenty law firms with the highest rankings on profits per partner in 1986 maintained their positional status through 2005. Finally, the notion that high profitability is associated with having a corporate model as opposed to a traditional professional partnership model appears to be quite questionable – many of the most profitable firms have more of a traditional partnership model.

Research implications

The gradual, equivocal, less clearly threatening change in identity that occurred in large law firms might seem uninteresting to organizational researchers because it does not have a shock factor to it. Given that this type of change is likely to be very common, however, and it is difficult to know a priori what effects it has, research needs to address the following sorts of questions.

---

[6] Anthony Angel, the current managing partner at the British law firm Linklaters, argues compellingly that truly global firms such as Linklaters have succeeded not by dismantling the traditional partnership model but by building on it (Angel, 2007).

(1) What has been the history of various law firms in relation to their organizational identity?

    (a) What did firms carry forward from their past identity?

    (b) How did firms drift away from their past?

(2) Do organizational members see their organizations' identities as the same or changed from the past?

(3) If organizational members see them as different, when and how did that occur?

    (a) Were there precipitating incidents, either positive or negative, in their own dealings with their organizations that led to the realization?

    (b) Were there thresholds or tipping points for individuals that led them to perceive a changed identity?

(4) Do particular organizational attributes, such as size or geographical expansion, predict perceptions of a changed organizational identity (for example, it might be that, as a firm grows in size or locations, partners have a more difficult time getting to know one another by names, and the central identity of the firm becomes less clear)?

(5) Do organizational members identify more or less with their organizations' changed identity?

    (a) Does the degree of identification vary by different cohorts of partners and by different categories of lawyers?

    (b) If so, why does it differ?

Organizational identity research on law firms also needs to examine the linkage of identity to that of firm competitive advantage. Collins and Porras argue that an enduring identity is central to achieving extraordinary success.[7] They summarize their argument as follows:

Companies that enjoy enduring success have . . . [identities] that remain fixed while their business strategies and practices endlessly adapt to a changing world. The dynamic of preserving the core while stimulating progress is the reason that companies such as HP, 3M, Johnson & Johnson, P&G, . . .

---

[7] Collins and Porras (1996, p. 66) do not actually use the term "organizational identity," but it is captured in their definition of a core ideology: "[T]he enduring character of an organization – a consistent *identity* [emphasis added] that transcends product or market lifecycles, technological breakthroughs, management fads, and individual leaders . . . "

Nordstrom became elite institutions able to renew themselves and achieve superior long-term performance. (Collins and Porras, 1996, p. 65)

Collins and Porras's argument seems to hold with large law firms. As figure 6.6 shows, firms with the highest sustained profitability per partner, such as Cravath, Wachtell, and Sullivan Cromwell, have maintained more of their identity. Thus, a key to gaining further insight into the most successful law firms will come from understanding what can and cannot change in their identities in order for them to maintain their sense of continuity and progress.

Variation in HRM systems within firms

Strategic HRM research examines the effects of different bundles of HRM practices – called HRM systems – across and within firms. Most strategic HRM research has examined variation across firms, seeking to understand the determinants for firms' HRM systems or their effects on financial and other key outcomes (Becker and Gerhart, 1996; Sherer and Leblebici, 2001). As David Lepak and Scott Snell (1999, p. 32) argue, little in the way of empirical research exists on the variation in HRM systems within firms:

In reality, organizations utilize a variety of approaches to allocate human capital and often use these forms simultaneously ... Yet, the literature on how firms can manage their employment modes remains sparse. From the point of view of strategic human resource management (HRM), researchers need to investigate how various combinations of employment modes ... lead to competitive advantage ... To date, most strategic HRM researchers have tended to take a holistic view of employment and human capital, focusing on the extent to which a set of practices is used across all employees of a firm as well as the consistency of these practices across firms ... By ignoring the possible existence of different employment practices for different employee groups within a firm, much of the strategic HRM literature may seem some-what monolithic.

Various models

Core/periphery model
Theoretical interest in the variation in HRM management within organizations has focused almost exclusively on a core/periphery model (Atkinson, 1987). It involves a core composed of well-rewarded and

protected employees alongside a periphery of casual employees or independent contractors. The argument typically made is that the periphery provides lower-cost labor and protects the core by buffering it from the vagaries of the product market.

The core/periphery model is only one possible arrangement that a firm can use. A number of other arrangements potentially exist that involve multiple HRM systems operating simultaneously. These combinations could involve multiple cores, multiple peripheries, and HRM systems that are intermediary to the polar extremes of cores and peripheries (Sherer and Lee, 1992). The large law firm illustrates the greater variation that exists and can be the basis for theory building and empirical assessment.

The "up or out" system in large law firms

In the large law firm, partnership was built around the Cravath model and had as its central tenet an "up to partner or out of the firm" ("up or out") system. Named after its originator, Paul Cravath, this model had two tiers of lawyers, with the "lower" tier of associates feeding into the "upper tier" of partners (Galanter and Palay, 1991; Gilson and Mnookin, 1988; Swaine, 1946, 1948). Lawyers entered the firm through law school as associates and served a probationary period of approximately seven years before a decision was made whether to invite them into the partnership or ask them to leave the firm. The lawyers who entered the firm as associates were leveraged in that they generated revenues that, after salaries and overhead costs, were used to boost the profits for partners (Hitt *et al.*, 2001; Sherer, 1995). Associates were by no means peripheral in that they had opportunities to make it up to partner.

The Cravath model had certain dictates that kept the firm lean in its categories of lawyers and HRM systems (Galanter and Palay, 1991; Gilson and Mnookin, 1988). Firms would avoid the past practice of renting space to lawyers, effectively having them operate as independent contractors inside the firm, and instead would have only partners and associates on partner track. The model precluded, with certain exceptions (to be discussed later), the acquisition of partners from other firms and instead meant that firms would develop partners internally from the ranks of their associates. The firm would not have a complicated hierarchy but, instead, a lean hierarchy of partners and associates. The firm would avoid treating partners vastly differently.

Since all lawyers that made it up to partner went through and passed the same hurdles, partners tended to be treated equally. In many firms partners received an equal voice and vote in firm matters, and there were share systems in which partners' draws on profits were based on lockstep seniority.

By the 1980s cracks, if not gaping holes, were appearing in the Cravath model (Galanter and Palay, 1991; Gilson and Mnookin, 1988; Sherer and Lee, 2002). A scarcity of law school graduates from elite schools had arisen because of the Cravath model's need for additional lawyers to leverage and because of growth in the demand for legal services (Sherer and Lee, 2002). Highly prestigious firms such as Davis Polk began to experiment and challenge the Cravath model, adding tiers or different categories of lawyers, leading to variation internally in their approaches to human resource management. Later these changes could be seen as tempering the Cravath model and ensuring its further survival (Sherer and Lee, 2002).

Variation in the management of lawyers in large law firms

Figure 6.7 examines a number of arrangements used by law firms that either have lawyers neither up nor out or never enter into the up or out system. Firms have created tracks for lawyers who did not make it up to partner but were asked to stay on as employees, called senior or permanent attorneys, in which they were neither in or out of the up or out system (Gilson and Mnookin, 1988; Sherer and Lee, 2002).

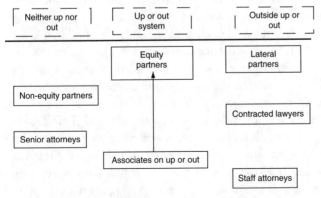

Figure 6.7 Variation in the management of lawyers within law firms

Firms have also created new tracks for lawyers who never entered into the up or out system, called staff attorneys. The position of non-equity partner has been established in order to delay lawyers receiving draws on profits or to create another tier in firms for those who never became full equity-sharing partners (Gilson and Mnookin, 1988). Firms have used the position of counsel, which had once been an honorific position designated for retired partners or politicians, to hire lawyers to do contract work on a long-term or continuous basis (Galanter and Palay, 1991; Sherer, 1995; Wagner, 1986).

The multifaceted variation in HRM systems within large law firms is particularly valuable for conducting research that examines its effects on attitudes, behaviors, firm capabilities, and firm performance. Since research has been carried out that examines the attitudinal effects of having different HRM systems in a single organization, that research provides a valuable starting point for studying the variation in the management of lawyers within law firms.

Research on the attitudinal effects of two-tier wage systems

Cappelli and Sherer (1990) examine the effects on employee attitudes of two-tier wage systems, which create a lower pay tier for new employees over a temporary period, or permanently, as compared to an upper pay tier for employees hired before a specified date. Two-tier wage systems more generally act as different HRM systems, with the lower tier having wages tied more directly to the external market and the upper tier having wages that are more internalized or buffered from the external market (Doeringer and Piore, 1971). Additionally, two-tier wage systems often have more than just different pay scales, with different employment security, benefit plans, and so forth for the different tiers. Cappelli and Sherer (1990) find that lower-tier employees hired for at most one year had more positive attitudes on organizational commitment and job satisfaction than upper-tier employees. They argue that the more positive attitudes of lower-tier employees could be explained by their self-selection into their jobs, their being on the job for no more than one year and therefore still experiencing something of a honeymoon with their organization, and their comparing themselves to referent groups outside the organization. They argue that the more negative attitudes of more senior employees could be explained by their having previously made concessions.

Research on attitudinal differences of employees versus independent contractors

Jone Pearce (1993) examines the difference in attitudes among employees and independent contractors doing similar work in an aerospace company. What makes Pearce's study particularly fascinating is that the employees and independent contractors worked together. Pearce does not find that the independent contractors were less satisfied or committed than the employees of the same firm. What she does find, however, is that employees who worked alongside independent contractors experienced greater mistrust of the organization.

Research implications

Given the theoretical arguments and empirical findings in Cappelli and Sherer (1990) and Pearce (1993), what might we expect in examining the different tiers of lawyers in the large law firm? Staff attorneys, lawyers who are not on the up or out track of the firm, might not otherwise have had the opportunity to work in the larger and more prestigious US law firms. The following quote by Tamar Lewin (1987, p. D3) from the managing partner at Jones Day, the firm that acted as the first mover in the adoption of staff attorneys, is suggestive of a self-selection effect: "[W]e went to local schools to see if there was anyone who wanted a chance to work at Jones Day for a while, in a temporary kind of position. Hundreds of résumés poured in, from people who seem ecstatic to get a chance to work with us." Thus, we might expect that, particularly since staff attorneys never lost or conceded anything ex ante, they would show high levels of job satisfaction and organizational commitment.

Firms historically required associates on the up or out system who were not "partnerable" to leave the firm. Cravath believed that associates who were passed over would be unhappy and would do poor-quality work (Swaine, 1948, p. 7). Therefore, we would expect that senior attorneys, associates who did not make it up to partner, would be less committed, less satisfied, and the like. Unlike Cappelli and Sherer's (1990) lower-tier employees who were new employees, senior attorneys have lost out on partnership and have seen others make partners and their own careers plateau. There is the possibility, however, that these lawyers are simply happy to have their jobs and the ones who stay have self-selected, thereby not suffering the fate that Cravath had warned about. Moreover, there has also been a growing sense, since the short-term decline in law firm profitability in the early 1990s (see figure 6.1) and the increase during that time in the dissolution of firms, that making partner does not mean as much as it did in the past. An associate at a firm that dissolved in the early 1990s was quoted by Alison Cowan (1992, p. D1) as saying that "my biggest nightmare is not making partner, and my second biggest nightmare is making partner."

Making partner at a large US law firm offers both income and prestige, however, especially with the growth in profits per partner that has occurred over the years. Younger partners might particularly be highly satisfied and committed because of the recent gains in profitability, and in that sense mirror Cappelli and Sherer's (1990) privileged group. Older partners might suffer from a "concession effect." Partners who have been with firms since the early 1990s have witnessed changes in the way firms have been managed since that time. Bradford Hildebrandt, a principal consultant to large law firms, was quoted by Cowan (1992, p. D1) in *The New York Times* as saying: "Partnership is a much different thing today . . . There's no question that young partners, who in the past would have gotten down on their hands and knees and thanked the Supreme Being in the law firm if somebody said they could be a partner, are asking tougher questions." Partnership over the period from the early 1990s has become more of a business, with firms more freely giving partners the equivalent of "pink slips." In fact, some of what is called "free agency" is anything but free as firms are pushing out partners. Additionally, "de-equitized" partners in firms, those who have lost rights to a draw or share of profits, would be expected to be particularly dissatisfied given the concession they have made, voluntarily or involuntarily.

Associates relative to senior and staff attorneys are presumably more satisfied and committed. Unlike these other categories of lawyers, they have the option of going up for partner. Yet, as Pearce (1993) finds, it might be the case that associates on the up or out track are more distrustful of the organization to the degree that a firm has senior attorneys. Ronald Gilson and Robert Mnookin (1988) argue that senior attorney tracks lead to moral hazards, because firms can cheat associates out of partnership and still make use of them. Additionally, associates might be in competition with senior attorneys for legal work that requires more expertise and experience.

The context of the large law firm shows that organizations have multiple options in combining HRM systems that transcend the notion of a core/periphery model and that these options have potential attitudinal effects. The variation in HRM systems within organizations additionally has the potential to affect behaviors, the portfolio of capabilities in an organization (Sherer, 1996; Sherer, Rogovsky, and Wright, 1998; Wernerfelt, 1984), and, ultimately, firm performance (Becker and Gerhart, 1996). Such research is clearly needed.

The acquisition of lateral partners

The acquisition of lateral partners by large law firms raises two important and interrelated questions. First, how did lateral partner acquisitions go from being exceptions to the rule to become accepted fact for most firms? The question ties in to critical issues in institutional theory on the origins and diffusion of practices. An additional issue raised by this question is why a small number of firms never moved to treating lateral partner acquisitions as accepted fact. Second, given the many lateral partner acquisitions by firms, what are the financial, strategic, behavioral, and attitudinal effects on the acquiring firms? The question ties in to critical debates in the business strategy and strategic HRM literature on the value of acquiring external assets.

From exception to the rule to accepted fact

The dominant view in institutional theory is built on the notion of an "iron cage" in which firms in an organizational field become "imprisoned" and forced to act the same way (DiMaggio and Powell, 1983). Firms adopt innovative practices and these practices then gain legitimacy as "the right way to do things." As these practices gain momentum, they reach a threshold at which they come to dominate over other alternatives. There is, then, a complete or very near-complete adoption of practices in organizational fields, and firms all have the same practices – what is referred to as "isomorphism." In the theoretical imagery of an iron cage, isomorphism means not only that all or almost all firms have the same dominant practices but that there is complete or near-complete adherence to those practices, in the sense that there are no exceptions to get around using them. Is the imagery of the iron cage really an accurate or even useful view, however? Christine Oliver (1991) has argued that there is often a lack of complete adoption with practices, and studies conducted on the diffusion of HRM practices find a significant percentage of non-adopters even after significant diffusion of practices (Baron,

Dobbin, and Jennings, 1986; Jacoby, 1985). Sherer (2003) argues that, within an organizational field, forces favoring conformity and isomorphism often face off with forces pushing organizations toward individualization and uniqueness. As I suggest below, the image of complete adherence to practices – even when there is seemingly complete isomorphism – is questionable. Exceptions to rules play an important role in refocusing the imagery. Moreover, I show that certain firms hold out and do not adopt a practice even when it seems to most organizations in the organizational field to be accepted fact.

The Cravath model and lateral partners as an exception to the rule
The Cravath model was the basis for the view that lateral partner acquisitions are an exception to the rule. In this model, lateral partner acquisitions interfered with promotion to partner from within, which was the key incentive for associates to work hard. By bringing in partners from outside, Cravath believed that associates would become discouraged (Swaine, 1948, p. 8). Equally important, Robert Swaine says that Cravath saw advantages to developing one's own lawyers (1948, p. 2): "Cravath believed that a staff trained within the office would be better adapted to its methods of work than a staff recruited from older men who, in practice elsewhere, might have acquired habits inconsistent with Cravath methods, and hence he insisted that the staff should be recruited, *so far as possible* [emphasis added], from men just out of the law schools." It is important to note that Swaine (1948) uses the words "so far as possible." Even Cravath, early on, made exceptions to the rule of acquiring laterals by hiring what appear to have been partners in the areas of real estate and litigation – areas in which the firm at that time lacked expertise or experience (Swaine, 1948, p. 4).

Erwin Smigel (1969) studied large New York law firms in the 1960s and finds that these firms generally abided by the rule of not acquiring partners.[8] He does, however (p. 42), find specific circumstances in which firms made exceptions to the rule:

---

[8] Smigel (1969, pp. 57, 58) also talks about firms having non-competitive agreements: "Competition for lawyers among the large firms in New York is limited in two ways: the firms will not hire an employee from another law office [firm], and they maintain a gentlemen's agreement to pay the same beginning salary, commonly called the going rate." These agreements do not appear to apply to partners, however, for Smigel refers specifically to employees, who are the

Occasionally the firm takes in partners who have not come up through the ranks. These men [sic] are generally well known, mostly from the world of politics, and/or business getters. Some, however, are taken into a firm because of their special training in an area of law. This is especially true when a new department is being developed or a specialty is needed which has not been previously covered ... The partners brought in from the outside are *the exception rather than the rule* [emphasis added].

Transition period

While there are no precise estimates on when exception to the rule became accepted fact for large law firms across the United States, the evidence suggests that the period from the 1970s to the 1980s was the transition phase. In a study of eighty-eight large Chicago law firms, Nina Shah (2005) finds that the proportion of firms that acquired lateral partners was 17 percent in 1975, dropping to 10 percent in 1976, then jumping to 50 percent in 1986.[9] Similarly, Robert Whitfield (1988, p. 2) suggests that there was a change from the 1970s to the 1980s: "Ten years ago [1977], lateral recruiting was regarded as a questionable practice by the legal profession. Lawyers were reluctant to recruit from competing law firms and equally reluctant to pay search fees. Now, all that has changed." David Kaplan (1982, p. 1) uses an analogy to Major League baseball and the advent of free agency to suggest just how much things had changed from the 1970s to 1980s:[10]

Being a partner in a law firm used to be like being a baseball player before the advent of free agency. You had come up through the farm system [the associate

associates in the firm. Moreover, the second part of his statement directly refers to associates' beginning salaries.

[9] I used data from the National Law Journal's *Directory of the Legal Profession* (Gerson, 1984) to get estimates of the percentage of large law firms (which would later appear in one or more years in the Am Law 100) that acquired laterals in the early 1980s. The figures indicate that over the four-year period from 1980 to 1983 approximately 80 percent acquired one or more laterals, 50 percent acquired four or more laterals, and about 20 percent acquired no laterals.

[10] There is clearly some hyperbole here. Large law firms did not have the equivalent of Major League baseball's reserve clause that expressly banned players from changing teams. Even in baseball, however, teams did not develop their own players only before Curt Flood's challenge to the reserve clause opened the floodgates to free agency; they got players through trades and acquisitions from other teams. One has only to think of the curse put on the Boston Red Sox for selling Babe Ruth to the New York Yankees to see that there were exceptions to the rule of developing only one's own players.

track], paid your dues. You finally had made the major leagues and were rewarded handsomely: prestige, respect, and a fat paycheck. The team owned you, but you did not mind – fidelity and tradition counted. But that's all changed. Free agency came to baseball. And so too its equivalent has come to the law. Hundreds of partners nationwide are migrating from one firm to another, according to surveys conducted for the National Law Journal, Directory of the Legal Profession . . .

By 1990 Jean Fergus (p. 1) was referring pejoratively to the avoidance of hiring lateral partners as an "old fashioned idea." Toward the end of the 1990s Hillman (1999, pp. 1:2, 1:3) observes: "Increasingly, law firms are but temporary resting places for their partners. Lateral hiring, once confined largely to junior lawyers, now extends through all levels of a partnership." Hillman notes (1999, p. 1:3, footnote 5) too, in a statement attributed to the New York Court of Appeals, that the "revolving door" is seen as a "modern day law firm fixture." These impressions are confirmed by data from *The American Lawyer* indicating that approximately 6 to 8 percent of partners from firms in the Am Law 200 (the top 200 US law firms in terms of revenues) moved to or from a firm, be it law firm or other type of firm, during 2000 to 2004 – out of a universe of approximately 30,000 partners each year (Braverman, 2001; Sherer, 2005).

First movers of change

Considerable interest in institutional theory lies also in understanding which agents, in relation to their organization's place in an organizational field, are the first movers of change. Huseyin Leblebici, Gerald Salancik, Anne Copay, and Tom King (1991) show how marginal or peripheral players in radio broadcasting in the early part of the twentieth century were the first movers for change. Leblebici *et al.* argue that the marginal players had everything to gain and nothing to lose from deviating from accepted practice. Peter Sherer and Kyung Mook Lee (2002) find that it was the highly elite players in the field that were the first movers in adopting certain practices, such as senior attorney tracks, that were departures from the standard of the Cravath system. They argue that, while many firms in the field suffered from a scarcity of talented associates, it was the firms with the most prestige that could "pull off" making innovations that were departures from the standard. What these studies suggest is that organizations of different status can serve as the first movers and that status can be an enabler or a constraint on first moves.

Which agents were first to treat lateral acquisitions as accepted fact instead of as exception to the rule? While old-line and highly prestigious firms such as Davis Polk, what are referred to as "white-shoe" firms (Safire, 1997), were first movers in adopting senior attorney tracks, they did not see lateral partner acquisitions as anything but an exception to the rule: Kaplan (1982, p. 24) quotes Henry L. King, head of Davis Polk's managing committee at the time: "Our partners are home grown ... We don't want to go outside *except* [emphasis added] under very narrow circumstances. It's a function of the age and success of the firm." Kaplan also quotes Samuel Butler, the Cravath firm's managing partner at the time: "There's no chance of us going outside. We'd never even consider it in any context, *barring a calamity* [emphasis added]." Thus, as the italicized portions of the quotes show, Davis Polk would make an exception to the rule only under narrow circumstances and Cravath under calamitous circumstances.

Effectively ruling out the old-line elite firms does not necessarily mean that the marginal players in the field drove change. The marginal players in the organizational field of large law firms did not have the resources or clients to draw lawyers from other firms, no less the elite firms. Another group of firms, those high in status but younger, were quite possibly the first movers, and, in so doing, made lateral partner acquisitions an accepted fact.

Skadden is the likely candidate here, particularly given its prominence. Skadden acquired lateral partners very selectively. As Andrew Longstreth (2006, p. 105) states about Skadden: "And unlike some of its New York-based competitors [e.g. Cravath], Skadden has never been too proud or too conservative to hire laterally." S. Nelson (1985) reports: "In small bites [small acquisitions of partners] ... the DC office has digested a lot of lawyers in a lot of practice areas. Ever since the securities lawyer Neal S. McCoy and antitrust specialist John C. Fricano opened the door in 1976, the office has been expanding – into such areas as communications, energy, environment, and international law" (p. 12). Kaplan (1982) reports that Skadden was involved in acquiring partners from elite firms to start up its bankruptcy group in 1980 and its real estate group in 1981. The highly publicized success of Skadden, its very visible DC office, and the emergence of its bankruptcy and real estate groups opened competitors' eyes and helped to make lateral partner acquisitions an accepted fact.[11]

---

[11] Alison Frankel (2006, p. 96) reports that Skadden also broke away from other elite firms in finding associates during the associate scarcity in the 1980s: "Twenty years ago, Skadden, Arps, Slate, Meagher & Flom pioneered the

Another influence: *The American Lawyer*
Considerable speculation exists on what role an additional agent had in
the rise of lateral partners in the early 1980s. While Brill (1996) suggests
that *The American Lawyer* adeptly tapped into the times and found a
willing audience, claims have been made that *The American Lawyer's*
reporting of firms' profits per partner helped to cause the growth in
lateral partner movements. Brill (1996, p. 5), responding somewhat
sarcastically yet acknowledging these claims, states:

After all, it wasn't until the Am Law 100 and similar stories in this magazine
[*The American Lawyer*] about partner earnings and law firm finances ... that
we began to see the most destabilizing, indeed traumatic, phenomenon ever
to hit the law firm world: the end of law firms as partnerships built on loyalty
and unity and the beginning of the lawyer-partner as a perpetual free agent
jumping from place to place, or threatening to, whenever the money looked
better across the street.

Current state of lateral partners
The American Lawyer's Partner Mobility Data provides insight into
firms' more recent practice in acquiring lateral partners. *The American
Lawyer* has been collecting data on individual partner movements
(arrivals and departures) among the top 200 revenue-producing
firms, the Am Law 200, since 2000. The figures are compiled from
public sources, including firm announcements, press releases, and news
reports. In addition, firms are surveyed as to partner arrivals and
departures (Braverman, 2001). Aggregating the data from the individual or partner level to the firm level of analysis provides information
on the acquisitive activity of the law firms.

Table 6.1 provides data on lateral acquisition activity for select law
firms from 2000 to 2004. The figures show that the law firms vary a great
deal in the extent to which they acquire partners. There are only a few
firms that do not acquire or make very little use of laterals. As Paul
Braverman (2001, p. 93) states: "Time was, hiring laterals was *déclassé*,
and some firms didn't want to get their hands dirty. But the number of
firms that can still lay claim to such exclusivity is dwindling ..." The firms

recruiting of top ranked law students from second tier law schools ..." The
effect of that pioneering effort is captured in Frankel's (2006, p. 96) subsequent
point: "Today, every Am Law 100 firm is recruiting and hiring from far more
schools than it did 20 years ago."

Table 6.1 *Incidence of lateral partner acquisitions for selected firms, 2000–4*

Firm name	2000–4
Akin Gump	102
Cadwalader Wickersham	22
Cravath	0
Dickinson Wright	9
Duane Morris	160
Finnegan, Henderson, Farabow, Garrett and Dunner	13
Gibson, Dunn and Crutcher	43
Greenberg Traurig	304
Hogan and Hartson	116
Holland and Knight	228
Hughes Hubbard and Reed	11
Jones, Day, Reavis and Pogue	174
Kirkland and Ellis	26
Latham and Watkins	119
Lord, Bissell and Brook	10
O'Melveny and Myers	62
Reed Smith	200
Shearman and Sterling	55
Skadden Arps	26
Wachtell	0
White and Case	152
Wilson Sonsini Goodrich and Rosati	28

that make little to no use of lateral partner acquisitions are among the most highly prestigious and highly successful firms, such as Cravath, Cleary Gotlieb, Wachtell, and Sullivan Cromwell. Robert Lennon (2001) quotes H. Rodgin Cohen, chairman of Sullivan and Cromwell: "On paper and from a strictly economic point of view, it may have made sense [to acquire a partner who wanted to join the firm], but given our firm philosophy, the choice was simple [not to acquire him/her]." Similarly, Lennon quotes Robert Joffe, presiding partner of Cravath, Swaine, and Moore: "We have a very deep culture here. Everyone trusts, knows, and can depend on one another ... You would not bring someone into that situation, who you had not grown up with ..." Lennon also quotes Peter Karasz, managing partner of Cleary Gottlieb: "Taking in a partner from outside the firm would be a measure of last resort . . ." What is striking about these managing partners' statements is that they mirror what managing partners in some of these same firms said in the early 1980s to Kaplan (1982).

There are also highly prestigious firms that make very selective use of lateral partner acquisitions, such as Skadden, Cadwalader Wickersham, and Kirkland and Ellis. These firms treat lateral partner acquisitions as accepted fact and have the resources and status to gain a great deal by selectively acquiring partners.

Other firms have a zeal for lateral partner acquisitions. Greenberg Traurig leads in the acquisition of laterals and notes on its website its ranking of number 1 on *The American Lawyer*'s 2005 Lateral Report, Top Gainers List (Greenberg Traurig website, 3 July 2005). Carlyn Kolker (2004, p. 73) describes a similar approach by Duane Morris: "As soon as Duane Morris gets as big as it can [through lateral hires], it turns around and gets bigger . . . Growth like this usually comes by way of mergers." These two highly acquisitive firms were in the middle in size and status, paralleling Shah's (2005) findings as to which Chicago law firms were the most acquisitive. These two firms used lateral partners acquisitions as part of a growth strategy.

Research implications
The study of lateral partner acquisitions thus invites research that examines the change from exception to the rule to accepted fact for most firms. Since organizational status and prestige appear to play such an important role in first moves and, ultimately, which organizations acquire more or fewer or no partners, research needs to incorporate a role for status and stratification in understanding both the rise in the popularity of partner acquisitions and the more recent acquisitive activity of firms (Podolny, 1993). Just as there are strategic groups (Caves and Porter, 1977) that are argued to explain firms' actions in the product market, I suggest that there are "status groups" that have effects on firms' actions in the labor market and in the management of human resources.

The value of external acquisitions

The question of what value firms gain by making external acquisitions is at the heart of important theoretical debate in the business strategy and strategic HRM literatures. The debate centers on whether firms can truly gain competitive advantage through human assets that are not developed inside the organization and are instead acquired outside, in the market. The study of lateral partner acquisitions provides a valuable context in which to build on recent research that suggests that the way to reconcile the different views to the debate is through seeing that certain firms have greater internal acquisition capabilities.

The Barney (1986) versus Dierickx and Cool (1989) strategic factor markets debate

Jay Barney asked the question: do firms gain value from external assets such as those acquired through corporate M&As? His answer was "yes," but he cautioned that there were limited possibilities. He indicated that factor markets, such as labor markets, were open and assets were tradable, but firms could gain value only through luck or superior insight in the pre-acquisition phase in assessing the value of assets. Ingemar Dierickx and Karel Cool responded to Barney by arguing it was quite unlikely that a firm could gain competitive advantage through acquiring external assets because critical assets are non-tradable. They argued that critical assets are firm-specific, being internally accumulated and path-dependent, tied into the history of a firm. Such assets are not purchased by themselves as they are incorporated into the organization. For example, a firm cannot simply hire talent from another organization, because the individuals do not embody the total knowledge system of that organization. Thus, the acquiring firm has to take the entire organization and its social system with it, but that disrupts the social complexity of the organization and does not work either.[12]

Research on the financial effects of M&As

Research in business strategy on the financial effects of corporate M&As provides fodder for both sides of the Barney versus Dierickx

---

[12] Diercyx and Cool's argument is reflected in the following comment by Nathan Koppel (2005, p. 109): "With its Troop Steuber haul, Akin Gump learned the dangers of cherry picking ... 'Akin Gump was only interested in some of Troop Steuber's assets, but it failed to realize that its selective hiring would destroy the cohesiveness of the group that it inherited,' says Akin Gump's managing partner McLean. He adds: 'You shouldn't disassemble a firm without a clear eye as to what will happen to the internal synergies of the firm ...'"

and Cool debate. A number of studies (see, for example, King *et al.*, 2004, and Zollo and Singh, 2004) find either no effect or a small negative financial effect for acquiring firms, but that certain firms have been able to a greater or lesser extent to succeed financially at corporate M&As. Maurizio Zollo and Harbir Singh (2004, p. 1233) suggest that this variance should guide future research toward a more fine-grained analysis of acquisitions: "Whereas the evidence on the average magnitude of value created for the various counterparts is relatively uncontroversial, the explanation of the variance around the mean is still very much in need of both theoretical and empirical work."

Views among managing partners and partners on the value of partner acquisitions

Opinion on the value of lateral partner acquisitions in law firms also shows variety, although it has become weighted more favorably in recent years towards the benefits of acquisitions. The main rationale for making lateral partner acquisitions is captured by managing partner R. Bruce McLean of Akin, Gump, Strauss, Hauer, and Felds, who stated (Braverman, 2001, p. 93): "[I]n today's market, you've got to take laterals to be competitive ... The market is changing quickly, clients' needs are changing quickly. Firms can't develop resources organically fast enough to keep up. They have to go outside to get talent." Kaplan (1982, p. 24) quotes Robert J. Lipton, an executive recruiter who stated that "lateral hiring of partners often is the only practical way to get the desired new blood ..." David A. Richards, a partner who was acquired by Sidley Austin from Coudert Brothers in the early 1980s, was quoted by Kaplan (1982, p. 24) as saying that laterals are needed to start up a practice group because "you need instant credibility to go up against other big firms."

Not all the comments about lateral partner acquisitions are positive, however. Harkening back to Cravath's concerns with the attitudes of associates, Henry L. King, the managing partner in the 1980s of Davis Polk (Kaplan, 1982, p. 26), stated: "If they [associates] see slots being filled, it is terribly demoralizing ..." Kolker (2004, p. 75) reports that Duanne Morris firm chair Sheldon Bonowitz admits that the firm's growth through lateral partner acquisitions "cut into profits." Koppel (2005) discusses the difficulty a number of firms have had in retaining lateral partners and the financial losses involved; he reports, for example (p. 108), that Schnader Harrison lost 68 percent of the partners that it acquired between 1999 and 2003. Ben Hallman (2006, p. 120) questions whether highly sought-out partners that get significant bonuses are really worth it: "It remains an open question whether these partners provide a significant, long-term value or whether they serve as trophies for the mantel."

The debate in strategic HRM on the value of acquiring external talent

The study of lateral partner acquisitions is also important to addressing critical questions in the field of strategic HRM. The vast majority of research in strategic HRM assesses the value of high-performance or high-commitment HRM systems (Huselid, 1995; MacDuffie, 1995). They entail such HRM practices as long-term employment, firm-specific training, and strong socialization efforts. These practices mirror in many ways what the large law firm had into the 1980s, except that the law firm had them more so. For example, law firms did not have just long-term employment but virtual lifetime employment, as it took a two-thirds or three-quarters majority of the firm to terminate a partner; law firms groomed lawyers from their very first days in the firm, and socialization was based on a strong sense of collegiality (Brill, 1990).

Several studies in strategic HRM find that high-commitment HRM systems have positive effects on financial and other outcomes (e.g. Huselid, 1995, and MacDuffie, 1995). The studies provide a relatively weak test, however, in that the superiority of high-commitment HRM systems has largely been based on comparing the presence of high-commitment practices to the lack of them (Sherer and Leblebici, 2001). Thus, finding that firm-specific training provides value in these studies is really only saying that it does so in comparison to not having it. The crucial test of high-commitment HRM systems is in comparing them to their main competitor – free agency.

Recent strategic HRM research on the inter-firm movement of talent (Boeker, 1997; Kraatz and Moore, 2002; Phillips, 2002; Rao and Drazin, 2002) suggests that there are benefits to firms in acquiring external talent. Warren Boeker (1997) finds that organizations in the semiconductor industry that acquired top management with experiences in different products and strategies were more likely to enter into new product markets. Hayagreeva Rao and Robert Drazin (2002) find that mutual fund families were more likely to introduce new mutual funds if they had recruited an investment advisor from a fund family with that fund. Matthew Kraatz and James Moore (2002) find that liberal arts colleges were more likely to adopt professional programs if they had recently recruited a new college president that had come from a college with professional programs. Damon Phillips (2002) finds that the inter-firm movement of law partners (named or not) increased the probability of organizational survival for a start-up law firm. While these studies show positive effects of movements on strategic outcomes, they do not show whether firms gain a temporary or sustainable competitive advantage over their competitors.

Lepak and Snell (1999) argue that when organizations acquire talent from outside the firm it has the potential to be valuable but not unique and, therefore, can create only a temporary competitive advantage. Defining their concept of value, Lepak and Snell (p. 35) state that "[human] resources are valuable when they enable a firm to enact strategies that improve efficiency and effectiveness, exploit market opportunities, and/or neutralize potential threats ..." By uniqueness, they (p. 35) rely on the notion developed by Becker (1975), and further developed by Peter Doeringer and Michael Piore (1971) and Oliver Williamson (1985), that skills vary in their degree of firm specificity – the extent to which they are specific and idiosyncratic to a firm. While Lepak and Snell treat firm-specific skills as rare and general skills as not, many individuals in an organization might possess firm-specific skills and few people outside the organization might possess particular general skills. Alternatively, one can conceive of uniqueness as the extent to which particular skills are distributed in a labor or product market. By this definition, highly firm-specific skills as well as highly general skills can either be rare or common. Therefore, free agents can potentially have both valuable *and* unique skills, in that very few individuals in the market have that critical talent. Firms that can capture this type of talent can create value that is sustainable.

Toward a reconciliation: internal acquisition capabilities

While the above literature offers a sharply contested debate on whether firms achieve value through acquiring lateral partners, an emerging literature on corporate M&As holds considerable promise in reconciling the different views. This emerging literature suggests the notion of an internal acquisition capability as a way of seeing how firms can create or lose value through lateral acquisitions. Zollo and Singh (2004, p. 1237) argue: "[T]he outcome of the acquisition process is influenced by the degree to which the acquiring firm develops a

Figure 6.8 A process view of micro-M&As in large law firms

capability specific to managing the acquisition process." These acquisition capabilities are firm-specific, being built inside organizations and are, therefore, a potential source of competitive advantage.

A process model of internal acquisition capabilities and lateral partners

Wesley Cohen and Daniel Levinthal (1990) argue that firms vary in their internal acquisition capabilities to select, integrate, and apply external assets. As figure 6.8 suggests, there are three key processes in the acquisition of lateral partners: (1) selection, (2) integration, and (3) application (along with its appropriation).

Selection

Selection is the starting point in the acquisition of lateral partners. Its importance is measured in both its costs and time to firms. Duanne Morris, an admittedly heavy user, spent $10 million on legal recruiter fees over a five-year period (Kolker, 2004, p. 74). Managing partners at the offices of Duanne Morris are reported to spend close to fifty hours per month on recruiting and selecting (Kolker, 2004, p. 74).

Barney (1986) argues that firms must either be lucky or have superior insight in order to gain value through acquiring such external human assets. Luck, by definition, is unlikely to be repeated when firms make a number of selection decisions over time. Firms need superior insight over time in selecting lateral partners. What makes the issue of superior insight particularly relevant is that most law firms are not acquiring partners from more profitable and established firms. Rather, lateral partners are typically moving from lesser firms up to what Daphne Eviatar (2002, p. 92) refers to as "higher ground." Therefore, assessing talent is not obvious, and except for areas such as litigation there are no visible demonstrations of performance. The managing partner of Hunton and Williams, Thurston Moore (quoted by Fleischer-Black, 2003, p. 65), stated how intangibles play into insight:

It doesn't bother me that others are articulating similar-sounding strategies as ours. There are some real nuances that will separate those that succeed. It's going to come down to having the right people. It's not just the strategy, and the right C.V. in the area. It's identifying the people who, in flesh and mind, are more client-oriented and talented.

Royston Greenwood, C. Robert Hinings, and John Brown (1994) argue that concerns with strategic fit are typically given primacy over those of organizational fit in selecting targets in corporate M&As. They argue that concerns with organizational fit arise from differences between organizations, such as their management practices. At the level of selecting lateral partners, this translates into questions about the individual–organization fit. Research on individual–organization fit (e.g. Chatman, 1991) suggests that lateral partners selected by firms with individual values that are more congruent with the organizations' would have smoother adjustments and be less likely to leave. Eva Yaskiel, the co-managing partner of the Toronto office of Oglivy Renault, echoes this concern with fit (Belford, 2003):

Some firms recruit just for the book of business [clients] a lawyer might bring with him or her. We have always had a different view. To us, fit is more important than a book or practice. We have the clients; what we look for are lawyers who fit our own particular culture.

Her comment also suggests that better-positioned firms have the client base and status to have more options and, therefore, are able to be more concerned with fit.

The highly confidential nature of the vetting process makes matters more difficult for the law firm. Partners invariably do not want their firms to know they are looking elsewhere and, therefore, it is difficult to gain information about them in their current firms (legal recruiters and firms often check with past firms, but that does not help with first-time movers or those who have been with a firm a long time). One case that has been particularly visible illustrates a firm's "worst selection nightmare." Kolker (2002) reports that Frode Jensen III, an M&A specialist, was hired away from Pillsbury Madison by Latham Watkins, which "posted a press release on its web site heralding Jensen's move as a boon to Latham's corporate practice and touting Jensen as a 'great guy.'" Kolker (2002) reports that Pillsbury Madison followed with its own press release, stating: "Jensen ... had been accused of sexual harassment – accusations Pillsbury pointedly did not rebut – and had not been at work much since the beginning of the year" (p. 68).

Strategic fit, as suggested by Greenwood, Hinings, and Brown (1994), often has primacy in selection decisions. One way in which the corporate M&A literature suggests that firms can achieve strategic fit is to engage in M&As that lead to related rather then unrelated diversification. There is only limited to mixed evidence to show that related diversification leads to better financial performance, however (King *et al.*, 2004). Questions of related versus unrelated diversification arise in law firm lateral partner selection decisions over whether to deepen existing or add new practice area capabilities. Many law firms appear to be using laterals to add new practice areas, a particularly strong form of unrelated diversification, especially when it is done with talent from outside the organization. While this is a risky strategy, some firms have been able to make it work. For example, as noted before, Kaplan (1982) argues that Skadden created a successful bankruptcy and real estate practice in the early 1980s from scratch through acquiring lateral partners.

Even assuming that lateral partners are properly selected, the process does not end there. Some firms have clients for the partner, but that is not always the case. Moreover, while a lateral partner's clients have the right to follow the lawyer to the new firm, the lateral partner has legal and professional limits on getting the client to leave the old firm and join him/her at the new firm. The move is referred to as the "grab and leave" (Hillman, 1999). In many cases, the firm has to provide start-up money for the new partner, at least until he/she can generate new billings (Kolker, 2004).

Integration
Firms face challenges in integrating lateral partners into their new firms. Zollo and Singh (2004) find that firms are more successful when they develop and use explicit protocols for the purposes of integration in corporate-level mergers, and firms such as GE have gained a reputation for being particularly adept at their planning and execution of integration (Ashkenas, DeMonaco, and Francis, 1998). The opposite, a lack of integration capability, is reflected in the following comments by Matt Fleischer-Black (2003, p. 65) about Akin Gump: "Absorbing laterals has … tired Buchanan Ingersoll. In 2000, the Pittsburgh firm added 44 partners. Another seven came this year. But

27 partners have left over the past two years, including seven of the 2000 crop ..."

The challenge of integration plays out in a number of ways. Selection errors involving organization–individual fits make it more difficult to integrate lateral partners. The selection of partners from unrelated practice areas with different legal training will presumably also be more difficult to integrate. For firms that make larger-size acquisitions, acquiring laterals en masse or in big bites (Eviatar, 2002; Rovit, Harding, and Lemire, 2004; Voorhees, 2004) as opposed to onesies or twosies, face a more formidable challenge. A lateral partner by him-/herself might be reluctant to change and conform to his/her acquiring firms' culture and practices, but a large group of partners from another firm has the numerical power to resist change.

Integration has to be examined not only from the perspective of lateral partners but also from the view of existing partners, associates, and other lawyers in firms. There is potential for disruption when a lateral partner and, even more so, when two or more lateral partners join a firm. Associates on the partner track are the most vulnerable to the entry of lateral partners. Associates on the partner track might be looked over for partner with the arrival of lateral partners, not have lateral partners' backing when going up for partner, be affected by lateral partners bringing in their own associates and making them seemingly redundant, or come in with different approaches to law and legal areas.

Existing partners can be affected by the arrival of lateral partners as well. Rivalry can be caused by invidious comparisons. Greenwood, Hinings, and Brown (1994) and Laura Empson (2001) have found that integration is more difficult in corporate-level M&As in professional service firms when the acquiring and merging firms are more dissimilar in management practices and the status of the firms and their practice areas. Given the many lateral partners that come from lesser firms and, presumably, the different management practices at these firms, the integration of those partners represents a formidable challenge.

Law firms' efforts to integrate lateral partners are especially complex because they must be balanced with their need to safeguard themselves against claims of conflict of interests (Hillman, 1999). When a partner worked on a case at his/her former law firm involving the other side to a case or a competitor company, a process has to be established to isolate that lateral partner from other partners. Terence Belford (2003) says this process involves building a "Chinese wall."

Application and appropriation

The last phase in the acquisition of laterals is to get those partners to apply their expertise, often in concert or through leveraging other lawyers in a firm, and for the firm to appropriate economic value from the lateral partners. While the actions that firms take in properly selecting and integrating partners clearly play into this last phase, research needs to be carried out that examines whether firms successfully add to their practice portfolio, are able to leverage successfully through lateral partners, deepen their existing practice areas, and ultimately whether they achieve more clients, higher revenues, and greater profits per partner.

Research implications

The study of lateral partner acquisitions has the potential to provide insights that benefit business strategy researchers interested in corporate M&As as well as benefiting strategic HRM researchers interested in the value for firms of acquiring external talent. It is strictly human asssets that are being acquired with lateral partners, as compared to the mix of assets that are so commonly a part of corporate M&As. Lateral acquisitions thus allow for a precise specification of what is being acquired and for fine-grained analyses of the acquisition processes. Lateral partner acquisitions by firms occur with frequency, with many firms consistently involved in acquiring partners. Corporate M&As are often episodic activities on the part of a firm, separated by years and perhaps even occurring under different senior management (Haspelagh and Jemison, 1991; Zollo and Singh, 2004). Given too the short time frame involved in a lateral acquisition, key players in firms see the consequences of their actions and can readily gain feedback and learn from what they do. Researchers, therefore, can discern the planned or emergent patterns to firms' strategies in acquiring laterals, and also see their effect clearly.

The firm-level data sets used to address these issues come from a variety of sources. One main source that has already been discussed, *The American Lawyer's* Partner Mobility Data, allows researchers to examine the incidence and effects of lateral partner acquisitions on Am Law 200 firms beginning in 2000 and contains close to 14,000

partner movements from 2000 to 2005. A second source involves tra-
cing partner movements across firms using the *Martindale-Hubbell
Legal Directory*. While there is an online version for each current year
that is readily accessible, there is no such ready online access for earlier
years. The *Martindale-Hubbell Legal Directory* is, moreover, very time-
consuming to work with, in that, to find out the arrival firm of a partner
who has departed, the researcher potentially would have to search
through all other firms' list of partners across the United States (and
even across the world). Since the inter-firm movement of partners is very
often localized, researchers such as Phillips (2002) and Shah (2005)
have delimited their studies by examining a specific geographical area,
such as Silicon Valley or Chicago, and by examining only firms or
offices of firms in that city. With the data from the *Martindale-
Hubbell Legal Directory*, the researcher can examine partner mobility
over an extended period of time. Thus, Phillips examined Silicon Valley
law firms from 1946 to 1995 and Shah examined Chicago law firms
from 1975 to 1990. Researchers who use the *Martindale-Hubbell Legal
Directory* to examine offices or firms in a city or local labor market are
typically restricted on measures of performance to such outcomes as
survival, growth, and practice diversification. Financial data is generally not available on offices of firms, and small firms are not included in
the Am Law 100 and 200 financial data reports.

Both *The American Lawyer's* Partner Mobility Data and the
Martindale-Hubbell Legal Directory are important sources of data for
addressing key questions on lateral partner acquisitions. Questions arise
about how selection and integration matter. Answers to these questions
come through examining issues of organization–individual fit, identifying
where firms hire partners from, what practice areas of law lateral partners
are hired into and how these practice areas either deepen or add to the
existing practice portfolio, and the rate of lateral partner retention.
Questions arise too about whether firms are able to apply and appropriate
lateral partner expertise. Answers to these questions come though examining, for example, the extent to which firms successfully build practice
areas, add new clients, generate more revenues, and achieve higher profits.

Conclusions

My aim in this chapter has been to raise interest among organizational
researchers in the context of the changed world of the large law firm and

its lawyers by showing how the context both connects to and brushes up against important theoretical arguments and empirical findings in the fields of business strategy, human resource management, organizational behavior, and organizational theory. Large law firms allow us to look at the notion of organizational identity when change occurs gradually yet very significantly, when change is generally not threatening to positional status, and when something of the old is combined with something of the new. Large law firms allow us to examine variation in the HRM systems within an organization that is truly multifaceted, such that it transcends the imagery of the core/periphery model. Large law firms allow us to see how an exception to the rule of acquiring lateral partners provided a way out of the iron cage and later became the accepted fact for most firms. Large law firms allow us to reconcile the debate on the value of acquiring external assets through showing the importance of internal acquisition capabilities as reflected in the processes of selection, integration, and application/appropriation.

It has also been my aim to raise organizational researchers' interest in learning more about the context of the large law firm. Some of the learning will come easily, from seeing parallels in the trends in large corporate entities. Cappelli (2000), for example, shows how large corporations have taken to free agency with acceptance of the fact that there is a new deal. Some of the learning will come from having insights into business schools as academic institutions and other knowledge-based organizations (e.g. consulting firms), which share key management practices with large law firms. Nonetheless, the joy for me (and pain for others) of studying the large law firm, or any particular industry or population of firms, is the uniqueness of the institutional arrangements. The large law firm is a vestige of its past, the time in which it was formed, its emphasis on partnership, and law as a profession. That the large law firm has parallels to other organizational forms such as the large corporation yet has its uniqueness requires that organizational researchers show balance and perspective in understanding them.

I hope I have shown that methodological pluralism should not simply be tolerated but, instead, should be encouraged or even demanded, as it will be absolutely necessary. Researchers can avail themselves of many different methodologies in examining the large law firm and the topics addressed in this chapter. Many large law firms now have published histories, like Swaine's (1946, 1948) well-known account of Cravath, Swaine, and Moore. These histories capture views in print from the past, all the way back in some cases to the origins of the firm. Markers from the past can also be used to gain a sense of firms' identities from the past to the present (Webb *et al.*, 1966). These markers can be photos of firms and their partners, biographical information and death notices, legal briefs filed by firms, and the like. Numerous articles in legal trade journals such as *The American Lawyer* and *National Law Journal* date back to the late 1970s and directly quote partners.

Researchers can also conduct "oral histories" with key informants, some of whom will be retired partners. William Starbuck's (1993) wonderful account of what makes Wachtel unique illustrates the value of a key informant approach combined with analyses of Am Law 100 data. Ethnographic studies (Barley, 1990) are needed as well, in which researchers go into large law firms, learn the language of the lawyers, and come to understand issues from the perspective of these actors. The Stanford Project on Emerging Companies (SPEC) shows how qualitative data from retrospective accounts with key informants can be used to conduct quantitative studies (e.g. Baron, Burton, and Hannan, 1996, Baron and Hannan, 2002). Phillips (2002) and Shah (2005) show how a legal directory can be used to generate data on the inter-firm movement of partners. Sherer (2005) shows how *The American Lawyer* Partner Mobility Data can be used to assess the impact of different internal acquisition capabilities on firm performance. Thus, research should include single case histories of firms, comparative case historical analyses, ethnographic studies, survey research, and larger-scale quantitative studies. Moreover, since the evidence will often be "circumstantial," requiring researchers to connect pieces of evidence, researchers can weave a more powerful mosaic of evidence by using multiple methodologies in conjunction.

Large law firms deserve to be studied, because they are a place in which organizational researchers can build on and extend theoretical arguments and empirical findings that are based largely on large corporate entities. We should study the large law firm, because it is an important economic player along with the large corporation, a party to virtually every major business transaction in the US economy and in other economies, and with revenues that in a growing number of cases exceed $1 billion. We should study large law firms, because they provide variety in organizational form and, much as they may appear to coevolve with large corporations, they also seem to go their separate way. The large law firm is truly an opportune context for organizational researchers.

References

Albert, S., and Whetten, D. A. (1985). Organizational identity. In B. M. Staw and L. L. Cummings (eds.), *Research in Organizational Behavior*, vol. VII (263–95). Greenwich, CT: JAI Press.

Angel, T. (2007). Your challenge: sustaining partnership in the 21st century: the global law firm experience. In L. Empson (ed.), *Managing the Modern Law Firm: New Challenges, New Perspectives* (196–217). Oxford: Oxford University Press.

Ashkenas, R. N., DeMonaco, L. J., and Francis, S. C. (1998). Making the real deal: how GE integrates acquisitions. *Harvard Business Review*, 76(1), 5–15.

Asimow, M. (2001). Embodiment of evil: law firms in the movies. *UCLA Law Review*, 48, 1339–92.

Atkinson, J. (1987). Flexibility or fragmentation? The United Kingdom labour market in the eighties. *Labour and Society*, 12, 87–106.

Barley, S. R. (1990). Images of imaging: notes on doing longitudinal field work. *Organization Science*, 1, 220–47.

Barney, J. (1986). Strategic factor markets: expectations, luck and business strategy. *Management Science*, 32, 1231–41.

Baron, J. N., Burton, M. D., and Hannan, M. T. (1996). The road taken: origins and evolution of employment systems in emerging companies. *Industrial and Corporate Change*, 5(2), 239–75.

Baron, J. N., Dobbin, F. R., and Jennings, D. P. (1986). War and peace: the evolution of modern personnel administration in US industry. *American Journal of Sociology*, 92, 350–83.

Baron, J. N., and Hannan, M. T. (2002). Organizational blueprints for success in high-tech start-ups: lessons from the Stanford project on emerging companies. *California Management Review*, 44(3), 8–36.

Bartunek, J. M., Rynes, S. L., and Ireland, R. D. (2006). What makes management research interesting, and why does it matter? *Academy of Management Journal*, 49, 9–15.

Becker, B., and Gerhart, B. (1996). The impact of human resource management on organizational performance: progress and prospects. *Academy of Management Journal*, 39, 779–801.

Becker, G. (1975). *Human Capital: A Theoretical and Empirical Analysis with Special Reference to Education* (3rd edn.). Chicago: University of Chicago Press.

Belford, T. (2003). When law firms play musical chairs. *The Globe and Mail*, 23 December, B11.

Boeker, W. (1997). Executive migration and strategic change: the effect of top manager movement on product market entry. *Administrative Science Quarterly*, 42 (2), 213–36.

Braverman, P. (2001). In motion: lateral moves by attorneys in top 200 US law firms. *The American Lawyer*, February, 88–90, 93.

Brill, S. (1989). The end of partnership. *The American Lawyer*, December, 3, 35.
    (1990). The changing meaning of partnership. *The American Lawyer*, March, supplement.
    (1996). Ruining the profession. *The American Lawyer*, July/August, 5–6.

Cappelli, P. (2000). A market-driven approach to retaining talent. *Harvard Business Review*, 78(1), 103–11.

Cappelli, P., and Sherer, P. D. (1990). Assessing workers' attitudes under a two-tier wage system. *Industrial and Labor Relations Review*, 43, 225–44.

Caves, R. E., and Porter, M. E. (1977). From entry barriers to mobility barriers: conjectural decisions and contrived deterrence to new competition. *Quarterly Journal of Economics*, 91(2), 241–62.

Chatman, J. A. (1991). Matching people and organizations: selection and socialization in public accounting firms. *Administrative Science Quarterly*, 36(3), 459–84.

Cohen, W. M., and Levinthal, D A. (1990). Absorptive capacity: a new perspective on learning and innovation. *Administrative Science Quarterly*, 35(1), 128–52.

Collins, J. C., and Porras, J. I. (1996). Building your company's vision. *Harvard Business Review*, 74(5), 65–77.

Cowan, A. L. (1992). The new letdown: making partner. *New York Times*, 1 April, D1, D8.

Dierickx, I., and Cool, K. (1989). Asset stock accumulation and sustainability of competitive advantage. *Management Science*, 35, 1504–13.

DiMaggio, P. J., and Powell, W. W. (1983). The iron cage revisited: institutional isomorphism and collective rationality in organizational fields. *American Sociological Review*, 48, 147–60.

Doeringer, P. B., and Piore, M. J. (1971). *Internal Labor Markets and Manpower Analysis*. Lexington, MA: D.C. Heath.

Dutton, J. E., and Dukerich, J. M. (1992). Keeping an eye on the mirror: image and identity in organizational adaptation. *Academy of Management Journal*, 34, 517–54.

Elsbach, K. E., and Kramer, R. M. (1996). Members' responses to organizational identity threats: encountering and countering the *Business Week* rankings. *Administrative Science Quarterly*, 41(3), 442–76.

Empson, L. (2001). Fear of exploitation and fear of contamination: impediments to knowledge transfer in mergers between professional service firms. *Human Relations*, 54, 839–62.

Eviatar, D. (2002). Toward higher ground: a recession doesn't halt lateral moves. It makes them imperative as partners seek safety in ever-larger firms. *The American Lawyer*, February, 92–5.

Fergus, J. (1990). Seasoned lateral hires still sought. *National Law Journal*, 24 September, 1, 36, 38.

Fleischer-Black, M. (2003). Musical chairs: lateral moves never go out of style, even in this tight economy, the pace continues. But some firms are finding that the more they lure, the hungrier they get. *The American Lawyer*, February, 62–5.

Frankel, A. (2006). Growing pains. *The American Lawyer*, May, 94–8.

Galanter, M., and Palay, T. (1991). *Tournament of Lawyers: The Transformation of the Big Law Firm*. Chicago: University of Chicago Press.

Gerson, B. (1984). *Directory of the Legal Profession*. New York: New York Law Publishing.

Gilson, R. J., and Mnookin, R. H. (1988). Coming of age in a corporate law firm: the economics of associate career patterns. *Stanford Law Review*, 41, 567–95.

Glendon, M. A. (1994). *A Nation under Lawyers*. New York: Farrar, Straus, and Giroux.

Greenwood, R., Hinings, C. R., and Brown, J. (1994). Merging professional service firms. *Organization Science*, 5, 239–57.

Hallman, B. (2006). Trophy lawyers. *The American Lawyer*, May, 118, 120, 121.

Haspelagh, P. C., and Jemison, D. B. (1991). *Managing Acquisitions: Creating Corporate Value through Renewal*. New York: Free Press.

Hillman, R. W. (1999). *Hillman on Lawyer Mobility: The Law and Ethics of Partner Withdrawals and Law Firm Breakups* (2nd edn.). New York: Aspen Law and Business.

Hitt, M.A, Bierman, L., Shimizu, H., and Kochhar, R. (2001). Direct and moderating effects of human capital on strategy and performance in professional service firms: a resource-based perspective. *Academy of Management Journal*, 44, 13–28.

Huselid, M. A. (1995). The impact of human resource management practices on turnover, productivity, and corporate financial performance. *Academy of Management Journal*, 38, 635–72.

Jacoby, S. (1985). *Employing Bureaucracy: Managers, Unions, and the Transformation of Work in American Industry, 1900–1945.* New York: Columbia University Press.

Kaplan, D. A. (1982). The rush to laterals: a fundamental change. *National Law Journal,* 4 October, *1,* 24–6.

King, D. R., Dalton, D. R., Daily, C. M., and Covin, J. G. (2004). Meta-analysis of post-acquisition performance: indicators of unidentified moderators. *Strategic Management Journal, 25,* 187–200.

Kolker, C. (2002). Lateral manners. *The American Lawyer,* October, 19.

(2004). Running in place. *The American Lawyer,* March, 73–9.

Koppel, N. (2005). Hello, I must be leaving. *The American Lawyer,* February, 106–9, 134.

Kraatz, M. S., and Moore, J. H. (2002). Executive migration and institutional change. *Academy of Management Journal, 45,* 120–43.

Leblebici, H, Salancik, G., Copay, A., and King, T. (1991). Institutional change and the transformation of interorganizational fields: an organizational history of the US radio broadcasting industry. *Administrative Science Quarterly, 36*(3), 333–63.

Lennon, R. (2001). Help not wanted. *The American Lawyer,* February, 91.

Lepak, D. P., and Snell, S. A. (1999). The human resource architecture: toward a theory of human capital allocation and development. *Academy of Management Review, 24,* 31–48.

Lewin, T. (1987). Law firms add second tier. *New York Times,* 11 March, D1, D3.

Linowitz, S. M. (1994). *The Betrayed Profession: Lawyering at the End of the Twentieth Century.* New York: Scribner's.

Longstreth, A. (2006). How Skadden does it. *The American Lawyer,* May, 100–5.

MacDuffie, J. P. (1995). Human resource bundles and manufacturing performance: organizational logic and flexible production systems in the world auto industry. *Industrial and Labor Relations Review, 48,* 197–221.

Nelson, R. L. (1988). *Partner with Power: The Social Transformation of the Large Law Firm.* Berkeley, CA: University of California Press.

Nelson, S. (1985). Skadden, Arps D.C. office just keeps growing. *Legal Times,* 17 June, 12.

Oliver, C. (1991). Strategic responses to institutional processes. *Academy of Management Review, 16,* 145–79.

Pearce, J. L. (1993). Toward an organizational behavior of contract laborers: their psychological involvement and effects on co-workers. *Academy of Management Journal, 36,* 1082–96.

Phillips, D. J. (2002). A genealogical approach to organizational life chances: the parent–progeny transfer among Silicon Valley law firms, 1946–1996. *Administrative Science Quarterly*, 47(3), 474–506.

Podolny, J. M. (1993). A status-based model of market competition. *American Journal of Sociology*, 98, 829–72.

Rao, H., and Drazin, R. (2002). Overcoming resource constraints on product innovation by recruiting talent from rivals: a study of the mutual fund industry, 1986–94. *Academy of Management Journal*, 45, 491–507.

Rhode, D. L. (2000). The profession and its discontent. *Ohio State Law Journal*, 61, 1335–9.

Rovit, S. Harding, D., and Lemire, C. (2004). A simple model M&A model for all seasons. *Strategy and Leadership*, 32, 18–24.

Safire, W. (1997). On language: gimme the ol' white shoe. *New York Times*, 9 November, online version.

Schiltz, P. J. (1999). On being a happy, healthy, and unethical member of an unhappy, unhealthy, and unethical profession. *Vanderbilt Law Review*, 52, 871–951.

Shah, N. (2005). Change in institutions: the decline of the no-lateral-hiring norm among large law firms, 1974–1990. Paper presented at the Annual Meeting of the Academy of Management, Honolulu, 5–10 August.

Sherer, P. D. (1995). Leveraging human assets in law firms: human capital structures and organizational capabilities. *Industrial and Labor Relations Review*, 48, 671–91.

(1996). Toward an understanding of the variety in work arrangements: the organization and labor relationships framework. In C. L. Cooper and D. M. Rousseau (eds.), *Trends in Organizational Behavior*, vol. III (99–122). New York: John Wiley.

(2003). The tensions between best practices and different-from competitor practices in strategic HRM: fusing institutional and resource-based theories. Paper presented at the Annual Meeting of the Academy of Management, Seattle, 1–6 August.

(2004). Long waves of dominance: routines and path dependence in highly successful large law firms. Paper presented at the Clifford Chance Workshop on Professional Service Firms, Boston, 25–7 June.

(2005). Acquisition capabilities in large law firms: gaining value through lateral partners. Paper presented at the Clifford Chance Professional Service Firm Conference, Oxford, 3–5 July.

(2007). Your competitors: mapping the competitive space of large US law firms: a strategic group perspective. In L. Empson (ed.), *Managing the Modern Law Firm: New Challenges, New Perspectives* (162–85), Oxford: Oxford University Press.

Sherer, P. D., and Leblebici, H. (2001). Bringing variety and change into the study of strategic human resource management. In J Ferris (ed.), *Research in Personnel and Human Resources Management*, vol. XIX (199–230). Oxford: Elsevier Science.

Sherer, P. D., and Lee, K. M. (1992). Cores, peripheries, and more and less: mixes of labor relationships in firms. In *Proceedings of the 1992 Industrial Relation Research Association* 317–24 Madison, WI: Industrial Relations Research Association.

——— (2002). Institutional change in large law firms: a resource dependency and institutional perspective. *Academy of Management Journal, 45,* 102–19.

Sherer, P. D., Rogovsky, N., and Wright, N. (1998). What drives employment relationships in taxicab organizations? Linking agency to firm capabilities and strategic opportunities. *Organization Science, 9,* 34–48.

Smigel, E. O. (1969). *The Wall Street Lawyer: Professional Organizational Man?* Bloomington, IN: Indiana University Press.

Starbuck, W. H. (1993). Keeping a butterfly and an elephant in a house of cards: the elements of exceptional success. *Journal of Management Studies, 30,* 885–921.

Swaine, R. T. (1946). *The Cravath Firm and Its Predecessors, 1819–1947,* vol. I, *The Predecessor Firms, 1819–1906.* New York: Ad Press.

——— (1948). *The Cravath Firm and Its Predecessors, 1819–1947,* vol. II, *The Cravath Firm since 1906.* New York: Ad Press.

Voorhees, M. (2004). Go fish: how aggressive lateral hiring, a democratic culture, and casting a wide net put Fish & Richardson on top of the IP defense rankings. *The American Lawyer,* June, 63–5.

Wagner, D. (1986). Variations on the 'of-counsel' theme. *California Lawyer,* July, 59, 60, 62, 64.

Webb, E. J., Campbell, D. T., Schwartz, R. D., and Sechrest, L. (1966). *Unobtrusive Measures: Nonreactive Research in the Social Sciences.* Chicago: Rand McNally.

Wernerfelt, B. (1984). A resource-based view of the firm. *Strategic Management Journal, 5,* 171–80.

Whitfield, R. (1988). Lateral recruiting and the new economics. *Chicago Daily Law Bulletin,* 22 September, 2, 12.

Williamson, O. E. (1985). *The Economic Institutions of Capitalism.* New York: Free Press.

Zollo, M., and Singh, H. (2004). Deliberate learning in corporate acquisitions: post-acquisition strategies and integration capability in US bank mergers. *Strategic Management Journal, 25,* 1233–45.

7 | The upside of bureaucracy: unintended benefits for professional careers

FORREST BRISCOE

Introduction

There is a frequent refrain from scholars and practitioners alike that the professions are becoming ever more bureaucratized. If true, what does this trend imply for professional careers? Several volumes have been devoted to the implications of bureaucratization in general, nearly all of which see it negatively from the point of view of professional workers themselves (e.g. Derber, 1982; Leicht and Fennell, 2001; Freidson, 2001). In this chapter I advance another, perhaps less obvious, interpretation: that bureaucracy offers those in professional careers the kind of career flexibility that today is welcomed. I argue that bureaucratization is (largely unintentionally) creating a range of flexible career options that were previously unavailable – and that are increasingly valued by professional workers themselves. I advance this argument using data from a multi-method study of primary care physicians.

A review of the historical and current trends in professional organizations (e.g. law firms, medical practices) in the research literature shows that they are indeed becoming more bureaucratic. This process entails a greater use of formalized rules and procedures (Gerth and Mills, 1946), and more centralized control of professional activities and client relationships (Pugh *et al.*, 1968). Some of the resulting effects on careers are straightforward. For example, bureaucracy tends to increase the demand for professionals to take on managerial roles (see Rothman and Perrucci, 1970, and Raelin, 1985).

The link between bureaucratization and career flexibility follows a different logic, however: bureaucracy tends to standardize professionals' client-related activities, and in so doing makes it easier for professional workers to hand off clients amongst one another. That ability to make

client handoffs, in turn, helps to guarantee windows of time for professional workers to plan activities *other* than being available to clients,
including work or non-work career activities that would otherwise be
infeasible. In effect, bureaucratization allows schedule control, which in
turn permits workers to pursue more flexible career options.

The chapter proceeds as follows. I first define and identify professional service workers, and then review the literature on trends in
professional occupations and careers, including both historical and
contemporary developments. This is followed by a summary of my
own studies of primary care physicians (PCPs), focusing on details of
the career options and career flexibility found among PCPs in different
organizational settings. I introduce the elements of a model used to
understand why PCP career flexibility is greatest within the most
heavily bureaucratized medical practice organizations, and consider
the extent to which this model can be extended to other types of
professional service workers.

Who are professional service workers?

Professional service workers represent an important and growing segment of the economy. According to Andrew Abbott (1988), professional services are provided by "exclusive occupational groups that
apply somewhat abstract knowledge to particular cases." Those cases
usually originate with clients outside the profession (whether individuals or organizations), and the abstract knowledge applied to them is
usually codified and regulated to some degree by the profession. Expert
services provided to clients commonly require customization to fit
each situation (Greenwood *et al.*, 2005; Lowendahl, 2000; von
Nordenflycht, 2006). Because expert services are usually difficult to
evaluate for non-professionals, an information and power asymmetry
arises that favors the professional worker (Sharma, 1997). This power
relationship gives rise to the claim for a special fiduciary duty that
professional workers have toward clients and society (Freidson, 1970;
Nanda, 2003). Part of that duty involves responding to client issues in a
timely and thorough fashion – a factor that can place considerable
burden on professionals themselves (Zerubavel, 1979).

Though some controversy surrounds the exact scope of the professional service occupations, they generally include the "classic" professions, such as doctors, lawyers, accountants, architects, and scientists

(Freidson, 1970; Abbott, 1988), as well as the (partly overlapping) "professional service firm" professionals, such as management consultants, technical consultants, advertising and design professionals, bankers, and financial advisors (Greenwood, Hinings, and Brown, 1990; Mills *et al.*, 1983; Empson, 2007). The growing ranks of technical workers, whose expertise is typically rooted in understanding particular technologies, share many characteristics with professionals, in that they apply occupationally specified expertise to address issues presented to them by clients and others (see Zabusky and Barley, 1996).[1]

Depending on the definition used, professional services constitute or directly influence between 15 and 25 percent of the US gross domestic product (GDP). Following Joseph Broschak (2004), I used the 2004 US Service Annual Survey to estimate that the combination of professional, scientific, and technical services, health services (ambulatory care, hospitals, and nursing facilities), and securities and brokerage services amount to 23.7 percent of US GDP. Daniel Bell (1999) comes up with similar figures, and Stephen Barley and Julian Orr (1997) present comparable figures to suggest that professional and technical workers may constitute one of the most important and fastest-growing sectors of the modern US economy. These trends in the size and growth of professional services are found in other advanced economies as well (Empson, 2007).

Historical approach to professions and careers

A substantial literature on professionals has developed over the decades, particularly in sociology. In this section I review some of the general literature on professional organizations, the pattern of professional careers, and the links between professional organizations and professional careers. Though much of this research focuses on the US context, there are parallel traditions in other country contexts (Brock, Powell, and Hinings, 1999; Ackroyd, Muzio, and Chanlet, 2007).

---

[1] Professions that are not directly engaged in the economic sphere, such as soldiers and priests, are often excluded. Teachers, nurses, and social workers are often omitted or treated as cases of partial professionalization (Etzioni, 1969). Other traditional professions, such as academics and engineers, do not fit the client-driven theme in professional service work as easily.

Historically, studies of professionals have emphasized the uniqueness of professional occupations in comparison to other occupations. An orientation toward individual autonomy, rooted in occupational culture, gave rise to an observed tension between professionals and bureaucratic organizations. American and British sociologists, including W. Richard Scott (1965) and Richard Hall (1968), studied the co-occurrence of professionals and bureaucratic organizations, finding that traditional bureaucratic techniques fared poorly with key segments of the professional workforce. Henry Mintzberg (1979) suggested that the professional bureaucracy could do little to intervene in the work of the professionals, instead limiting the scope of organizational activities to providing administrative support. Gloria Engel (1970) and others soon modified the basic negative association between autonomy and bureaucratic intensity, but the general ideas persisted. Debates also developed as to whether this need for autonomy was a functional necessity in order to produce high-quality work or simply a privileged outcome of professional power (Larson, 1977; Abbott, 1988; Freidson, 1984).

The structure of professional careers was also thought to be unique, driven less by the needs of organizations than by the unique character of professional work. The career pattern was marked by lengthy apprenticeship-style training and socialization into occupational norms (Hall, 1948; Goode, 1957). Howard Becker, Blanche Geer, Everett Hughes, and Anselm Strauss (1961) studied the institutional socialization of physicians during medical school and medical residency, characterizing the key function of that career phase as one in which career values and expectations were crystallized and transmitted between generations. Chief among those career values was a primary commitment to the profession, placing employers or other work organizations second (see Wallace, 1995). That pattern of commitment led to careers in which professional success depended on relationships with clients and institutions, rather than on demonstrating commitment to an organization (see Gunz and Gunz, 1994). These are the "careers of achievement" that Stacia Zabusky and Stephen Barley (1996) contrast with the more traditional "careers of advancement" in non-professional occupations, in which organizational attachment and commitment were key elements in career success.

Careers within professional service organizations were characterized by minimal integration with the rest of the organization. For example, physicians maintained arm's-length relationships with hospitals by acquiring admitting privileges, a position that allowed them a considerable amount of control without ever becoming employees or managers (Starr, 1982). Lawyers, accountants, architects, and others were typically organized into professional partnerships of varying sizes, in which the partners enjoyed being owners with relatively high individual autonomy and minimal imposed structure. Indeed, partnerships have been seen as a way for accomplished professionals to pool certain risks and resources while maintaining their independence (Gilson and Mnookin, 1985). They also allow partners to leverage their knowledge, skills, and social capital by hiring junior professionals in apprentice-style positions, in which they are motivated to work hard with the possibility of one day becoming partners themselves (Galanter and Palay, 1991; Greenwood and Empson, 2003; see also chapter 6 in this volume). These junior positions, in turn, formed a key career phase for professional workers in occupations in which partnership is the norm.

Contemporary developments in professions and careers

The current portrait of professional organizations and careers contrasts with the historical image of exceptionalism. Some aspects of the current portrait were predicted by earlier scholars, who argued that professionals would, essentially, be transformed into ordinary workers through the successful bureaucratizing efforts driven by clients and various other forces external to the professions (Haug, 1973; Derber, 1982; McKinlay, 1982).[2] The theoretical literature on this issue is

---

[2] At the same time, others suggested that increasing expertise and knowledge content could lead many other types of workers to manifest increasingly profession-like qualities (Bell, 1976; Wilensky, 1964). Knowledge content in non-professional work may indeed be increasing, creating the need for more profession-like autonomy and discretion in a wide range of settings (National Research Council, 1999, pp. 105–63; see also Ichniowski *et al.*, 1996, and Blair and Kochan, 2000). In terms of careers, too, the generic worker literature is also increasingly emphasizing professional career concepts such as socialization (Van Maanen and Barley, 1984), mentoring and networking (Higgins and Kram, 2001), and participation in communities of practice (Lave and Wenger, 1991). Profession-like career patterns, such as project-based careers (Bielby and Bielby, 1999; Jones, 1996), independent contracting (Kunda, Barley, and Evans, 2002; see also chapter 5 in this volume), and organizationally detached careers, are gaining scrutiny (Cappelli, 1999). Anecdotally, even the *term* "professional" seems to be incorporated nowadays into an ever-expanding set of job titles from a wide range of occupations.

extensive (and beyond the scope of this chapter). For present purposes, I will summarize the key empirical trends in professional organizations and the professional workforce that have in fact transpired in recent years.

Changes in professional organizations

Professional organizations are changing in response to a wide range of external factors, such as deregulation, competition, globalization, the use of information technology and managerial practices taken from other sectors of the economy, and changes in the composition and demands of the clients whom professionals serve (Brock, Powell, and Hinings, 1999; Fennell and Alexander, 1993; Abel, 1989). In response to these forces, the organizational form for professionals is changing. For example, Laura Empson and Chris Chapman (2006) marshal evidence that the professional partnership, the traditional organizational form among many professional service occupations, is giving way to incorporation and even public ownership. Andrew von Nordenflycht (2007) documents a trend toward public ownership among advertising agencies, and explores the impact of this trend on professionals employed in those organizations. Royston Greenwood and Roy Suddaby (2006) describe the emergence of new professional organizations that combine multiple professions, such as accounting, consulting, and law. Shah (2005) shows how certain widespread hiring norms in law firms (only hiring associates at entry level, only creating partners through internal promotion) have given way to a more varied set of hiring practices; these practices, in turn, have come to be viewed more as strategic choices and less as taken-for-granted organizational norms (Malos and Campion, 2000).

Internal changes are also taking place in professional organizations, many of which entail increasing bureaucracy. For example, lawyers and professional consultants are using standardized knowledge management systems to encode and share insights across clients and projects (Davenport and Prusak, 1998; Hansen and Haas, 2001; Morris, 2001), and physicians increasingly use electronic medical records for some similar reasons (Weber, 2005). In addition, we are seeing within organizations the increased adoption of rules and procedures that standardize core professional work despite the long-recognized difficulties and dangers perceived in doing so (Laffel and Blumenthal, 1989). Professionals are also being asked to develop a more standardized and organizationally generic relationship with clients, away from the individual and idiosyncratic bonds linking professionals and clients in the traditional approach (Michelson, Laumann, and Heinz, 2000; Briscoe, 2006). Because many of these changes entail more administrative control and bureaucratic intensity from the perspective of professionals, they strike many scholars and practitioners as the fruition of earlier predictions that the professions would eventually succumb to bureaucratic control (Leicht and Fennell, 2001; Hafferty and Light, 1995; McKinlay and Marceau, 2002).

The implications for professional careers as traditionally conceived, then, could be quite negative. As a result, one might expect professionals to avoid these bureaucracies or to join them with reluctance, leading to greater conflict within organizations. In fact, some evidence exists to support this perspective. For example, some seasoned partners appear to be leaving professional service firms rather than give up personal autonomy and individualized client relationships (Hillman, 2001). In addition, some occupation-wide surveys of particular professional occupations suggest declining career satisfaction (Linzer *et al.*, 2000; Ranalli, 2003), though others do not (NALP [National Association for Law Placement] Foundation, 2004; Landau, 2003).

Concurrent changes in the professional workforce

One reason the trend toward greater bureaucratization may not produce the anticipated negative response is that the professional workers of today are not the professional workers of yesterday. Neither the demographic makeup nor the attitudes of young professionals appear to mirror those of earlier generations. Demographically, women have entered professions in large numbers, including medicine, law, academia, and accounting (see figure 7.1). Reflecting this trend, the division of household labor among workers in these occupations is shifting from one dominated by male breadwinners (with female homemakers supporting them at home) toward a diversity of family structures, including large numbers of dual-career families (Waite and Nielson, 2001). Racial and ethnic diversity are also increasing across the

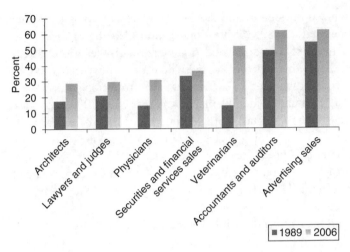

Figure 7.1 Rise in the percentage of women in professional occupations, 1989 and 2006
Source: Author's tabulation of Current Population Survey data (available from www.bls.gov).

professions, though at a generally slower pace (Wilkins and Gulati, 1996; Nickens, Ready, and Petersdorf, 1994).[3]

These demographic trends are bringing a range of new values and, in particular, a range of new career interests into the professional workforce that go beyond traditional conceptions of stratification (based on income, status, and autonomy). The old, homogeneous model of a professional committed fully to his or her work and clients – representing the

---

[3] Given these changes, many scholars have focused on understanding the degree to which increasing demographic diversity in the overall professional workforce is being translated into differential career attainment and stratification within the professions (Hull and Nelson, 2000; Sasser, 2005). For example, Lisa Cohen, Joseph Broschak, and Heather Haveman (1998) find that female bank managers were promoted only under certain conditions based on the gender composition of their work context, and Christine Beckman and Damon Phillips (2005) find that more women attorneys were promoted to partner in firms in which more of the clients were also women. Forrest Briscoe and Thomas Konrad (2006) find that black physicians were more likely to obtain practice positions as health maintenance organization (HMO) employees during the early 1990s, leading them to greater subsequent career disruption and dissatisfaction. Fiona Kay and John Hagan (1999) find that, even when female attorneys develop the necessary skills and relationships within law firms, they still do not achieve partnership status when compared with similar male attorneys.

"ideal-type" professional in many accounts – is no longer seen as feasible or desirable for many in this new professional workforce (Bailyn, 1993; Williams, 2000). Some professional workers who shoulder family responsibilities are seeking career options during certain phases of their life that accommodate more flexible work arrangements. This may include part-time work or extended leaves of absence followed by a resumption of their professional work roles. These career options represent, to some degree, curtailed commitment to professional work (see Valcour, Bailyn, and Quijada, 2007). Even beyond these work–life considerations, growing diversity within the workforce is increasing the range of career interests in younger generations of professionals (Hull and Nelson, 2000; Families and Work Institute, 2005).

Linking organizational bureaucratization and workforce changes through the career

In the preceding sections I have outlined two major trends at work in the professions: (1) professional organizations are becoming more bureaucratic in response to various pressures, especially the need to streamline client service; and (2) there is increasing diversity in the professional workforce, particularly with regard to the gender and family structure of professionals. The question is, how will these trends affect professional careers? To answer this question I present findings from an in-depth study of one occupational setting.

Field study: primary care physicians

From June 2001 to May 2005 I studied the work practices and careers of PCPs across a range of organizational settings in the United States. In essence, the findings show that *more* organizational bureaucracy was providing *more* personal schedule and career flexibility – while at the same time coming at some cost to the worker in terms of traditional career values such as autonomy and income.

I chose to study physicians in part because they lie at the extreme end of the spectrum in terms of the temporal demands placed on them by their patients. PCP work entails responding to unpredictably timed patient illnesses, and it involves a high level of "specificity" between physicians and their patients, creating a kind of sequential dependency in which the physician who treated a patient at one point in time often needs to be the one who treats him or her in subsequent episodes. This creates a context in which temporal flexibility is hard to achieve for any PCP. Within this context, I focused on aspects of work related to patients, seeing them as both the focus of PCP work and the root cause of PCP flexibility problems. My overarching aim was not just to understand this context better but also to make a contribution to theory that could be generalized to other client-based professional settings.

Despite a historical tradition of autonomy, the US medical profession experienced an expansion of bureaucratic practice organizations from the 1970s onward that diverged from the past tradition of private partnership (Starr, 1982; Robinson, 1999) – a trend witnessed in other professional occupations and country contexts as well (Leicht and Fennell, 1997; Brock, Powell, and Hinings, 1999). As a result, the current landscape includes physicians practicing in a range of settings, from solo independent practitioners (traditionally the norm), to medium-sized group practices, to large, bureaucratic medical practice organizations, and health care systems in which physicians practice as salaried employees.

At nearly the same time that these organizational changes were taking place, the PCP workforce was also radically shifting. The proportion of women among medical school graduates grew from 7 percent in 1970 to 24 percent in 2000 (American Medical Association, 2002), and among practicing physicians it rose from 9 percent to 44 percent (Barzansky, Jonas, and Etzel, 2000).[4] The division of household labor also moved away from a male breadwinner/female homemaker model. Lee Powers, Rexford Parmelle, and Harry Wiesenfelder (1969) find that, of male physicians who had graduated in the 1930s through the 1950s, 83 percent had wives who were not employed. By 2000 young physicians were more likely to marry or partner with individuals who also had demanding careers. In fact, Nancy Sobecks and colleagues (1999) find that 44 percent of female physicians and 22 percent of male physicians have married other physicians. These changes are bringing new career interests, including a growing interest in schedule flexibility, non-traditional career options, and personal quality of life (Moody, 2002).

---

[4] At the same time, the occupation itself expanded, from 156 physicians per 100,000 population in 1970 to 261 per 100,000 population in 2000.

Methods

To examine these issues, I conducted multi-method research combining both qualitative and quantitative data. The qualitative data was collected over the course of an eighteen-month field study including interviews, documents, and meeting observations from primary care physicians and administrators in a major US metropolitan region. The study followed an inductive approach, evolving over time from a generative process using semi-structured interviews to a confirmatory process using systematic survey data to evaluate the propositions generated earlier (Strauss, 1987; Eisenhardt, 1989).

I conducted over forty interviews, in six relatively formalized medical practice organizations and seventeen smaller and less formalized practice organizations. I focused the most effort on one of the formalized organizations, referred to here as HCO, where I conducted physician interviews, observed administrative meetings, and collected archival data relevant to the organization's rules and procedures governing physician work life. HCO is one of two large-sized medical practice organizations in its geographic region, the approximately 500 salaried physicians it employs representing approximately 5 to 10 percent of those practicing in the region. The non-formalized settings included solo practices and small-group practices. Most interviews lasted for approximately one hour and were conducted in person. The interviews were guided by a semi-structured protocol that sought to address individuals' personal flexibility and career activities, as well as their understanding of organizational processes and work coordination mechanisms.

The survey data comes from two parallel surveys of PCPs. The first survey was collected from a random sample of PCPs in the region, representing a range of different organizational arrangements. The second survey targeted HCO PCPs. Survey questions covered schedule and career activities, control at work, and other aspects of the physician's organizational context and personal characteristics. For both surveys, three rounds of paper surveys were sent to home addresses. The first survey sample was obtained through the state medical association, and led to a final response rate of 45 percent (usable n = 441). The second survey sample included all PCPs employed by HCO in 2002, from a list provided by the organization's administration, leading to a final response rate of 62 percent (usable n = 147).

Background: traditional physician careers and organizations

My interview informants from traditional private practices often reflected the careers and career values of the historical US medical tradition. That archetypal career took place in a small, stable practice that was either solo or in partnership with a few other physicians. In that setting, the logic of an individual physician's work and career was organized around the needs of sick patients. In addition to long hours in regularly scheduled appointments with patients, the doctor was on call for patient emergencies as they arose, day or night. As a physician's practice expanded over the years, so would clinical responsibilities and hours. Other myriad responsibilities involved in running a small business would also take substantial time and energy. Over the entire career, the demands on a physician's time were relentless (Starr, 1982; Laster, 1996). The physician in this archetypal career model was typically male, with a wife at home to raise his family – a division of household labor that was essential to permit the physician to have the availability to meet the demands of patients at all times.

Some PCPs I interviewed who were nearing retirement reflected on the profound constraints that the earlier career tradition and organizational context placed on them, even with a traditional breadwinner/home-maker family structure. One had practiced from the 1960s through the 1980s in a suburban solo medical office, and the demands of that setting were daunting. He reflected on the toll this took on his home life:

> And the worst thing about it wasn't so much the time constraint, although that was horrible, but it was that it made you unreliable. There were these long episodes, of which dozens occurred, when I called up and said: "Gee, I thought I was going to be home for dinner but something's come up, I'll be home in time to read a story to the kids," and an hour later you call up again and say: "I'll be home in time for bed," and then you didn't get home at all. Until the kids turn you off, and when you say: "I'll be home" your kids say: "Yeah, sure, dad."

Clearly, the inability to protect time from his patients was a dominant theme in this informant's work career, and, consequently, in every other aspect of his life, including his family and marriage. Another PCP reflected a similar sentiment at a more internal, psychological level:

[H]ow do you turn it off? You have patients out there in the world, and they have problems and you want them to be OK. After a while, you may not actually be in the clinic, but it's on your mind and you're not free of it – the responsibility.

This informant described an inability to "turn off" the demands of patients, even when she was not working. She went on to discuss the way this developed out of a common professional belief in full personal responsibility for patients, combined with a minimal organizational structure that provided little in the way of support for her to rely on anyone else in looking after those patients. She did, in fact, have other career interests that she wanted to pursue while practicing as a primary care physician, but she was prevented from ever pursuing them by the overriding fear of not providing adequate care for her patients.

The flexible careers of physicians practicing at HCO

In contrast to these solo or small-practice physicians, those at HCO described being engaged in a remarkable range of career activities beyond their core patient care responsibilities – while at the same time still seeing patients for part of their time. What makes this high level of non-traditional career activities all the more remarkable is that they all required those PCPs engaging in them to have protected windows of time in which they could be guaranteed that their patients' needs would not interfere with their other activities – and, at the same time, that those patients' needs would still be adequately and safely met.

The main career activities among PCPs at HCO can be categorized into (1) "true" part-time clinician, (2) clinician and administrator, (3) clinician with alternative role, and (4) exclusive, regular full-time patient care. Below, the typical character of each career path is summarized, along with a few examples drawn from my informant interviews. This is followed by a discussion of the quantitative frequency of these career activities in HCO based on surveys.

True part-time clinician

"Part-time" for physicians can include as many as forty weekly work hours, since the definition of regular full-time is commonly viewed as upward of fifty hours per week (Barnett and Gareis, 2000). I define a true part-timer as someone who self-identified as working part-time in patient care during a period of time, and was not engaged in other career activities that brought him or her up to full-time. In HCO, part-time clinicians were responsible for a reduced number of patients, and tended to report fewer weekly patient office visit hours. Pay was prorated and on-call schedules were scaled back in proportion to the diminished clinical load, though this was not always true in other bureaucratic medical practice organizations I studied. Part-time status was maintained by some PCPs for a period of months, and by others for much longer, including permanently.

Many physicians described their interest in coming to HCO as being based on the availability of a true part-time practice. These individuals wanted to see patients – the core client service activity for which they had trained – and still have something approximating a regular schedule that included time and energy away from work, particularly for family responsibilities. The ability to define and contain the workload, the level of schedule predictability, and the on-call burden were frequently mentioned by these respondents. For example, Brenda, a female PCP, was attracted to HCO right out of residency because she thought it would help her with the juggling act of simultaneously starting a family and starting her practice while her husband, a surgeon she had met in medical school, worked even longer hours during his (longer) residency and fellowship training. While Brenda liked working in an organization committed to innovation in the organization of medical care delivery, it was not the main reason for her decision to join. In fact, she confessed that when she had joined she was hoping privately not to become too involved in any activities beyond patient care.

Clinician and administrator
Many PCPs had also served as administrators with official managerial capacity in HCO. The most common such position was chief for a regional office and a particular medical specialty. Higher-level positions included medical specialty chiefs across all offices, and various other centralized roles including chief medical officer. These appointments varied in length, from around one year to much longer. Responsibilities in these posts included colleague evaluation, communicating with other departments and/or offices, and resolving conflicts among staff or occasionally between staff and patients (see also Betson, 1986, and Montgomery, 2001). Almost all physician-administrators in

the study maintained a clinical practice at some reduced level. As a result, the overall work hours for these administrators were often comparable to those of regular full-time PCPs. Physician-administrators received additional income for their additional responsibilities.

A large number of informants described involvement in administration, and most reported doing so as a result of a proactive interest in administration. One example is Adrian, a physician who joined HCO after an early career stint in PCP private practice, which he had found to lack stimulation. Adrian had an interest in public health, and at the time he joined he had believed that organizations such as HCO had the potential to revolutionize medicine. He explained that his interests were broader than just delivering patient care, and that he wanted to be part of the leadership that continued to advance the state of health care delivery; he thought that HCO was a unique setting for him to do that while still "being a real doctor" (i.e. seeing patients). From the start of his tenure Adrian had been involved in a string of different administrative roles, from office chief to more senior organizational governance activities in which he was able to help develop some of the standards and routines that contributed to the somewhat more bureaucratic feel of the organization. Adrian's latest activity along these lines was planning an organizationally sponsored experiment in which patients with chronic conditions would meet as a group to discuss the social/psychological issues related to managing their condition.

Clinician with alternative role

There were many other assorted roles that could be found among PCPs. One example is a relatively new position known as the "hospitalist" (Hoff, Whitcomb, and Nelson, 2002). In this role a physician representing the medical group is based in a hospital or hospitals where patients of that medical group are treated. Instead of the patients' regular PCPs coordinating their care through telephone calls and periodic visits to the hospital, the hospitalist takes over that coordinating role and serves as a liaison between the patients, their PCPs, and the hospital physicians carrying out treatment. PCPs also worked in nursing homes or other extended care facilities doing similar types of work, in addition to seeing their regular patients. These positions existed because they were intended to increase the efficiency and/or quality of health care services provided to patients. Often individual PCPs choosing to pursue them saw them as valuable sources of growth and renewal in the course of their own career trajectories, however. Other PCPs were engaged in roles outside the organization, such as involvement in public health research or patient advocacy. Some physicians had purposefully pursued these alternative roles, and others had ended up in them through more circuitous events, but seemed to have been pleased with their ability to juggle these new roles with their clinical patient care practice.

Full-time patient care
My finding is that true regular full-time patient care, though relatively straightforward in terms of career structure, was associated with two types of career orientations. Some informants professed a pragmatic orientation toward their work in HCO, recognizing the financial security and predictability of life in the larger, more bureaucratic organization when compared with traditional private practice. They had few idealistic conceptions of the differences between one organizational setting or another, but consistently recognized the value of being free from the headaches of private practice. For example, Peter, a young physician who had recently come to HCO, was anxious to begin paying his medical school debt. He did not want to haggle with colleagues in private practice over compensation, staffing, and other office policies. He just wanted to see patients, be paid without worry, and start enjoying some of the rewards of his long training.[5]

Frequency and pattern of flexible career activities in HCO

Perhaps even more surprising than the presence of these different career activities among practicing PCPs is the frequency of their use and ability to switch between them over time. Using survey results from those with at least ten years' experience in the organization, I find that 42 percent of HCO physicians reported undertaking a true part-time position in the past decade, 46 percent an administrative role, and 28 percent an alternative clinical or extra-organizational role (see table 7.1). It was actually rare for HCO physicians to have

---

[5] "Peter" generally reflected the norm, but some regular full-time patient care informants were more ambivalent about their organizational context. These individuals seemed more aware of the autonomy they had given up, and fit the more traditional professional ideal type. They expressed dismay regarding both the organization (HCO) and the wider heath care system.

remained exclusively in regular full-time patient care (only 7 percent fitted this description). The figures for surveyed physicians from comparable large medical practice organizations were of a similar magnitude. By comparison, the incidence of these career activities among physicians who had practiced in traditional small private practices was as follows: 16 percent reported a true part-time position, 33 percent an administrative position, and 15 percent an alternative role. These figures indicate considerably less involvement in activities beyond the core professional work of client service for those in traditional small private practices.

These non-traditional career paths within HCO appeared to be temporary engagements for some but more enduring for others. Of those who reported having been part-time in the past decade, nearly a half (45 percent) had subsequently returned to regular full-time practice. Among those who had reported an administrative stint, only 30 percent were currently working at least ten hours in administration. In short, some were using the part-time patient care option as a long-term career strategy, while others were making shorter-term use of it.

In some cases, informants had availed themselves of this career flexibility to a remarkable extent. Consider the comments of one informant:

> I worked full-time for the first couple years. Then I had two children . . . At first I was working just part-time and nothing else, but eventually I did a total array of other things they had to offer. I've been a chief of department, I've been on a board committee. In the late '80s I also did some national activities in quality measurement.

Throughout the time she was engaging in these activities, this informant continued to see patients. Other HCO informants discussed similarly dynamic changes in their careers over time. In sum, physicians had been in both part-time and administrative posts with frequency, and many had moved in and out of these positions over time.

Reasons for, and importance of, career flexibility

Non-traditional career paths (i.e. paths other than full-time regular clinical practice) were common among HCO doctors. My survey data suggests that individual physicians were most often choosing various career paths in order to accommodate their individual needs and interests rather than being forced into those options. First, consider the true

Table 7.1 *Frequency of career activities reported by individual physicians over the previous ten years*

	True part-time clinician (part-time patient care without additional administrative or alternative roles)	Clinician and administrator (administrative role within a medical practice organization held while also providing patient care)	Clinician with alternative role (alternative role inside or outside medical practice organization held while also providing patient care)
HCO (physicians working in HCO: number of physicians ~ 500, workplace control score = 1.18, n = 116)	42%	46%	28%
Other large organizations (physicians working in organizations other than HCO with at least 50 physicians: average number of physicians = 162, workplace control score = 1.19, n = 70)	28%	38%	26%
Small organizations (physicians working in practices with fewer than 10 physicians: average number of physicians = 5, workplace control score = 1.42, n = 252)	16%	33%	15%

Notes: Values reflect the percentage of physicians from each organizational category who reported ever engaging in that career activity during the past ten years. Many individuals did more than one of these activities during the time period, so columns sum to over 100 percent. Uniform data was not collected for regular full-time patient care, which is the default career activity for patient care physicians.

Fisher exact tests for difference in frequencies between the HCO sample and the small organizations sample, and between the other large organizations sample and the small organizations sample, are all significant at the 95 percent level, with one exception: the difference between the administrative frequency for other large organizations and small organizations is significant only at the 10 percent level.

The administrative frequency figure for small organizations includes responsibilities associated with practice ownership; a second estimate excluding those responsibilities yields an 8 percent involvement in administration among small private practice physicians.

Source: 2002–3 survey of Massachusetts PCPs (see Briscoe, 2003, for more details).

part-time position. The most common reason reported for undertaking this career option was an interest in having more family or personal time (77 percent). One informant encapsulated this view in this comment: "Although it was difficult to relinquish control of the day-to-day details of my practice, I have really appreciated the clinical support here and I love working part-time. I feel that I am truly able to enjoy both my work and my family." Other reasons, less commonly cited, included the hope of practicing better medicine (31 percent) and the excessive workload of the full-time position (29 percent). A small group (11 percent) indicated that the organization required them to take this position.

Interviewees also took administrative positions for a wide range of reasons, the most common of which was an interest in leadership (78 percent). One informant commented, "I have loved the opportunities to grow and expand all within one organization. I've changed my career here from primary care internist to oncologist to building and chiefing an oncology department." This comment reflects a sense of vertical growth, and an appreciation toward the organization for facilitating that growth. Many who had taken administrative posts also reported, however, that the organization needed them to do so (73 percent) – revealing a degree of organizational pressure. More than a half of the interviewees also indicated that they hoped the work would be more interesting (55 percent), and that they wanted to change the organization (54 percent). About a third hoped for greater autonomy in the administrative post (33 percent) or saw it as a step to other positions (29 percent). In sum, the reasons given for pursuing non-traditional career activities varied widely.

How does bureaucracy facilitate handoffs and, hence, career flexibility?

In HCO I observed a more organizationally sophisticated workplace that, from the perspective of PCPs, carried with it more bureaucratic constraint in the form of rules and procedures and authority structures. Key features were the required use of an electronic medical record, the standardization of clinical work processes, and the development of stronger organization-level (as opposed to individual-level) relationships with patients. What is the link between these generally more bureaucratic organizational practices and the career flexibility enjoyed by PCPs? The key to understanding this connection lies with

the importance of the patient handoff. All these "bureaucratic" organizational practices enhance the ability of PCPs to hand off their
patients amongst one another. Such handoffs serve organizational
ends, to the extent that they increase the flexibility of the organization
to allocate physician labor and other resources. In addition, however,
and largely by coincidence, those handoffs also open up a range of
career options and a wider scope for dynamic career flexibility over
time.

To see how this process of bureaucratization functions to enhance
the personal career flexibility of PCPs, it is helpful first to see why the
patient handoff event is a limiting step in the achievement of flexibility.
Without effective handoffs, one PCP has to be available to respond to
the demands of patients whenever they arise, including during times
when that PCP would otherwise be pursuing other career activities.
Hence, in the absence of effective handoffs, attempts at other career
activities beyond full-time patient care (or attempts to achieve part-
time practice in order to accommodate family needs) tend to be dis-
satisfying. The following account summarizes a theoretical model of
career flexibility and handoffs presented in Briscoe (2007), based on
fieldwork at HCO and the other large medical practice organizations
described in the methods section above.

A PCP (call her Dr. X) will hand off some of her patient responsibilities to another PCP (call him Dr. Y) during a year-long stint when
she is acting as chief of Primary Care. During that year-long period
many of Dr. X's patients will present complex problems that require
Dr. Y to make decisions about diagnosis and treatment. For those
diseases for which the organization has adopted clinical protocols –
standardized diagnosis and treatment plans – Dr. Y's decision may be
expected to be more similar to those that Dr. X would have made
herself. Standardizing guidelines for patient care therefore reduces the
scope for disagreement and misunderstandings between Drs. X and Y.

A second set of handoff issues arises when the patient's trust is based
on an individualistic relationship with one physician – Dr. X – making
that patient reluctant to trust Dr. Y when seen for medical problems
during the handoff period. Organizational processes that shift the
relationship and locus of trust to the organizational level can therefore
also enable handoffs. At HCO, this took place through organizational
efforts to communicate a positive and consistent organizational identity that transcends individual physicians.

A third set of handoff issues arises from the sequential dependence of patient care interactions. Many patient interactions depend greatly on knowledge of the patient and his/her medical problems garnered from past interactions. When Dr. X hands off to Dr. Y, that knowledge needs to be codified in some way. The electronic medical record system at HCO provides a vehicle for such knowledge transfer. The system provides a common syntax for communication, and requires a certain degree of record completeness from those who use it. In addition, because Dr. X knows that her records are likely to be used by Dr. Y or someone else at some point, she may elaborate more than if her notes were simply for herself. Again, this can improve handoffs by heading off disputes stemming from associated patient care decisions.

In sum, in those organizational contexts in which I observed these bureaucratic processes to a greater degree, handoff capabilities were accordingly enhanced. From the perspective of PCPs, this, predictably, influenced their autonomy (negatively); more interestingly, however, it also influenced their career flexibility (positively).

Extending the model of bureaucracy, handoffs, and career flexibility to other industries

The handoffs-based model of career flexibility takes as its starting point the reality that client service work impedes career flexibility, since client demands are likely to hamper any attempts at reserving time for career activities *other* than full-time regular client service. When handoffs are enabled through organizational processes such as those outlined above for PCPs, options for combining client service and other career activities are revealed.

If it can be generalized, this career model has the potential to offer valuable insights into understanding the ways that workers respond to the increasingly prevalent bureaucratic organizational forms spreading across other professional service settings. There are several considerations to take into account in transferring the model across settings, though. First, there are boundary conditions associated with the nature of the work that underlie the model. These are (1) the tendency of clients to make unpredictably timed demands on workers, and (2) the one-to-one specificity between clients and workers that limits the scope for handoffs whenever clients' needs arise. In occupations in which the nature of the work hews closely to these boundary conditions, we should expect a positive role for bureaucracy in enhancing client hand-offs and enabling flexibility for professionals. Likely examples include many medical specialties, corporate lawyers, laboratory scientists, financial advisors, investment bankers, university professors, accountants, architects, management consultants, and advertising and design professionals. The exact nature of the work varies across and within these occupations, yet, to the extent that the above conditions are met, temporal flexibility problems should exist and the model of career flexibility based on client handoffs should apply.

The model may also generalize further beyond client-based occupations. Conceptually at least, the logic of specificity limiting handoffs could be extended to two other categories of professional work: project-based work and internal service work. In project settings, which are common in technology organizations, a worker seeking flexibility has to orient toward the project team much like the physician does toward his or her patient. The worker has to be responsive to demands that arise from others on the team at unpredictable times, and he or she cannot hand off those demands to someone else because of his/her unique role in the team. Internal service workers, such as computer network administrators, endure similar constraints, in the sense that they must be responsive to unpredictably timed demands and cannot easily hand off those demands to another person. Here, too, greater bureaucratization may provide increased flexibility.[6]

Alternative models of career flexibility in professional service organizations

A few alternative routes to career flexibility have been suggested in professional services, though each appears to be limited in feasibility and few have been explored systematically. One example is the possibility of limiting or changing the composition of the clients to whom the organization (or individual professional) provides services. In

---

[6] Another factor influencing the model's relevance to other professions relates to the degree of labor market power that workers possess. Power matters in order to ensure that organizational handoff capabilities are made available for workers' own purposes, rather than being usurped by organizational leaders in the service of other goals.

practice, this strategy would appear to be limited to certain narrow types of client work, in which career flexibility is less of a problem to begin with.

Another alternative is to alter the service expectations of existing clients, particularly around the importance of worker availability for high-quality services. Cynthia Fuchs Epstein, Carroll Seron, Bonnie Oglensky, and Robert Saute (1999, p. 135) suggest that this may be feasible in certain areas of legal practice. Again, however, the extent to which this approach would be tolerated by clients is unclear. It may sometimes also be possible to alter the *timing* of clients' demands, though many professional services are valued precisely because they guarantee the timely address of unforeseen problems as they arise for clients.

Of course, many professional organizations themselves perpetuate an unnecessarily hostile stance toward the notion of career options beyond client service (Perlow and Bailyn, 1997). In many organizations, cultural barriers present themselves to those seeking alternative career activities and career flexibility, and addressing those cultural factors may itself go some way toward opening up career options. Yet again, it is unclear how far a culture shift can address the real underlying dangers presented when a professional blocks off windows of time away from clients and says, "At this point in my career, I am only going to be available for clients during certain times ..." When clients are buying timely expert services, it would seem that limits on professional worker availability have to be matched with (organizational) systems that can ensure that the clients are guaranteed access to high-quality services during those off times.

Costs and benefits of the career flexibility model

As with any model, there are likely to be costs and benefits associated with a career flexibility model based on client handoffs. Some of these costs and benefits can be identified for the employees, organizations, and clients involved, and also for society at large.

Employees

In terms of advantages for employees, the model offers a way for professional workers to combine a career of client service with the flexibility to pursue many other work and non-work activities. This possibility appears to match the changing career interests in the work-force that I outlined above. If organizational leaders view the ability to offer this flexibility as a human resource capability that they can use to attract and retain valued professionals, this may further solidify access to career flexibility among professionals in organizations.

The central cost of the model is probably the declining level of individual autonomy that appears to be inextricably linked to greater schedule and career flexibility. This tradeoff complicates the historical portrait of uniform alienation arising from increasing bureaucracy (see Adler and Borys, 1996). An additional potential cost to employees is the loss of labor market power associated with weakening the specific bond between an individual client and an individual worker. This is a benefit to companies, however, as it removes some of the threat that a professional worker may leave the organization and steal away clients. In the extreme, the combination of enhanced worker substitution and diminished worker power may open the door for organizational leaders to reallocate labor strictly in line with organizational needs – and in so doing restrict the career flexibility made possible by those handoff-enabling organizational processes in the first place.

In my research, some informants noted another implication: a sense of emotional loss because they no longer had such long-term connections to clients (in this case, patients and their families). This and other changes in the work itself raise important questions about which types of individuals may be more attracted to, and capable of, working in an organization in which handoffs are routine.

Organizations/employers

A key attraction of the career flexibility model for organizations would seem to be the strategic HR advantage in attracting and retaining young professionals of diverse backgrounds. In my field research, however, I came across only a nascent recognition of this potential in the medical field. Instead, the advantages identified with the types of organizational processes that enabled handoffs were more focused around direct impacts on the efficiency and effectiveness of professional service work.

There may be other positive and negative impacts for organizations. For example, increasing the number of handoffs within an organization leads to new learning triggered by the increased necessity for interaction between otherwise isolated professional workers. My fieldwork uncovered instances in which PCPs had made discoveries about their colleagues' work practices only as a result of discussing handoff cases. Those discoveries could lead, in turn, to beneficial changes in individual work practices or organizational policies. This process resembles the kind of dynamic professional reflection that Donald Schon (1983) finds to be central in professional learning – but that he speculated would be attenuated under increasingly bureaucratic organizational conditions.

Clients

The impacts on clients are as yet unclear. A primary concern is that the enabling of handoffs will be associated with lower-quality services for clients. The organizations I studied that enabled handoffs showed no public evidence of lesser quality, however, and in fact HCO had received national quality awards. Further, within HCO an unpublished study concluded that part-time physicians compared favorably to full-time colleagues, spending longer with each patient on average, receiving higher patient satisfaction scores, and scoring similarly on measured health outcomes. Nonetheless, there clearly may be situations in which the quality of service delivery is affected by handoffs, and, given the difficulty that clients have in evaluating service quality in professional settings, many are likely to be concerned with the added uncertainty associated with organizations engaging in handoffs (Miller, Kochan, and Harrington, 2003).

Even if handoff systems are developed further in organizations that serve a wide range of clients, high-end clients seeking professional services may always demand timely personalized attention. Professional work conducted in that market segment may continue to be organized along traditional lines, and the careers of those engaged in that segment would therefore probably follow the more traditional professional career model with relatively little flexibility.

Society

There are two themes in the career flexibility model that hold implications for society in general. The first is the potential value in helping to retain talented current and future workers in the professional service occupations. Some evidence suggests that exit rates are increasing across a wide range of professions, and that women in particular are leaving professions even after considerable training investments

(Preston, 2004; Landon *et al.*, 2006; Kay, 1997). To the extent that the career flexibility model provides an avenue for more workers to remain in these occupations, at varying levels of involvement over the course of their careers, this may be seen as socially beneficial – all the more so given the unique and valuable activities conducted by professional service occupations.

The second societal theme is closely related: professional organizations can play a key role in accommodating "family time" for those in the growing professional workforce. The rise of the dual-earner (and dual-professional) family has placed heavy limits on family involvement in this segment of the workforce (Bailyn, Drago, and Kochan, 2000). Through the career flexibility model, professional organizations may support worker involvement in high-quality professional work while also keeping that work from overflowing into all other corners of the worker's life, facilitating a positive work–life balance (Moen, 2003). To the extent that professional service work is becoming the template for organizing and managing other types of workers as well, the presence of a viable career flexibility model in that sector may be viewed as even more vital.

Concluding remarks: implications for career theory

Career theory has begun to address the need for individual flexibility. Throughout much of the recent literature, however, there is a pervasive notion that bureaucratic organizations are inherently part of the problem. For example, the observation that careers have become less attached to particular organizations is often interpreted as an opportunity for individuals to chart their own courses, including their own balance between work and family, and between various career "projects" (Arthur and Rousseau, 1996).

My research tells a different story. For PCPs, bureaucratic organizational processes are themselves the key ingredients to career flexibility, and firmly embedding oneself into an organization that is capable of effective handoffs is the key to achieving flexibility. This turns on its head much of the thinking by career theorists about organizational attachments. For example, instead of part-time work implying less attachment to an employer, here achieving part-time careers requires greater attachment to an employer. Future research needs to explore this surprising link between career flexibility and bureaucratic organizations, and document the implications for professional workers as well as their clients.

References

Abbott, A. (1988). *The System of Professions: An Essay on the Division of Expert Labor*. Chicago: Chicago University Press.

Abel, R. L. (1989). *American Lawyers*. New York: Oxford University Press.

Ackroyd, S., Muzio, G. D., and Chanlet, J. F. (2007). *Redirections in the Study of Expert Labour*. Basingstoke: Palgrave Macmillan.

Adler, P., and Borys, B. (1996). Two types of bureaucracy: enabling and coercive. *Administrative Science Quarterly, 41*(1), 61–89.

American Medical Association (2002). *Socioeconomic Characteristics of Medical Practice*. Chicago: Center for Health Policy Research.

Arthur, M. B., and Rousseau, D. M. (eds.) (1996). *The Boundaryless Career: A New Employment Principle for a New Organizational Era*. New York: Oxford University Press.

Bailyn, L. (1993). *Breaking the Mold*. New York: Free Press.

Bailyn, L., Drago, R., and Kochan, T. A. (2000). *Integrating Work and Family Life: A Holistic Approach*.

Barley, S. R., and Orr, J. E. (1997). *Between Craft and Science: Technical Work in US Settings*. Ithaca, NY: Cornell University Press.

Barnett, R., and Gareis, K. (2000). Reduced-hours employment: the relationship between difficulty of trade-offs and quality of life. *Work and Occupations, 27*(2), 168–87.

Barzansky, B., Jonas, H., and Etzel, S. I. (2000). Educational programs in US medical schools, 1999–2000. *Journal of the American Medical Association, 284*, 1114–20.

Becker, H. S., Geer, B., Hughes, E. C., and Strauss, A. L. (1961). *Boys in White: Student Culture in Medical School*. Chicago: University of Chicago Press.

Beckman, C. M., and Phillips, D. J. (2005). Interorganizational determinants of promotion: client leadership and the attainment of women attorneys. *American Sociological Review, 70*, 678–702.

Bell, D. (1976). *The Coming of the Postindustrial Age: A Venture in Social Forecasting*. Harmondsworth: Penguin Books.

 (1999). The axial age of technology: forward 1999. In D. Bell (ed.), *The Coming of Post-Industrial Society* (ix–lxxxv). New York: Basic Books.

Betson, C. (1986). *Managing the Medical Enterprise: A Study of Physician Managers*. Ann Arbor, MI: UMI Research Press.

Bielby, W. T., and Bielby, D. D. (1999). Organizational mediation of project-based labor markets: talent agencies and the careers of screenwriters. *American Sociological Review*, 64(1), 64–85.

Blair, M., and Kochan, T. A. (eds.) (2000). *The New Relationship: Human Capital in the American Corporation*. Washington, DC: Brookings Institution Press.

Briscoe, F. (2003). Bureaucratic flexibility: large-scale organizations and the restructuring of physician careers. Unpublished doctoral dissertation. MIT Sloan School of Management, Cambridge, MA.

(2006). Temporal flexibility and careers: the role of large-scale organizations in the practicing physician labor market. *Industrial and Labor Relations Review*, 60(1), 67–83.

(2007). From iron cage to iron shield? How bureaucracy enables temporal flexibility for professional service workers. *Organization Science*, 18(2), 297–314.

Briscoe, F., and Konrad, T. R. (2006). HMO employment and African-American physicians. *Journal of the National Medical Association*, 98(8), 1318–25.

Brock, D., Powell, M., and Hinings, C. R. (1999). *Restructuring the Professional Organization: Accounting, Health Care and Law*. London: Routledge.

Broschak, J. P. (2004). Managers' mobility and market interface: the effect of managers' career mobility on the dissolution of market ties. *Administrative Science Quarterly*, 49(4), 608–40.

Cappelli, P. (1999). Career jobs are dead. *California Management Review*, 42, 146–67.

Cohen, L. E., Broschak, J. P., and Haveman, M. A. (1998). And then there were more? The effect of organizational sex composition on hiring and promotion of managers. *American Sociological Review*, 63, 711–27.

Davenport, T., and Prusak, L. (1998). *Working Knowledge: How Organizations Manage what They Know*. Cambridge, MA: Harvard Business School Press.

Derber, C. (ed.) (1982). *Professionals as Workers: Mental Labor in Advanced Capitalism*. Boston: G. K. Hall.

Eisenhardt, K. M. (1989). Building theories from case study research. *Academy of Management Review*, 14(

Empson, L. (2007). Professional service firms. In S. Clegg and J. Bailey (eds.), *International Encyclopedia of Organization Studies*. Thousand Oaks, CA: Sage.

Empson, L., and Chapman, C. S. (2006). Partnership versus corporation: implications of alternative forms of governance for managerial authority and organizational priorities in professional service firms. *Research in the Sociology of Organizations*, 24, 145–76.

Engel, G. V. (1970). Professional autonomy and bureaucratic organization. *Administrative Science Quarterly*, 15(1), 12–21.

Epstein, C. F., Seron, C., Oglensky, B., and Saute, R. (1999). *The Part-time Paradox: Time Norms, Professional Lives, Family, and Gender.* New York: Routledge.

Etzioni, A. (1969). *The Semi-Professions and Their Organization: Teachers, Nurses, Social Workers.* New York: Free Press.

Families and Work Institute (2005). *Generations and Gender in the Workplace: An Issue Brief.* Watertown, MA: American Business Collaborative.

Fennell, M. L., and Alexander, J. A. (1993). Perspectives on organizational change in the US medical case sector. *Annual Review of Sociology*, 19, 89–112.

Freidson, E. (1970). *Profession of Medicine: A Study of the Sociology of Applied Knowledge.* New York: Dodd Mead.

(1984). The changing nature of professional control. *American Review of Sociology*, 10, 1–20.

(2001). *Professionalism: The Third Logic.* Chicago: University of Chicago Press.

Galanter, M., and Palay, T. (1991). *Tournament of Lawyers: The Transformation of the Big Law Firm.* Chicago: University of Chicago Press.

Gerth, H. H., and Mills, C. W. (eds. and trans.). *From Max Weber: Essays in Sociology.* New York: Oxford University Press.

Gilson, R. J., and Mnookin, R. H. (1985). Sharing among the human capitalists: an economic inquiry into the corporate law firm and how partners split profits. *Stanford Law Review*, 37, 313–92.

Goode, W. (1957). Community within a community: the professions. *American Sociological Review*, 22, 194–208.

Greenwood, R., and Empson, L. (2003). The professional partnership: relic or exemplary form of governance? *Organization Studies*, 24(6), 909–33.

Greenwood, R., Hinings, C. R., and Brown, J. (1990). "P^2-form" strategic management: corporate practices in the professional partnership. *Academy of Management Journal*, 33(4), 725–55.

Greenwood, R., Li, S. X., Prakash, R., and Deephouse, D. L. (2005). Reputation, diversification, and organizational explanations of performance in professional service firms. *Organization Science*, 16(6), 661–73.

Greenwood, R., and Suddaby, R. (2006). Institutional entrepreneurship in mature fields: the Big Five accounting firms. *Academy of Management Journal*, 49(1), 27–48.

Gunz, H., and Gunz, S. (1994). Professional/organizational commitment and job satisfaction for employed lawyers. *Human Relations*, 41, 801–27.

Hafferty, F., and Light, D. (1995). Professional dynamics and the changing nature of medical work. *Journal of Health and Social Behavior, 35* (Extra Issue), 132–53.

Hall, O. (1948). The stages of a medical career. *American Journal of Sociology, 53,* 327–36.

Hall, R. (1968). Professionalization and bureaucratization. *American Sociological Review, 33*(1), 92–104.

Hansen, M., and Haas, M. (2001). Competing for attention in knowledge markets: electronic document dissemination in a management consulting company. *Administrative Science Quarterly, 46*(1), 1–28.

Haug, M. (1973). Deprofessionalization: an alternative hypothesis for the future. *Sociological Review Monographs, 20,* 195–211.

Higgins, M., and Kram, K. (2001). Reconceptualizing mentoring at work: a developmental network perspective. *Academy of Management Review, 26*(2), 264–88.

Hillman, R. W. (2001). Professional partnerships, competition, and the evolution of firm culture: the case of law firms. *Journal of Corporate Law, 26,* 1061–7.

Hoff, T., Whitcomb, W., and Nelson, J. (2002). Thriving and surviving in a new medical career: the case of hospitalist physicians. *Journal of Health and Social Behavior, 43*(1), 72–91.

Hull, K., and Nelson, R. (2000). Assimilation, choice or constraint? Testing theories of gender differences in the careers of lawyers. *Social Forces, 79,* 229–64.

Ichniowski, C., Kochan, T. A., Levine, D. I., Olson, C., and Strauss, G. (1996). What works at work: overview and assessment. *Industrial Relations, 35,* 299–333.

Jones, C. (1996). Careers in project networks: the case of the film industry. In M. B. Arthur and D. M. Rousseau (eds.), *The Boundaryless Career: A New Employment Principle for a New Organizational Era* (58–75). New York: Oxford University Press.

Kay, F. M. (1997). Flight from law: a competing risks model of departures from law firms. *Law and Society Review, 31*(2), 301–35.

Kay, F. M., and Hagan, J. (1999). Cultivating clients in the competition for partnership: gender and the organizational restructuring of the law firm in the 1990s. *Law and Society Review, 33,* 517–56.

Kunda, G., Barley, S. R., and Evans, J. (2002). Why do contractors contract? The experience of highly skilled technical professionals in a contingent labor market. *Industrial and Labor Relations Review, 55*(2), 234–61.

Laffel, G., and Blumenthal, D. (1989). The case for using industrial quality management science in health care organizations. *Journal of the American Medical Association, 262,* 2869–73.

Landau, Z. (2003). The road taken. *The CPA Journal*, 73(2), 80.

Landon, B., Reschovsky, J., Pham, H., and Blumenthal, D. (2006). Leaving medicine: the consequences of physician dissatisfaction. *Medical Care*, 44(3), 234–42.

Larson, M. (1977). *The Rise of Professionalism*. Berkeley, CA: University of California Press.

Laster, L. (1996). *Life after Medical School*. New York: W. W. Norton.

Lave, J., and Wenger, E. (1991). *Situated Learning: Legitimate Peripheral Participation*. Cambridge: Cambridge University Press.

Leicht, K., and Fennell, M. (1997). The changing organizational context of professional work. *Annual Review of Sociology*, 23, 215–31.

(2001). *Professional Work: A Sociological Approach*. Malden, MA: Blackwell.

Linzer, M., Konrad, T. R., Douglas, J., McMurray, J. E., Pathman, D. E., Williams, E., Schwartz, M., Gerrity, M., Scheckler, W., Bigby, J. A., and Rhodes, E. (2000). Managed care, time pressure, and physician job satisfaction: results from the physician worklife study. *Journal of General Internal Medicine*, 15, 441–50.

Lowendahl, B. (2000). *Strategic Management of Professional Service Firms*. Copenhagen: Copenhagen Business School Press.

McKinlay, J. B. (1982). Toward the proletarianization of physicians. In C. Derber (ed.), *Professionals as Workers: Mental Labor in Advanced Capitalism* (37–62). Boston: G. K. Hall.

McKinlay, J. B., and Marceau, L. D. (2002). The end of the golden age of doctoring. *International Journal of Health Services*, 32(2), 379–416.

Malos, S. B., and Campion, M. A. (2000). Human resource strategy and career mobility in professional service firms: test of an options-based model. *Academy of Management Journal*, 43(4), 749–60.

Michelson, E., Laumann, E., and Heinz, J. P. (2000). The changing character of the lawyer–client relationship: evidence from two Chicago surveys. In W. Raub and J. Wessie (eds.), *The Management of Durable Relations: Theoretical and Empirical Models for Households and Organizations* (106–7). Amsterdam: Thela Thesis.

Miller, B., Kochan, T. A., and Harrington, M. (2003). *Beyond the Part-time Partner: A Part-time Law Firm?* Working Paper WPC 100. Cambridge, MA: Massachusetts Institute of Technology Workplace Center.

Mills, P. K., Hall, J. L., Leidecker, J. K., and Margulies, N. (1983). Flexiform: a model for professional service organizations. *Academy of Management Review*, 8(1), 118–31.

Mintzberg, H. (1979). *The Structuring of Organizations*. Englewood Cliffs, NJ: Prentice Hall.

Moen, P. (ed.) (2003). *It's About Time: Couples and Careers*. Ithaca, NY: Cornell University Press.

Montgomery, K. (2001). Physician executives: the evolution and impact of a hybrid profession. *Advances in Health Care Management, 2*, 215–41.

Moody, J. (2002). Recruiting generation X physicians. *New England Journal of Medicine, Recruiting Physicians Today, 10*(1), 1–2.

Morris, T. (2001). Asserting property rights: knowledge codification in the professional service firm. *Human Relations, 54*(7), 819–38.

NALP Foundation (2004). *After the JD: First Results of a National Study of Legal Careers*. Chicago: American Bar Foundation.

Nanda, A. (2003). *The Essence of Professionalism: Managing Conflict of Interest*. Working Paper 03–066. Harvard, MA: Harvard Business School.

National Research Council (1999). *The Changing Nature of Work: Implications for Occupational Analysis*. Washington, DC: National Academy Press.

Nickens, H., Ready, T., and Petersdorf, R. (1994). Project 3000 by 2000: racial and ethnic diversity in US medical schools. *New England Journal of Medicine, 331*(7), 472–6.

Perlow, L., and Bailyn, L. (1997). The senseless submergence of difference: engineers, their work, and their careers. In S. R. Barley and J. E. Orr (eds.), *Between Craft and Science: Technical Work in US Settings* (230–43). Ithaca, NY: Cornell University Press.

Powers, L., Parmelle, R., and Wiesenfelder, H. (1969). Practice patterns of women and men physicians. *Journal of Medical Education, 44*(6), 481–91.

Preston, A. E. (2004). *Leaving Science: Occupational Exit from Scientific Careers*. New York: Sage.

Pugh, D., Hickson, D., Hinings, C. R., and Turner, C. (1968). Dimensions of organization structure. *Administrative Science Quarterly, 13*(1), 65–105.

Raelin, J. (1985). *The Clash of Cultures: Managers Managing Professionals*. Boston: Harvard Business School Press.

Ranalli, R. (2003). Pleas of frustration: lawyers questioning, abandoning their profession. *Boston Globe*, 18 August, A1.

Robinson, J. (1999). *The Corporate Practice of Medicine*. Berkeley, CA: University of California Press.

Rothman, R., and Perrucci, R. (1970). Organizational careers and professional expertise. *Administrative Science Quarterly, 15*(3), 282–93.

Sasser, A. (2005). Gender differences in physician pay: trade offs between career and family. *Journal of Human Resources, 40*(2), 477–504.

Schon, D. (1983). *The Reflective Practitioner: How Professionals Think in Action*. New York: Basic Books.

Scott, W. R. (1965). Reactions to supervision in a heteronomous professional organization. *Administrative Science Quarterly*, 10(1), 65–81.

Shah, N. (2005). Change in institutions: the decline of the no-lateral-hiring norm among large law firms, 1974–1990. Paper presented at the Annual Meeting of the Academy of Management, Honolulu, 5–10 August.

Sharma, A. (1997). Professional as agent: knowledge asymmetry in agency exchange. *Academy of Management Review*, 22(3), 748–98.

Sobecks, N., Justice, A., Hinze, S., Chirayath, H., Lasek, R., Chren, M.-M., Aucott, J., Juknialis, B., Fortinsky, R., Younger, S., and Landefeld, C. S. (1999). When doctors marry doctors: a survey exploring the professional and family lives of young physicians. *Annals of Internal Medicine*, 130(4), 312–19.

Starr, P. (1982). *The Transformation of American Medicine*. New York: Basic Books.

Strauss, A. L. (1987). *Qualitative Analysis for Social Scientists*. New York: Cambridge University Press.

Valcour, M., Bailyn, L., and Quijada, M. A. (2007). Customized careers. In H. P. Gunz and M. A. Peiperl (eds.), *Handbook of Career Studies* (188–210). Thousand Oaks, CA: Sage.

Van Maanen, J., and Barley, S. R. (1984). Occupational communities: culture and control in organizations. *Research in Organizational Behavior*, 6, 287–365.

Von Nordenflycht, A. (2006). What is a professional service firm . . . and why does it matter? Paper presented at the Clifford Chance Professional Service Firms Conference, Barcelona, 11–13 June.

(2007). Is public ownership bad for professional service firms? Ad agency ownership, performance and creativity. *Academy of Management Journal*, 50(2), 429–45.

Waite, L., and Nielson, M. (2001). The rise of the dual-earner family, 1963–1997. In R. Hertz and N. Marshall (ed.), *Working Families: The Transformation of the American Home* (23–41). Berkeley, CA: University of California Press.

Wallace, J. (1995). Organizational and professional commitment in professional and nonprofessional organizations. *Administrative Science Quarterly*, 40(2), 228–56.

Weber, D. (2005). The state of the electronic health record in 2005. *Physician Executive*, 31(4), 6–10.

Wilensky, H. (1964). The professionalization of everyone? *American Journal of Sociology*, 70, 137–58.

Wilkins, D., and Gulati, M. (1996). Why are there so few black lawyers in corporate law firms? An institutional analysis. *California Law Review*, 84(3), 493–625.

Williams, J. (2000). *Unbending Gender: Why Family and Work Conflict and What to Do about it.* Oxford: Oxford University Press.

Zabusky, S. E., and Barley, S. R. (1996). Redefining success: ethnographic observations on the careers of technicians. In P. Osterman (ed.), *Broken Ladders: Managerial Careers in Transition* (185–214). Oxford: Oxford University Press.

Zerubavel, E. (1979). Private time and public time: the temporal structure of social accessibility and professional commitments. *Social Forces, 58*(1), 38–58.

Index

257